First Hand

My Life and Irish Football

EOIN HAND, born in Dublin, won twenty caps with the Republic of Ireland while playing for Portsmouth. As player-manager of Limerick United, he won the League of Ireland title in 1980 and the FAI Cup in 1982. After managing the Republic of Ireland team and clubs in England, Saudi Arabia and South Africa, he worked as a career guidance officer for the Football Association of Ireland. Now retired, he lives in Kerry.

Ghostwriter **JARED BROWNE** had trials with Manchester United a
and represented the Republic of Ireland at schoolboy level b
football for a university education. His first book was *Dunphy: A*
(2012). He is Irish correspondent for UK football magazine *BA*
lives in Kerry.

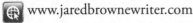 www.jaredbrownewriter.com   @Browne_Jared

First
Hand

My Life and
Irish Football

Eoin Hand
with Jared Browne

The Collins Press

First published in 2017 by
The Collins Press
West Link Park
Doughcloyne
Wilton
Cork
T12 N5EF
Ireland

A CIP record for this book is available from the British Library.

Paperback ISBN: 978-1-84889-323-8

Typesetting by Carrigboy Typesetting Services
Typeset in Adobe Garamond Pro
Printed in Poland by Białostockie Zakłady Graficzne SA

In memory of my mother, Monica, and my brother Eamonn

Contents

Foreword

Eoin Hand is a survivor – and more: Eoin has turned surviving into an art form. Every time he is struck a blow, back he comes, stronger than ever. He has often been on the ropes and has taken some punishment but he has never been rightly knocked out.

The job description of a footballing man covers a multitude and Eoin's life and times reflect his versatility. He is steeped in the game he loves and cares about so much. Eoin has been player for both club and country. He managed the Republic of Ireland and later in life became a football analyst. There was a long stint spent helping teenagers to make the transition from home to away when Eoin worked for the Football Association of Ireland.

Yes, there have been controversies and setbacks. His is a lively story. You can take what you may from it and make up your own mind. And it is true too that since he first left his beloved Drumcondra, he has never held a steady job or a cushy number. Eoin's life reflects the precariousness of his chosen career. He has had to travel to make a living. There were times when his health and his family life suffered. This book is as much a travelogue as a football book, with an insight into such diverse cultures as Limerick, Saudi Arabia, South Africa, Drumcondra in north Dublin and Moyvane in north Kerry. There have been massive highs and terrible lows.

Eoin is brave and resilient, both on and off the pitch. That is the real story behind all the years of controversy and derring-do. Eoin saw each setback as an opportunity to start again. He has a wonderful sense of humour. He can make the transition from down to up faster than any other man I have ever known.

Eoin is always philosophical. He doesn't forget or at times forgive, but he never lets the vicissitudes of life define him. It is the old footballing philosophy coming to the fore: there is always a next game or a next day. He is one of life's optimists.

But there was one ongoing challenge he could never seem to master. Eoin has spent more than thirty years attempting to learn to play the banjo. He is still learning and if as a football player he was bold and brave, his banjo-playing is slow and tenuous. But will he give up? Never.

He is a wonderful singer. Hand can lift the mood in a pub in seconds as he has often done in John B's. Eoin never has to be forced to sing and when he gets the crowd going, you can see the inspirational qualities that made him such a success in the dressing room, both as player and manager.

Jack Charlton's wonderful team was nurtured during the reign of Eoin Hand. Just like John Giles before him, Eoin's teams suffered from some truly awful refereeing decisions. The team that Eoin built was the foundation for the glory days of Irish football. The old football axiom applies: 'you have to lose one to win one.'

Eoin also had wonderful success with Limerick United. He is still a cult figure in the city. And sometimes we forget his career as a player. Eoin never let his country down in times when some were bullied by their club managers into feigning injury. He was brave and a leader on the field in times when the game was tougher and wages were but a fraction of the vast sums paid now. Eoin always played for the jersey. Money was never his god.

He is content now here in Kerry with his beloved Pauline. She is his rock and yes, there is a 'happy ever after'.

Billy Keane

1

'Boxing the Fox'

The Early Years: 1946–1968

It was August 1997. I had just received the last rites. I was a patient in the intensive care unit of Dublin's Mater Hospital and in a few hours I would undergo emergency surgery to try to save my life. Although I drew strength from the family members and friends who had come to my side, my odds of dodging an early meeting with my maker were not good.

On one level, I knew why I was in the Mater – in the previous months my personal life had threatened to fall apart at the seams and my solution had been to drink my way towards an early grave – but, still, I could not understand how it had all come to this. I lay there reflecting on my life. Little more than a decade earlier I was at the peak of my football career, managing the Republic of Ireland's national side. Now I was picking over the broken pieces of my life and hanging on to what was left of it by a thread. I had no idea how things were going to turn out. My life was in the hands of the gods.

I hold only two memories of my father: one good, the other not so good. In one scene I am four years old and playing at home on the floor. My father comes in and gives me a plastic toy bus. I smile and feel delight. In the other – I am still no more than a small boy – I take a knife to a plastic ball because I am intrigued to find out how it can bounce. I want to discover what magic is inside. For this moment of innocent vandalism, I get a clatter around the head and finish in tears. My father, Bernard Hand, whom I rarely saw, died when I was ten years old. I did not have an ordinary childhood.

I was born on 30 March 1946 in Ireland's oldest pub, The Brazen Head. Since the twelfth century the pub has sat close to the banks of the Liffey. It was a historic place in which to begin my life's journey, but of course I was oblivious of it at the time. My mother, Monica Hand (née McHugh), held the licence on the pub, having inherited the business from her grand-aunt.

My father had moved to England for work in the early 1950s, leaving my mother, myself and my three older brothers, Frank, Brian and Eamonn, behind in Dublin. It was not an ideal situation for anyone but there was simply no work in Ireland for my dad. He went to London, found employment as a salesman, and, after that, made only infrequent visits to Dublin to see us.

I won't easily forget the day in 1956 when I found out that my father was gone – for good. I came downstairs and looked into the kitchen. It was the afternoon, and my mother was cooking for the family before going out to work. There was nothing unusual in that; it was her daily routine. What had kept me rooted to the spot, however, was the fact that – all the while running to and fro – my mother had tears streaming down her face. She was cooking and crying. 'What's wrong, Ma?' I asked. She looked at me – nothing more than a kid – and, struggling to get the words out, told me 'Your father is dead, Eoin.'

That summed up my mother's life. She had just discovered that her husband had died, yet there was no time to stop and gather herself. That was a luxury for other people to enjoy, for people with choices. For my mother, there was work to be done, endless lists of things to tend to. She could not even attend my father's funeral in London.

With my dad now dead, my mother suddenly faced the daunting task of raising four young boys alone in the economically tough times of 1950s' Dublin and without any welfare state system to fall back on.

By the early 1950s my mother had already sold The Brazen Head and moved to Drumcondra on the city's northside. She managed The Beehive Bar in Clerys on O'Connell Street from 3 p.m. to midnight, six days a week. Sunday was her only day off. For extra income we kept boarders, or, as my mother preferred to call them, 'paying guests'. She had bought our three-storey home in Drumcondra with this plan in mind.

Having non-family living in our home was an unusual experience but it served to open me up to the world at a young age. One particular man, Gerry McHugh, from County Donegal, was a father figure to me. During

My mother, Monica, and I in 1953 on the day of my First Holy Communion. In the economically difficult times of 1950s' Ireland, my mother showed tremendous courage to bring up myself and my three brothers as a single-mother.

his time with us he taught me how to swim and showed me the basics of driving.

Another boarder, a young woman from County Kerry who worked for the civil service, would turn out to be a very significant person in our lives. My mother befriended Ms Josie Kirby and so began my lifelong fondness for Kerry. It soon became a routine for my brother Eamonn and me to visit Glenalappa, Moyvane, in the north of the county each summer. Here the Kirby family would look after us in order to give our mother a break. This continued for about six years from my seventh birthday onwards. I have special memories of the carefree, outdoors existence that we enjoyed in the Kerry countryside. We were inner-city boys and, with the exception of these holidays, we saw little or nothing of nature – outside of local Dublin parks and Dollymount Strand – from one end of the year to the other. We swam in a stream at the edge of Ms Kirby's parents' farm and ran in the fields surrounding the old cottage.

Josie's brother Jimmy showed us the country ways and we needed all the help we could get. There were so many little things that we did not understand. On one occasion, I inadvertently landed myself in trouble through sheer naivety. One Sunday morning, after having attended Mass with the Kirbys in Moyvane, I went outside, untied the donkey and – thinking I was being a good boy – sat up on the trap to wait for everyone else to get on. Of course, donkeys being creatures of habit, the untying of the rope was the animal's signal to take off for Glenalappa. There was nothing in the world that I could do to stop him. The donkey and I went all the way to Glenalappa. I don't remember exactly how my hosts made it home but I certainly remember them being none too pleased with me when they finally arrived back at the farm.

It was here, in what seemed to me and Eamonn to be a little corner of paradise, that my competitive spirit was born. I took part in the local community games in Knockanure and discovered the thrill of competition and athletic activity. I loved my time in Kerry.

Being the youngest of four boys had its challenges. With my mother working every weekday afternoon and evening, my brothers and I spent a lot of time on our own. Inevitably, mischief would rear its head. My brothers, being bigger and stronger than me, usually came out on top in any of the disagreements that would break out among us. One day, when I was twelve, one of my brothers was pushing me around and I lost control.

With my mother and brothers in 1961. (*L–r*): Frank, Eamonn, Monica, me and Brian, with our dog Bing.

Although it was nothing more than a minor altercation, with me kicking him on the knee, my brother came off the worst. Convinced that I was in serious trouble, I fled. I just kept running, certain that I could not go home after what I'd done. I had no real plan but knew that I had to go somewhere safe. In my thoughts, the one place where I felt comfortable was the home of the Kirby family in Glenalappa. And so I set out for Kerry.

I began thumbing lifts in Dublin's city centre. After being picked up by numerous drivers across the country, I finally made it to Listowel at about midnight. I was dropped off on a pitch-black country road and began walking the last eight miles towards the house. I was terrified. I had never seen such darkness and I could hear all kinds of strange sounds coming from the night-time undergrowth. Every now and then, a cow would stick its huge head out from a ditch. I would see it only at the last moment and give a start. Eventually I made it into the Kirbys' yard. The dogs began to bark wildly at the intruder. I feared how the Kirbys would react to seeing me on their doorstep and what they would think of my outlandish adventure. The oil lamps went on and scared, questioning faces began to peer out of the darkness. I made myself known. They were stunned. A twelve-year-old boy had just traversed half the country on his own! Thankfully, they took me in and looked after me. The next day we travelled the one-and-a-half miles by donkey and trap to Moyvane village and the Kirbys rang my mother to explain that I was with them, safe and sound. Arrangements were made for me to travel home to Dublin a few weeks later.

Although nobody had much money and everyone was forced to be resourceful in order to get by, I have fond memories of growing up in 1950s' Drumcondra. My friends and I played football on the streets, or in Griffith Park, until we were dropping from exhaustion. In what were difficult times, football was a great diversion. Playing on the streets, in particular, was formative for me. In hectic and frequently crowded games, with players coming at you from multiple angles, you quickly developed awareness and ball control. Also, because you were playing around the various obstacles that the urban environment threw up, you dealt with extra challenges: you avoided lamp posts, adjusted to freakish bounces and coped with unpredictable ricochets off kerbs and walls.

When we were not kicking a ball about, we were 'boxing the fox' – local slang for robbing orchards. The Clontarf baths and the cinema on Drumcondra Road, when money allowed, were exceptional treats. At other times we would scrounge some ball bearings from one of the garages in the area and attach them to the bottom of a piece of wood. We would then take this makeshift sledge to Griffith Park and use it to slide down various slopes. You were making do, in whatever way you could.

At the age of ten, music first entered my life. My mother bought me a banjo, and eventually, once I had some basic ability, I was ready for my first concert, at the age of twelve. It was a disaster and a painful enough experience to put me off the instrument for years. I was playing as part of a variety concert at O'Connell Street's Ozanam Hall, opposite the Gresham Hotel. When I finally got my turn, I nervously walked out in front of the audience and steeled myself to play a few pieces. I began, but something was very wrong. The sound coming from the banjo was awful and the longer I went on the worse it became. A silent crowd looked on expectantly. I was a child and it was my first time performing in public. I had no clue what to do except to freeze and gaze around helplessly. One of the women organising the event finally put me out my misery and chaperoned me off-stage. It was humiliating. I discovered afterwards that a prankster had deliberately untuned my instrument. I gave up the banjo, a decision I regret to this day.

Throughout my youth, whatever went wrong, my mother's reassuring presence held everything together. She was a wonderful, strong woman. She worked at a demanding day job, ran a guest house, raised four boys – all on her own. She also managed to put my three brothers through university, and they all qualified in their respective fields. My mother sacrificed so much – more than I can imagine.

My beginnings in organised football were with the north Dublin nursery, Stella Maris Football Club. Because of my pace, I started out as a right-winger. The club was noted for producing professional players. The most celebrated former player was John Giles and when he visited the club in 1959 I was in awe of him. I was only thirteen years old. John, then a Manchester United player, was himself only eighteen but what worlds there were between us! He was about to make his debut for the Republic of Ireland against Sweden at Dalymount Park. He would go on to inspire the Republic to a 3-2 victory over the Swedes, scoring one goal himself. Giles, a Stella lad and so one of us, was living proof that you could make it to the very top. He was an inspiration; I knew where I wanted to be but I never dreamed that one day I would play alongside John for Ireland.

Although I also played hurling and Gaelic football, playing football for Stella Maris was my greatest joy. In 1960s' Ireland, however, that did not make me popular. Like many other young footballers of the 'wrong' persuasion, I received regular beatings at school from a particularly zealous Christian Brother, nicknamed 'the Bull', who used a leather strap to show his disapproval of so-called 'foreign games'. The punishment stopped only when my mother went to the school and confronted him. After that, although the beatings stopped, they were replaced by psychological warfare. The Brother isolated me in the class by forbidding all classmates to sit next to me. I sat there, with empty desks all around me.

Later when I was Ireland manager the school invited me to a dinner as the guest of honour. They asked if I would like to sit next to the very same Christian Brother who had beaten me all those years ago. I made it clear that under no circumstances would I go anywhere near the man.

Throughout my teenage years in Dublin, aside from indulging in my love of sport, I also tried to work, where possible, to get some spending money. My first job was at the Bolands Mill in the Grand Canal Dock area of the city – a large bakery that made bread and, most famously, biscuits. It was part-time summer work and it did not pay a whole lot, but, still, I was determined to impress. Although I was hired to accompany the delivery drivers on their daily rounds, on the first day I was not needed for that work. My manager, instead, gave me a large brush and asked me to sweep the bakery floor for the day. Of course, after about an hour, I had swept every inch of the place. However, I still needed to look busy, so I just pushed the same pile of dirt around for the rest of the day. It worked, at least for that one time anyway.

Work, however, was always in short supply; if it came your way, you had to use whatever cuteness you could muster to land the job. In the summer of 1963 a friend told me of an opportunity to work with the frozen food company Birds Eye at its Great Yarmouth depot in Norfolk, England. The only snag was that, as a seventeen-year-old, I would have commanded poor wages. On the other hand, if there was a way of convincing Birds Eye that I was twenty-one, I would receive the much larger wage of an adult worker. The solution: by securing a fake ID in Dublin, Eoin Hand, the wet-behind-the-ears teenager, became Barry Byrne, the seasoned 21-year-old.

Myself and my brother Eamonn travelled to Great Yarmouth to work for the summer months. Our work involved registering the arrival and departure of Birds Eye delivery trucks at one of the company's depots. We had to get up very early every morning, which was fine in theory, but I had one very practical problem: how to wake on time. Being without an alarm clock – a luxury item in those days – I asked a colleague for help. Thankfully, he had an alarm clock but he was staying in a different house, as was my brother Eamonn. We devised an ad hoc morning routine to wake me from my slumbers. Before turning in every night, I would attach a piece of string to my toe and throw the slack out from my first-floor window. Then, in the morning, once my co-worker was up, he would come by and yank the string until it woke me.

Aside from the pay, with which I was delighted, the job came with its perks: if the drivers were ever late delivering their load, they would bribe us with cans of beer to enter them on the log as having arrived on schedule. We were young and naive and probably not aware of the full consequences

A twelve-year-old sportsman: here I am posing for a team shot in 1958 with my school's Gaelic football team.

of our actions. We were away from home and keen to enjoy ourselves. With enough tardy truck drivers to tide us over, stockpiling cans of beer became a mini cottage industry. After a few arrivals, we would usually have enough for a party. Those were innocent days. We were footloose and fancy free and in the final years of our youth.

At the end of the summer I returned home with money in my back pocket – a first for me. I bought a fridge for my mother and a Honda 50 motorcycle for myself. With my sleek new Honda underneath me, I thought I was the business driving around Dublin. On one occasion, I got what was coming to me. After finishing playing a game with Stella Maris, I was leaving to go home on my Honda when I spotted a group of girls across the road. I'd had a good game and even scored, so I was feeling pretty good about myself. I decided that I would impress the girls by tearing away on my new set of wheels. I ran, jumped onto the seat and turned the key. Unfortunately for me, in my eagerness to show off in front of my female audience, I had forgotten that the bike's steering was locked and so I made the fatal move of hitting the accelerator. Instead of majestically scorching down the road, the bike, rooted to the spot, simply flew around in circles with me astride it like a desperate rodeo rider struggling with an unruly mount until I was thrown over the handlebars and unceremoniously dumped on my backside. Of course, it did have an effect on the girls, although not the intended one. They were doubled over with laughter. Tail between my legs, lesson learned – the painful way – I gathered my things and, this time, pulled away nice and carefully.

From Stella Maris, at the age of seventeen. I moved to the amateur club Old O'Connell's. My performances on the right wing earned me a trial with the Republic of Ireland under-18s and it was here that I was spotted by a Swindon Town scout. I'd had a good day: my side had won 4-0 and I'd scored all four goals. As a result, I was also capped by the Irish youths at a tournament in the Netherlands. Although my football career looked to be going places, my mother encouraged me to complete my Leaving Certificate exams. I wanted to fly but my mother wisely kept my feet on the ground.

Subsequently, John Givens, the older brother of the future Republic of Ireland international Don, and I were invited to Swindon for a trial. I passed the test. Although John was not offered terms, he went on to have a successful career in the League of Ireland. In later decades, he was also instrumental in the formation of the Players' Football Association of Ireland (PFAI), as well as ultimately becoming a sports agent, representing Jack Charlton among others. Swindon's manager, Bert Head, offered me a professional contract on £8 a week. To put that in context, my digs cost £5 and, in those days, a pint of stout cost about one shilling. The dream had begun. At the age of eighteen, I was a professional footballer.

My move to Swindon caused a minor commotion in Dublin. Shelbourne alleged that I was registered as their player and not as an Old O'Connell player, and so they demanded a transfer fee from the English club. Although there had been some suggestion of my moving to Shelbourne, it had never

The Swindon Town squad in the 1964/65 season. The Wiltshire club gave me my first break in the English game. I am in the front standing row, fifth from left. Bert Head is fifth from right, seated row. (L. Maylett, Swindon)

materialised and, sure enough, unable to prove their case, the club ultimately dropped their claim and the matter ended. When this minor incident was reported in one of the Irish newspapers, the odd coincidence of names in the finished article was almost of more interest than the story: the player was Hand, the manager was Head and the journalist covering the story was (Arthur) Legge.

In the 1964/65 season, Swindon Town was playing in the Second Division and was a club on the rise. Only two seasons earlier, playing in the second tier of English football for the first time in its history, the club had finished runners-up to Northampton Town. This was not the top division but, for a youngster from Dublin getting his first break in the English game, it was a very exciting place to be.

The club manager, Bert Head, was old-school and strict, but fair. He had been Swindon's manager since 1956 and had revived the club's fortunes in

Me in 1964.
The Fifth Beatle?

the early 1960s with a pioneering youth policy which targeted local talent. His young squad had earned the nickname 'Bert's Babes' and the conveyor belt would produce numerous Swindon greats, such as Mike Summerbee, Ernie Hunt, Bobby Woodruff, John Trollope and Don Rogers. I too was now benefiting from Head's continued belief in recruiting young players.

At first I found being away from home daunting. Living in digs with a family called the Radways, I was suddenly separated from family, friends and everything that was familiar. The inevitable homesickness and loneliness descended on me very quickly. All the same, I tried to make the best of what the town had to offer. One evening, in 1964, I saw an advert for a young Irish singer who was performing in a barn outside the town. His name was Luke Kelly. I went along and enjoyed his singing and banjo-playing immensely. Afterwards, I introduced myself as a fellow Dub. Luke and I clicked straight away. It was the start of a long friendship and one that became a memorable part of my life. At this time Luke was on a two-year break from The Dubliners and touring Britain as a solo artist. Later, when I was playing for the Republic of Ireland football team, under John Giles, in the early 1970s, Luke, before ill-health restricted him, would often travel with the team. John, a close friend of Luke's, began this tradition. With his music, Luke led the celebrations or raised our spirits, depending on the result of the particular match.

I was enjoying playing for Swindon. This was English football. It was the place you wanted to be to test yourself. The learning curve, however, was steep. In my debut for the Swindon reserves, I got a special welcome to the professional game – old-style. Because I was a right-winger, I lined up against Queens Park Rangers' left back, Ray Brady. Ray, also a Dub and an older brother of Liam's, the latter of whom would go on to become one of Ireland's greatest ever players, laid on the fellow-Irishman act thick. With a look of sincere fatherliness, he came to me before the game. 'Listen, son, I know it's your first game and you could do with a dig-out, so here's what we'll do. When you get the ball for the first time, if you feign to go on the inside, I'll buy the dummy, and then I'll let you go past me on the outside.'

Grand job, I thought, and what a great tip! I was ready. The moment came. Just as we agreed, I went inside, then out and … *bang*. Ray sent me flying into the air with a crunching tackle. Still lying on the turf, I looked up, dazed, to see him glowering over me and shouting: 'Let that be your first fucking lesson in football.' I took the hint: don't trust anyone.

At Swindon, I befriended a young Mike Summerbee. Mike, an old-fashioned, direct winger, would go on to play for Manchester City in the First Division and earn eight caps for England. He was in the Swindon first team at this point, while I was in the reserves. We enjoyed a good-natured competitiveness and Mike was always one for a challenge. He came up with the idea that we would have a race on foot, followed by me getting on my Honda 50 motorbike and Mike into his car. The chosen route would be from Swindon's County Ground to the town hall. I was well up for the contest. Mike was sure he'd win. We met at the agreed time in front of some of the other lads and went for it. After the foot race, we were more or less neck and neck. Then came the next leg. I jumped onto my bike, but it would not start. I knew what was happening, though. I looked down to see the spark plug hanging out. This was Mike's handiwork, for sure. He thought that his bit of friendly sabotage would have this Paddy kicking the pedal for eternity while he disappeared into the distance. I reattached the spark plug and took off down the town's alleyways, while Mike continued down the nearby main road. I knew the Swindon back streets and was able to cover the distance far quicker than Mike. I won easily. For once, Paddy had got the upper hand.

Even though I was now playing professional football in England, I also continued to play Gaelic football. During the summer of 1964, I came home whenever I could to represent Scoil Uí Chonaill in the Dublin Under-21 County Club Championship. Although I was only an average Gaelic football player, I was good at free-taking and was able to knock the ball over the bar from most angles. We won that year's championship but, with the infamous Rule 27, or 'the Ban', still very much in force, I, a player of 'foreign games', was denied a medal. I attended the medal ceremony with the other players, fully expecting my honour. However, I was simply told by a partisan club president, 'there is no medal for you.' After that, although I retained my interest in the game, I gave up playing Gaelic football and focused on football alone.

My time in England would prove frustratingly brief. At the end of the 1964/65 season, Swindon Town was relegated to the Third Division and the club hierarchy made the decision to sack the long-serving Bert Head and drop the majority of the young players from the wages bill. I was being let go, and with my career only barely begun! When I left, I had not yet played for the Swindon first team. Any appearances that I made were restricted to the reserves. I was a young player in the development phase; unfortunately, that development was abruptly cut short.

When I came back to Dublin in 1965, I hit a low point. I had tasted the excitement of being a pro, but after only a year it was all over and here I was, back at square one, looking for work again, as if nothing had changed. It was not easy to find myself kicking stones around Dublin with only a few bob in my back pocket. Although it was the club's relegation that had sealed my fate at Swindon and not necessarily my own form, I did not take failure well. Being told that I wasn't good enough, no matter what the circumstances, was a huge blow.

I first tried a job as a Fiat car salesman with a company called Sweeney & Forte on Dublin's northside. That lasted about a year. Then I became a trainee accountant at the Wavin pipe company. It was all a bit aimless. I was trying out different things but really not knowing where I was going.

The one thing I was sure of at this time was my love of music. In mid-1960s' Dublin the so-called 'Ballad Boom' was in full swing and my future brother-in-law, John Lawless, and some friends had formed a traditional music band called The Irish Rovers. They needed a manager. I got the job but only because I had a car (a creaky, second-hand Fiat 1100 that had seen better days) to ferry around the band members, and a phone, at work in Sweeney & Forte, to book gigs for them. With the five of us (and an array of instruments) shoehorned into my tiny Fiat, we hit the burgeoning music scene. At work, whenever I had a spare minute, I would ring around to hotels and pubs to get bookings and then, in the evening, if we had secured one, we would head out to play. With live music in demand and so many venues seeking new talent, it wasn't too difficult to get a gig. For me, it was a joy to be immersed in this world. I was, after all, the frustrated banjo player who was determined, one way or another, to be involved with music. It was during these years, between 1966 and 1968, that I first met the Wolfe Tones, the Dubliners, the Dublin City Ramblers, the Fureys, Paddy Reilly and many other great folk bands and musicians. I have been lucky enough to enjoy lifelong relationships with many of these great names of Irish folk music.

Certain music venues were good to us and gave us a regular slot on the schedule. The Old Shieling Hotel on the Howth Road in Raheny was, for a long time, one such venue. The relationship, however, would ultimately turn sour. The owner of the hotel was not happy with the salty language of the band members. She made it clear to me that if they cursed once more on stage, it would be the last time we performed in The Old Shieling. One member, Seán Óg McKenna, brother of the Dubliners' Barney McKenna, was a particularly bad offender. Although I could understand the lads' situation – they were relaxing, playing some tunes, having a few pints – I had to insist that the bad language stop. The warning was especially directed at Seán Óg. 'Yeah, of course, Eoin, of course. Nothing to worry about, I'll be on my best behaviour.' Five minutes in and one of Seán Óg's banjo strings snaps in front of a full house: 'Ah, for fuck's sake, the stupid fucking string!' That was the end of us and The Old Shieling.

Although they were carefree times, every now and then the outside world would intrude on our innocence. One night, in March 1966, when we were driving back from a gig, on Dorset Street, we heard an extraordinary bang. Nelson's Pillar on O'Connell Street had just been blown to pieces by the IRA.

Even though I had to continue to hold down a day job to pay the bills, I was still trying to keep my football career alive. Dundalk, then playing in the League of Ireland's First Division, signed me in August 1965. A spate of injuries, however, would ensure that it was not a fruitful venture. Owing to a recurring hamstring tear, I could not build any momentum and so made only a limited number of appearances for the club. Although Dundalk gave me a chance to revive my career, because of the injuries it never worked out. The result was that, once new manager Alan Fox took over in the summer of 1966, I was deemed surplus to requirements at Oriel Park. I had played sixteen times for Dundalk and scored four goals.

Whatever about my own ill fortune at the County Louth club, I was lucky enough to play alongside the late Jimmy Hasty, the so-called 'one-armed wonder'. Hasty managed to be a prolific goal scorer despite having, as his nickname suggests, only one arm. He died tragically in Belfast in 1974 when he became an innocent victim of the Troubles, murdered by Loyalist paramilitaries while walking to work one morning.

I was quickly picked up by Shelbourne that August. Shelbourne, throughout the 1960s, was a strong force in the League of Ireland, while in European football it had faced sides like Barcelona and Atlético Madrid. I was more than happy with the move.

Yet the Shelbourne stint would prove to be no better than my time at Dundalk and I did not exactly get off to a good start with the club's Scottish manager, Gibby McKenzie. At this point I was working in the Smithfield Market in Dublin with a fruit and vegetable supplier, Torney Bros. and McCann. Because I had to start my shifts early in the morning, I decided to make use of being up and about at that time. Before work, I began going for jogs in the Phoenix Park. One morning, after my run, I was driving back down through Phibsboro towards the market when McKenzie crossed the street right in front of my car. I saluted him and thought nothing more of it until that night at training when it suddenly became an issue. 'Where were you last night?' Gibby started accusingly. 'I saw you coming down Phibsboro looking an awful mess this morning. You were on the lash all night, weren't you?'

I was taken aback. It took me a few seconds to figure this one out. It then dawned on me: I had jumped into my car that morning, sweating and scruffy-looking after my run. Evidently Gibby had a different take: he interpreted my dishevelled state as the telltale sign of someone who was

Me, on the right, in action for Drumcondra against Shelbourne in 1967. My two seasons at Drumcondra saw me shifting to centre half. My performances for the League of Ireland club ultimately led to me being signed by Portsmouth in October 1968. (Independent Newspapers)

wearing the effects of an all-night bender. Thinking that I might turn this situation to my advantage and impress him with my dedication, I tried to explain that I had actually been doing extra fitness work in my spare time, and that I followed this same demanding routine most mornings. 'Are you having a laugh?' he scoffed and walked off, thoroughly convinced of my guilt.

After making only three appearances for the Shelbourne first team, I moved on to Drumcondra FC. Drums was my local club and, at that time, a League of Ireland side. It was with Drums that the positional switch was made that was to define the course of my career, and the chief reason why I ultimately got back into English football. At the start of the 1966/67

With the legendary Bobby Charlton (*left*) at a post-match dinner in 1968.

season, our manager, Royden Prole, had a defensive crisis at centre half. His regular option, Brendan Masterson, was injured and so he called me aside in training for a chat. There was a pre-season tournament coming up, called the President's Cup, and he said, 'Look, we're going to try you at centre half in this tournament and we'll see how you get on.' I was certainly surprised but willing to give it a try. Up to that point, in all my time as a footballer, I had never played as, nor ever even considered myself to be, a defender. I had always been an attacking player, usually a right-winger. The manager's reasoning was simple: I was tall. In the preceding year or so I had shot up from 5 feet 9 inches to over 6 feet. I could see his point, even if I remained sceptical.

What began as a stop-gap measure soon became permanent, however. I took to the position quickly. Stationed at the back, I could suddenly see the whole game being played in front of me and found myself able to read it very well. Compared to playing out wide, where my view of the game was generally limited, centre half almost seemed easy – as a converted attacker, stepping out from the back with the ball came naturally to me.

In the 1966/67 and 1967/68 seasons I went on to play forty-three games for Drumcondra as a defender. I had the honour of playing alongside the legendary Bunny Fullam. Fullam, a hard-as-nails full back and then in the twilight of his long career, had won four League of Ireland titles and turned down numerous offers from English professional clubs. He was an ardent believer in his own abilities and, in general, chronically unimpressed with big-name players. No matter who you mentioned, invariably he had a ready-made withering assessment on hand. 'What about Pelé, Bunny?' 'Pelé!' he would answer. 'Don't get me started on Pelé. Fucking useless. I'd have him in me pocket.'

Bunny was a character all right and, as everyone knew, if he offered you a lift anywhere and you wanted to get to your destination in anything like reasonable time, you turned it down. 'Take the bus. Take the bus,' was the hard-earned advice of those who had made the mistake of innocently sitting into Bunny's passenger seat. Bunny would say: 'Hop in, I'm going your way,' but, of course, he wasn't. He was usually going anywhere but, and then there were the unscheduled stops. 'Hang on a minute there now, will you? I just have to pop in here for a few minutes to see this guy.' Or: 'I've a thing in the back there and I need to deliver it to a fella. Won't be a jiffy – you'll be grand, won't you? Yeah. Good man.'

A highlight of my time at Drums was a pre-season game that we played against Manchester United on 4 August 1968 at a packed Dalymount Park. United – with their greats such as George Best and Bobby Charlton on show – were the newly crowned European champions and this was their first match after that famous victory over Benfica at Wembley. With Matt Busby's agreement, the game was arranged as a testimonial for Drumcondra player John Whelan, brother of the late Liam, one of the legendary Busby Babes who had died in the Munich air disaster in 1958. As a mark of respect, the Manchester United players wore an all-green

Me, diving to block the ball, in action for Drumcondra in a friendly against Manchester United at Dalymount Park on 4 August 1968. George Best wears the No. 7 shirt. I was not the first, and certainly not the last defender, to be left on their backside by George.

kit. I was a young, aspiring League of Ireland player. To face such brilliant opposition was thrilling. Best, in particular, was exceptional. Throughout my entire playing career I would never again play against anyone with such natural ability and flair. Despite the gap in quality between ourselves and Manchester United, we kept the score respectable and narrowly lost 2-1.

2

'Hand, you think you're Georgie Best'

Portsmouth and International Playing Career: 1968–1979

In the early stages of the 1968/69 season I got the breakthrough that would take me back to English professional football. It was in my new centre-half position that Portsmouth noticed me in September 1968, playing for a League of Ireland selection against our Scottish counterparts.

Portsmouth manager George Smith offered Drumcondra £7,500 for my signature the next month. Although, in the context of Irish football, it was already a dream come true for me to line up for my local club Drumcondra (as a child I had been carried over the turnstiles to watch them perform at a packed Tolka Park), getting another break in English professional football was obviously hard to ignore. Still, the decision was not a straightforward one.

I had a dilemma. I had applied for what I believed was a good job in Dublin and now I had to weigh up the gamble of returning to the English game, with all its risks, versus making a steady living in Ireland. The position was as a trainee cameraman at RTÉ. I saw the role being advertised in a local newspaper. After applying, to my surprise, I was called for an interview. I never actually thought that I would get the gig but was going to give it my best shot. I hastily completed a few weeks' crash course on how to operate a camera. I was also aided by having an inside man in RTÉ, who tipped me off on all the likely questions they would ask at the interview. Once the day came, I confidently asserted that I knew plenty about cameras and had abundant experience to boot. I got the job! But it was not enough to turn my head. I had unfinished work in England: I was going to Portsmouth to play in England's Second Division.

Although I knew that I wanted to sign for Portsmouth, I subsequently discovered that I knew very little about the business of football. Brimful of enthusiasm, I signed for the club but without asking for any signing-on fee. No one told me that I should be looking for such a fee, so I never thought to ask. I had no adviser or agent – or a father – who might steer me in worldly affairs. Once I got to Portsmouth, players began to ask me what kind of a signing-on fee had I managed to wangle from the club (a favourite topic of professional footballers). When I said that there was none, they couldn't believe it.

At twenty-two years of age I was returning to English professional football – old by the standards of most players. Luckily, however, I did not have to wait long to make my debut. Within weeks I was in the first team and, happily, I stayed there. My debut came on 9 November 1968 against Fulham at Craven Cottage. I was marking the young, pacy forward Vic Halom. In the second half a dangerous ball was played in behind me. The race was on between Halom and me. Although he had a head start, I made it to the ball first and cleared. In isolation, it might have seemed like a minor incident, but for me, in my first game for the club, it represented a huge confidence boost. I knew then I would be all right.

Coming to the end of the 1968/69 season, I could look back on a successful beginning to my Portsmouth career. I was feeling very good about myself, and it was about to get a whole lot better. On 3 May 1969 I took a call from Charlie Hurley, the then player-coach and captain of the Republic of Ireland national team. Charlie was not exactly the manager because, as is well known, at that point in Irish football history there was no such position. Instead, a cabal of Football Association of Ireland (FAI) officials, known as 'the Big Five', selected the squad and picked the team. It was management by committee. Charlie, like all who went before him, was simply handed a team and told to go and get a result. With local, factional interests rife in the committee, Hurley often found himself having to field one of the committee's own men, usually an inexperienced League of Ireland player plying his trade in their neck of the woods.

The next day I joined up with the squad in Dublin for a home match against Czechoslovakia, to be played at Dalymount Park. It was a qualifying match for the 1970 World Cup. I was the wide-eyed greenhorn suddenly finding himself surrounded by top players like John Giles, Shay Brennan and Charlie Hurley himself. I was nervous and, and having had only a day to acclimatise to the idea of turning out for Ireland, very much feeling that I was in at the deep end. There was precious little time for fretting, however. The squad received me as a new player without any great fuss and everyone got down to the business of focusing on the game.

I began the match as a substitute but, after forty minutes, with Ireland one up, courtesy of an Eamonn Rogers goal, centre forward Mick Leech went down injured. Charlie ran over to me on the sideline and said. 'Get yourself ready, Eoin, you're going on up front.' 'Up front?' I exclaimed. 'But I've never played as a centre forward in my entire life. I'm a centre half.' Charlie was unmoved. 'Ah, you'll be grand, Eoin. Don't worry. Run around up there and make yourself busy.'

I was not sure at all how this was going to pan out but, considering that I was on the cusp of being capped for my country, I wasn't going to protest too much. I joined Ray Treacy as a stand-in striker and did my best for the rest of the match to at least give the Czechoslovakian defence something to worry about. We ultimately lost the game 2-1.

When I returned to Portsmouth for pre-season training in the summer of 1969, it was a new Eoin Hand who greeted his teammates. I was chuffed with myself. There were not too many international footballers in the Second Division but I was one of them.

George Smith, however, was not buying what I was selling. He was a demanding manager; anyone who wanted to be in his team knew that they would have to sweat blood for the cause. A former sergeant-major in the British army, Smith did not tolerate any nonsense. I began training with a swagger in my step and, evidently, it was all too apparent. Feeling every bit the international player, I began showboating with a few flicks and tricks. Smith was having none of it and clipped the wings of this budding maestro in quick time. Calling an abrupt halt to training, he roared: 'Hand, you think you're Georgie Best. You will never be a skilful player so long as you have a hole in your backside.'

Smith's military background inspired some eccentric training routines. In one particular season, he got it into his head that we were not hard

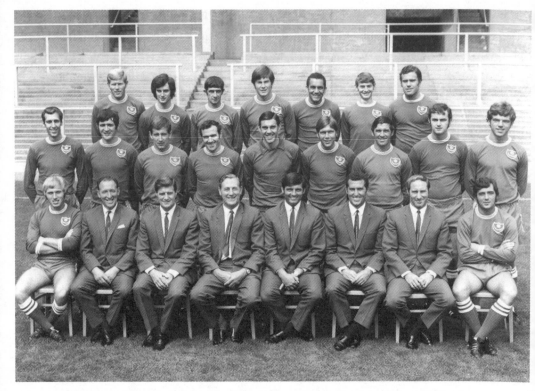

With my Portsmouth teammates in 1969 (I am second from left, middle row). My time at Portsmouth would represent the vast majority of my club playing career. I played with the then Second Division club from 1968 to 1976 and again from 1977 to 1979. In the back row, first left, is Ray Pointer. Ray, a striker, would be capped three times for England. In the front row, fourth from left, is Jimmy Dickinson. Jimmy, then the club secretary, was a celebrated former England international and Portsmouth player. (Angus MacNee, *The News,* Portsmouth)

enough, so, to deliver some much-needed toughening up, he had a boxing ring built in the club's gym. You might have thought that there was a subtler reason for the exercise – perhaps a chance for us to develop our footwork as we danced around the ring – but there wasn't. Smith simply believed that twenty-odd footballers pounding each other around on a weekly basis would soon sort the wimps from the hard men.

Smith pushed it too far, though. He became convinced that our defender George Ley was bone lazy and badly in need of a good shake-up. This was nothing that a few bracing rounds in the ring couldn't solve, or so he thought. He ordered Ley to join him in the ring for a fight, with the squad looking on. 'Now, listen to me, Ley. I want you to hit me as hard as you can. You are not to hold back. Now, all the rest of you, watch this.' Smith had no idea who he was inviting to take a swing at him in such a cavalier manner. Ley, unbeknownst to Smith, was an accomplished amateur boxer. The result was not pretty. Smith duly got hammered around the ring for his troubles, and with the whole squad as attentive and amused witnesses.

For all his gruffness, Smith could be surprisingly tender when the moment called for it. When he learned that I was engaged to be married, he took me aside in training one day, and with a paternal arm around me, said, 'Eoin, you're getting married, so remember this one thing: you are not giving up your freedom; you are sharing it.' That close season, I married Pat Lawless in 1969 and two years later our first son, Gary, was born. I first met Pat, who was from Whitehall in north Dublin, at a dance in the Olympic ballroom in Dublin in 1966. We had become engaged in 1968.

Although, as a player, you generally felt a strong togetherness with your teammates, the relationship was complex because your colleagues were the ones threatening to put you out of the team. At least with the opposition, the situation was straightforward: you knew where you stood with them: they were your adversaries and you had a ball to argue over. When the ninety minutes were done, the fair fight was over and there was nothing more to it. With your teammates, however, things were much more ambiguous: they were your pals, sure, but they were pals with whom you were effectively competing. This was always something difficult to come to terms with, and in the 1960s and 1970s, when the money was average and your contractual situation frequently uncertain, whether you found yourself in or out of the team made a big difference to your pay packet.

Financially, it does not matter a jot to modern professionals in the top two divisions: win, lose or draw; sit on the bench all season; star in the team; go out on loan; whatever – they still have a contract guaranteeing that they are paid handsomely week in, week out. This luxury was not there in my playing days. My basic salary would have been about £50 a week. But, when I was in the team, that figure would rise to maybe £60; and then the win bonus, if it applied, could take you up to £80. That's a big difference, compared to the guy who spends his Saturday afternoon warming the bench, and it created a lot of internal rivalry.

This uncertainty also turned getting injured into a much dicier affair, especially the longer-term lay-offs. Although my primary concern was always to get back playing football, I had a serious worry about my financial future. While you were laid up, twiddling your thumbs in boredom, some other guy – as fit as a fiddle – was running around the pitch in *your* place. As soon as I ended up on the treatment table and saw my replacement doing well, the fears (irrational or not) flooded in. You just felt helpless. I always immediately thought: 'God, this guy is going to take my place for good. I'm not getting back into the team.' Ultimately, if you were talented enough, you would get back in, and I generally did, but the sense of occupational insecurity was never truly banished.

Being an Irishman in England was not always the easiest of assignments in the 1970s. The political turmoil of the times was never far away – even on the football pitch. With the IRA pursuing a steady bombing campaign on British soil, from 1974 onwards you were all too conscious of your nationality. Soon after the Birmingham pub bombings in November 1974, I remember one scary game against Aston Villa, played in Birmingham. In the days before the match, the West Midlands Police had made official contact with Portsmouth to advise the club to take precautions because, being Irish, I could be a target at Villa Park. I did not know whether they were acting on concrete information or not, but I was very worried. While staying in Birmingham the night before the match, the options were churning over in my mind. Should I play? Should I pull out? Is the risk all that great? Eventually I steeled myself: 'I am going to play.'

I was not quite as brave the next day, however, when, before kick-off, the referee signalled a minute's silence for the victims of the city's recent bombings. It was only sixty seconds but it felt like an hour. Standing there, in the middle of the pitch, a sitting duck, I was thinking, 'Bloody hell, is some anti-Irish nutter going to take a pot shot at me?' I was honestly afraid that the air might crackle with a rifle shot at any moment. I was being a bit melodramatic but, still, someone from that large crowd could have sought retribution and I would have been the convenient Irishman, on hand, to take the brunt.

More so than any fear, though, my pervasive feeling during those years was just one of embarrassment. And, although as a footballer I mostly lived in a bubble, the situation would sometimes intrude on my comfortable world: you were working in an English environment; you were earning your money in the United Kingdom; you were privileged to be part of a professional football set-up; fans admired your ability as a player; and then, suddenly, certain of your compatriots had killed some of their friends. That was not easy.

Portsmouth v Arsenal, FA Cup tie 1971 at Fratton Park. The result was 1-1 in front of a crowd of 45,000. (*L–r*): John Milkins (goalkeeper), me, George Ley, George Armstrong (Arsenal), Colin Blant and Jon Sammels (Arsenal). (*The News*, Portsmouth)

Playing for Portsmouth, *c.*1972.

Being Irish also sometimes made you the target of cheap insults from the opposition. No provocation was too low for some players, especially if they felt they might get a rise out of you. The worst abuse that I experienced was when a Hull City player spat in my face and called me an 'Irish c**t'. The old Second Division was no place for shrinking violets.

We did things differently in the 1960s and 1970s. Although we always trained hard and were generally fit, by today's standards some aspects of our match preparation would seem alien, to say the least. Drinking was deeply entrenched in the weekly routines of footballers, with a fairly crude 'work hard, play hard' philosophy buttressing it all. There was no education on the damage that alcohol can do to your body and no analysis of its effects on a professional footballer's performance. It was part and parcel of your life – the glue that held together a sense of team spirit. At Portsmouth, the club even arranged weeknight darts sessions in various pubs around the city. They were seen as community nights where the players and fans could mingle freely and enjoy a few pints. It's not that we were getting drunk every night – it was more a consistent pattern of frequent social drinking – but it all added up.

The psychology was upside down. The club always held a particularly brutal day of training on a Wednesday, called 'stir the blood', because they knew that we would have been out drinking for a few nights before. They would say: 'Right. We are going to really knock the shit out of you today.' And they always did, except that it had the reverse effect on our behaviour. With our imagined boozing credit squirrelled away in the bank, we would be drinking even more heavily in the days leading up to the dreaded Wednesday session. You abused your body for three or four nights in the false belief that hard running would somehow magically make everything all right again.

Again, on match day, even in the dressing room, alcohol played its part. There was always a bottle of whiskey laid out on a table and each player was encouraged to take an 'invigorating' swig just before charging out for battle. If there was any scientific thinking behind this, it was presumably that the shock of downing the whiskey would stoke the fire in your belly. And this was not just a recipe cooked up at Fratton Park; Portsmouth was simply following common practice.

Smoking was another oddity that was simply accepted as part of many players' lives. It was common at half-time, for example, for any smokers to light up during the manager's team talk. The five or six smokers would always go to the shower area for a few precious, restorative drags on a cigarette. Then it was back out to hear what the boss had to say.

I, like many of the players in those days, had my little superstitions about preparing for each match. One pre-match routine that I slavishly observed involved getting the newspaper on the Saturday morning and then feverishly trying to complete the crossword before kick-off. I had it in my head that I could play well only if I succeeded in finishing the crossword. Like most superstitions, it had an anxious quality to it and probably served only to work me up, more than anything else.

Managers in earlier decades were also sometimes a different breed. John Mortimore, Portsmouth manager for the 1973/74 season, was a case in point. Mortimore was from a bygone era: flawlessly polite, never less than gentlemanly and possessed of an outrageously posh accent. In the rough-hewn world of professional football, Mortimore's stiff bearing stood out and could often lead to unintentional hilarity. One run-in I had with him proved the point. We were playing Brighton and Hove Albion and the player I was marking gave me a deliberate, sneaky kick in the balls while I was lying on the ground. I was in agony and, when I finally made it to my feet, I was furious. Like a man possessed, I spent the rest of the game chasing this guy around, like the hound after the hare, determined to get my revenge. We lost the game and, in the dressing room afterwards, Mortimore was none too pleased with my shenanigans. 'What were you doing out there chasing that player around? Please explain yourself.' I was not in the mood for debates. 'How would *you* like a kick in the balls?' I retorted. Mortimore, clearly not spotting the rhetorical question, was appalled. 'How dare you threaten to do such a thing to me? I'll see you in my office tomorrow.' He thundered out, with peals of laughter erupting from the players in his wake.

The next day, I showed up at Mortimore's office intent on dispelling the confusion. I told him that it was all a mistake and that he had taken up my message the wrong way. A Brighton and Hove Albion player had kicked me in the balls, I explained. 'What?' he said, with a genuinely startled tone, and in his typically posh delivery, asked: 'You mean to say that he kicked you in the testicles?'

In the dressing room, just before we were ready to go out onto the pitch, Mortimore was, again, formal to an almost bizarre degree. Like a public school teacher overseeing his young charges, he would usually shout out:

'OK, boys, does anyone need to use the toilet now before we go out and play?'

Mortimore was out of touch with footballers' mentality; sometimes it was hard to believe how naive he could be. In the winter of 1974, the team was staying overnight in a hotel in the north of England. Myself and my room-mate decided to have a couple of cans of beer. It was not unusual for players from that era to have a beer the night before a game. There were no fixed rules, but, generally, a manager didn't mind, provided no one abused it. Not long after we had begun to relax with our beer, there was a knock at the door. I opened it to find a stern-looking Mortimore standing in front of me. He noticed the beer cans – we were not trying to hide them. 'How long has this been going on?' he wanted to know. I cheekily answered back: 'A few years, Boss.' The next day we played well and won the game.

Despite being able to regularly attract large crowds for home matches, Pompey was never really a glamorous destination for players. The club suffered throughout the late 1960s and early 1970s from a chronic lack of investment and an almost complete absence of any youth policy. It was usually run with one eye over its shoulder on the bank manager. In the 1973/74 season (the club's seventy-fifth season), however, serious investment was made in the squad. The new chairman, John Deacon, bankrolled the biggest spending spree in the club's history. Portsmouth spent a combined £200,000 on Ron Davies, the veteran Southampton and Wales international centre forward, Peter Marinello, Arsenal's talented if troubled Scottish winger, and the promising Bristol Rovers and Wales under-23 full-back, Phil Roberts. Public interest was huge, and suddenly Portsmouth, a mid-table Second Division club, was getting gates of over 20,000. In early December, Deacon loosened the purse strings again and spent a further £200,000 on a new centre-half pairing: Paul Went arrived from Fulham and Malcolm Manley was brought in from Leicester City. With these two signings directly competing with me for a place in defence, now, for the first time in five seasons, I found my opportunities at centre half limited, and by December, with the club again in financial peril, I, along with many others, was transfer-listed. Thankfully, soon after Christmas, I managed to re-establish myself and get back in the manager's plans. I was taken off the transfer list and regained my place in the team, this time at left back.

Without a doubt, Marinello, the so-called 'George Best of the south', was the marquee signing. Unfortunately, despite his talent, Marinello's career was already on the downward slide at this point, having failed to set the north London club alight in his three years there. It was clear that Peter had genuine skill and natural dribbling abilities. The only problem with him was that, sometimes, he did not know when to look up and take the best option. He was the kind of player, you felt, who would nearly take on the linesman.

Although the new John Deacon line-up captured the public's imagination, it did not capture too many points. By the end of the season, we finished, once again, in our habitual comfort zone: towards the foot of the table in fifteenth place.

In 1973 I began what would become a regular summer routine. I started guesting for South African club sides in the English close season. During my first stint I played for the Port Elizabeth-based club, P. E. City and, in subsequent summers, for Durban Celtic, and the Johannesburg club Lusitano. The arrangement suited Portsmouth since they didn't have to pay my wages for the time I spent in South Africa. It was through one of these games that I got to know George Best in 1974. Best, whom I had first met in 1968, was at this stage guesting for Jewish Guild in Johannesburg.

I had seen the trappings of football stardom up close before but George was something else. He lit up every room he walked into and, of course, everyone wanted a piece of him, especially the ladies. When he was staying at his hotel room in Johannesburg, they constantly showed up in the lobby begging the receptionist to let them meet him. George, safe in his citadel on the top floor, came up with a solution to manage the numbers. For every lady who enquired, the porter was asked to rate their looks out of ten and tell George. If it was an eight or a nine, George would be informed.

George, despite all the controversy surrounding his unorthodox lifestyle, was a remarkable person. Even though he lived under the weight of incessant media and public attention, he maintained incredible composure. I saw at first hand the challenges he faced on an almost daily basis. On another occasion, I was having a quiet drink with him and Shay Brennan in a Manchester hotel in 1975 when a group of Manchester City fans steamed in. They were rowdy and clearly had a few drinks on board. Once they spotted us, they made a beeline for George. 'Hey you, you Irish bastard,' one of them bellowed. To my amazement, George did not stir. He was a picture of serenity. I, however, could not tolerate the abuse. I stood up to get stuck in but George wouldn't have it. He just motioned me to sit back down. With their provocations falling flat in the face of an unflappable Best, the aggressors gradually backed off. I was taken aback by the nastiness of the incident and I asked George if this happened to him regularly. 'Ay, sure,' he said, with a dismissive wave of his arm. It was depressing. He was so inured to such abuse that it had become a meaningless commonplace in his life. Fame haunted him.

It was also through the South Africa connection that I became acquainted with Bobby Charlton in 1976. Bobby travelled to make three guest appearances for Arcadia Shepherds, a Pretoria-based club I was now playing for. Because I was the club captain, I picked Bobby up at the airport. The first stop was a convention centre where a huge welcoming ceremony had been laid on for him. A large crowd was packed into the room and a suitably boisterous MC had been booked to drum up an atmosphere. Bobby may have been a bona fide star but not everyone in the room had been swotting up on their footballers. Bobby and I took our seats as the host began his big introduction. 'Ladies and gentlemen, will you please give a huge round of applause for the legend, the one, the only [Charlton starts to get up], the brilliant, the incomparable, the World-Cup-winning hero … Bobbyyyyyyyy MOORE'. Charlton sits down again awkwardly, waiting for the correction. A dig in the ribs to the MC: 'Bobbyyyyyyyy CHARLTON.' Bobby finally took to the stage and, to his credit, laughed it off.

By the mid-1970s, my time with Portsmouth was not going well. In September 1974, the former Liverpool and Scotland centre forward Ian St John became our new manager, replacing John Mortimore. Although St John was unveiled as a messiah figure who would cure all ills, it was quickly obvious to most of us that he was struggling. He had been a major player, of course, and we respected that, but football management brings its own set of challenges. St John's management experience before coming to Fratton Park was not extensive: in his only season in management, in 1973/74, he achieved a ninth-place finish with Motherwell in Scotland's First Division.

Our first season under St John was yet another poor one. We crashed out of the FA Cup in the third round, losing 3-1 to Notts County, and barely escaped relegation with a seventeenth-place finish.

St John would let his assistant, Billy Hunter, do most of the work from Monday to Thursday and then, on a Friday the Scot would appear at the training ground and try to motivate us for the next day's game. It would often be something like: 'Hey, this lot we're playing tomorrow, we're better

With George Best in 1987 before playing alongside each other in a charity match. I first met George in 1968 and got to know him better in 1974, when both of us were guesting for clubs in South Africa. (Sporstfile)

than them.' Although the Portsmouth job was not an easy one, and, to be fair to St John, he had no money to spend on new players, the general opinion was that he was trading on the fame of his playing days.

In the 1975/76 season my relationship with St John unravelled rapidly. In training, he had bizarre instructions for me. He insisted that, for set pieces, I should defend by standing *in front* of my man. This was contrary to even the most basic principles of defending. Any defender, whether amateur or professional, will tell you that your starting position should always allow you to see man and ball. If you cannot, your positioning is bad. It's that simple. I had to object. 'That's fine but is someone going to mark him behind me?' 'No', was St John's curt response. 'Do as you're told,' he insisted.

St John's shaky logic was going to get a trial run sooner than he thought. When we played Fulham in our next match, on 1 November 1975, the third corner kick we attempted to defend was a mess. I *did* do as I was told and, despite deep reservations, took up my position in front of my man. Sure enough the corner flew in, sailed over my head, and was hammered home by the Fulham midfielder Alan Slough – the man I was supposedly 'marking'. At half-time, the simmering tensions erupted. St John read me the riot act in front of the whole team and accused me of letting my man score. I defended myself and a very nasty row broke out. I knew that was the end of my time at Fratton Park. Call it career suicide, but I could not take St John's managerial style. In the week after the game, his reaction was to put me running up and down the empty terraces at Fratton Park for a few days after normal training had finished, as a punishment. I then involved the Players' Football Association and the punishment quickly ended.

I needed to get back playing and so I decided to part ways with Portsmouth after seven years, and head for South Africa. I had no future at this club while St John was manager. Ultimately, I believe that St John saw me as a threat because I was, at that point, one of the more experienced players in the squad and the club captain. I do not think he was sorry to see the back of me and the feeling was mutual.

My last game came in an FA Cup third-round replay on 6 January 1976, with Pompey winning 1-0 away to Birmingham City.

Portsmouth undoubtedly represented the key part of my career and it was here that I also gained all my twenty international caps. After making my debut in May 1969, I had to wait another year before receiving a second cap.

By this stage, Ireland had a new man at the helm: Mick Meagan. Mick, who had mainly played with Everton and Huddersfield, was also a retired Republic of Ireland international, having received seventeen caps. He was the first man to actually manage Ireland, as opposed to merely coaching the players. In 1969, before his appointment, the FAI, responding to a player revolt led by John Giles, Eamon Dunphy, Frank O'Neill, Tony Dunne and

Alan Kelly, finally moved to end the reign of the controversial Big Five. From now on, the Ireland manager would have full powers, the same enjoyed by all other international managers.

My second game for Ireland was a friendly match away to Poland on 6 May 1970. I will never forget my first conversation with Mick Meagan and the bizarre way in which I discovered that I was being capped again. He rang me in Portsmouth and, while I was certainly delighted to take a phone call from Meagan, my boyish excitement was replaced with confusion when I heard the casual-sounding voice at the other end of the line. Now Mick was a real gentleman, and one of the major Irish players of the 1960s, but he did not do dramatic. 'I was just wondering if you're doing anything tomorrow, Eoin,' he asked, in an almost throwaway manner. 'If you're free, sure why don't you maybe join up with us?' What did he mean? Had I just been selected to play for my country? Mick's manner was so low-key, you would swear that I was being invited to the Phoenix Park for a Sunday kick-about, and not to join the international squad. 'What – are you saying you want me to play for Ireland, Mick?' I asked. 'Yeah, that's it, Eoin. Why don't you fly out with us?' he said. 'Well, of course I'm free, Mick. I would be absolutely honoured.' The news was not exactly delivered with all the pomp and circumstance of 'Your country needs you', but did I care? I was far too busy being overjoyed.

Although Poland beat us 2-1, I was pleased with my own performance and very happy to be back in my normal position of centre half. Three days later it was followed by what would be my third cap, this time against West Germany in Berlin's Olympic Stadium on 9 May.

Both games were part of the same tour and, for me, making my first few appearances for Ireland, the experience was an eye-opener. I saw at first hand the class distinction that existed between the FAI officials and the players, and the way in which, when it came to travel arrangements, anything was good enough for the footballers. After playing Poland in Poznan, the squad and officials were scheduled to travel by train to Berlin on 8 May. When we gathered at the station there was a hitch. The train was overbooked and there were not enough seats for our full complement. The solution: the players were asked to get into the train's luggage van; and there we remained for the full journey. There did not seem to be any question that any of the large contingent of FAI officials might sacrifice their seats in standard class for players who were going to line up against West Germany twenty-four

Ireland v West Germany in 1970. Shay Brennan is in the dark shirt (*far left*), the referee is restraining Franz Beckenbauer. I am in the No. 4 shirt.

hours later. You could say that we were in third class, except it was far worse. We were just bunked up on top of piles of baggage.

The next day we put in a creditable performance against a world-class West Germany side led by Franz Beckenbauer, but lost 2-1. The Germans were on their way to the 1970 World Cup and eager to put on a show for the 70,000 home fans. Beckenbauer, who was class through and through, and normally a level-headed player, seemed to be a bit too pumped up for the encounter. When he went in uncharacteristically high on Shay Brennan, I lost it, and in the ensuing fracas, ended up punching Beckenbauer in the chest. It was handbags, really, and we were quickly separated with no punishment coming from the referee. Many years later, in late 1997, when Beckenbauer was getting an International Merit award from the FAI, and I was receiving a Special Merit award, we found ourselves sitting next to each other at the same function. I reached over, gave him my hand to shake, and said: 'Franz, I'm the fella who hit you.'

In Berlin, May 1970, with members of the Irish international squad. (*L–r*): Jimmy Conway, Don Givens, John Dempsey, Paddy Mulligan, Terry Conroy and me. The following day we lost 2-1 to a World Cup-bound West Germany side led by Franz Beckenbauer.

Franz Beckenbauer (*left*) and me in 1997 at a FAI awards ceremony. In a stellar career Beckenbauer both captained and managed West Germany to World Cup glory.

In October 1970 Ireland began an unhappy European Championship qualification campaign that would see us finishing bottom of our group on just a single point. When Austria beat us 4-1 at Dalymount Park on 30 May 1971, in the second-last game of the campaign, the FAI brought Mick Meagan's reign to an end. The game was not a pleasant experience for any of us but, for me, it was particularly uncomfortable. Since my teenage years my eyesight had been worsening, and by the time I began playing with Drumcondra in 1966, I was very worried about its impact on my playing career. I was beginning to notice in games that my vision was not perfect. It was then that I got contact lenses to solve the problem. The only thing was that they were not the sleek, comfortable lenses of today. They were a much cruder affair and not that well suited to sport.

Before the Austrian game, when I stupidly tried to reposition one of the lenses, it became dislodged and, try as I might, it would not go back into place. Being young and still fairly new to the Ireland squad, I was too nervous to tell Mick Meagan, so I soldiered on. I had no choice but to play the game with half a pair of eyes. It was torture. I could not judge the flight of the ball properly, so every time I went up for a clearing header, I could only use the back of the Austrian forward's head as a marker. Sometimes, in a desperate attempt to thwart my opponent, I would head the back of his head. At least I was stopping him from heading the ball!

On the whole, Mick Meagan's tenure was not a memorable one: Ireland did not register a single win under his guidance and failed to qualify for the 1970 World Cup and the 1972 European Championship. But was it any wonder? In the 1960s and early 1970s, all Ireland's home games, and even many away games, were played on a Sunday, a day after all the English-based players would have turned out for their club in various far-flung corners of Britain. It was ludicrous. There was no official international break at the time, whereby club football would stop for international fixtures, so it was up to individual associations to suggest a workable solution. The FAI's attempt certainly could not have been called workable.

The result was that English clubs often blocked their Irish players from participating. Usually word might come from, say, Manchester United or Leeds United, that big names like Shay Brennan, Noel Cantwell, Tony Dunne or John Giles had picked up knocks and so could not make the international fixture. Clubs did not want their players playing two games in as many days, and they were right.

All managers know that injuries happen when players have not had an adequate recovery period after a game. The English clubs were not going to risk some of their star players just because the FAI could not figure out how to schedule a game of football sensibly. It is well documented that the Manchester United manager Sir Matt Busby, for example, would simply tell his fully fit Irish players 'You're injured', when they told him at five o'clock on a Saturday afternoon that they intended travelling to Dublin that evening. In my own case, thankfully, Portsmouth never had any problem with me travelling for international matches.

On one occasion, I can recall playing with Portsmouth away to Hull City, in east Yorkshire on a Saturday afternoon, and at the final whistle, about 4.45 p.m., I made a beeline for the dressing room, hastily changed and got a train across England to catch the overnight boat from Liverpool to Dublin. It was a ten-hour journey and, of course, you always hoped that it was not going to be a rough crossing. The next day, I lined up for Ireland. You were in no state for any kind of football match, let alone an international fixture. You were knackered. It was utterly unsustainable and in large part responsible for Ireland's terrible international record at that time.

In the summer of 1971, the then Shamrock Rovers manager and former Ireland international, Liam Tuohy, was appointed national team manager in place of Mick Meagan. Under Liam, with his professionalism and infectious passion for the game, the national side made strides for the first time in almost a decade. Liam was a straight-up Dub with a great sense of humour. We discovered that early on. Since he came from a League of Ireland background, some of the English-based players would have been suspicious of his pedigree. Was he an FAI yes-man, deliberately drawn from the ranks of the Irish domestic game, so that he would be all the more pliable for meddling officials? Not likely. Liam knew well that the players held the FAI in disdain and he made sure to let us know that he was not far behind us on that score. On one occasion, when Liam, a group of players and a handful of FAI delegates were chatting on an away trip, he got the message in under the radar. Discussing the kind of interaction that he had with his bosses, he said: 'I have the perfect relationship with the FAI. They love me and I fucking hate them.' Everyone laughed, including the officials who were present. It was said as a joke, but Liam meant it.

Tuohy's head and heart were in the right place: Liam was both an astute tactician and a natural motivator of men. In his playing days, he had been a tricky left-winger both with Shamrock Rovers and with Newcastle United in the English First Division. It was also under Liam's management that I began to be capped more regularly. He would play me at either centre half or in the midfield anchor role.

It would take Tuohy to finally stand up to the FAI and insist that the nonsensical practice of playing international matches on a Sunday must end. His first match in charge on 10 October 1971, away to Austria, in the last game of the European Championship qualifiers was a joke too far for Liam. After a mass no-show from the English-based players, Liam was forced to travel to Vienna with a squad assembled at the last minute and made up almost entirely of League of Ireland players. He was able to call on only one full-time professional, Chelsea's Paddy Mulligan. Although Paddy never had a bad game in an Ireland shirt, his presence alone could not change the outcome. Ireland was ignominiously thrashed 6-0. The result held no competitive significance for us because Ireland could not qualify either way, but still, for Liam, it summed up everything that was wrong with the Ireland set-up.

He had had enough. For the next campaign, the 1974 World Cup qualifiers, Liam was going to do things right. He went back to the FAI and demanded that international matches be switched to Wednesday nights, thus giving players a chance to recuperate after their weekend club action. The FAI conceded and finally Ireland had a fighting chance in future games, and at least the possibility of fielding its best team.

The English clubs, however, still needed convincing because midweek internationals potentially meant clashes with midweek European club football. For the bigger clubs, like Arsenal, Manchester United and Leeds United, who obviously had ambitions in Europe, this was an issue. To persuade the clubs, Liam spent the next few months travelling to England and he finally managed to get their support for the measure and their word that they would release players when needed.

With sanity prevailing and new structures in place, matters slowly improved on the pitch. When, in Liam's second match, on 4 January 1972, Ireland defeated the West Germany Olympic team 3-0, the country registered its first victory since 22 November 1967. It was not much, but in the context of the barren years that had preceded it, it was a start. Ireland was winning games again. This was followed by away friendly wins against Iran (2-1) and Ecuador (3-2) in a close-season tournament in South America in June 1972. I was not selected for these games but, by October of that year, I was back in the squad and featuring in the first eleven.

For our next campaign, the 1974 World Cup qualifiers, we were drawn in a tough three-team group alongside France and the Soviet Union. Although we defeated the French 2-1 at home on 15 November 1972 and drew 1-1 with them in Paris on 19 May 1973, two defeats to the Soviets saw us missing out on qualification. The victory against France was a historic win and one of the Republic of Ireland's first wins against a major opposition.

On a personal note, it was also my finest performance for Ireland. I made our second goal by chasing a lost cause into the left corner of the French half and crossed for Ray Treacy to score a late winner. I was not normally the creator. Playing in the midfield-holding role, my job had been to get amongst the opposition and to break up French attacks. At one stage, in the interests of reminding the French goalkeeper that he was in a game, I shoulder-charged him to the ground after he had collected the ball. My moment of rashness did not, as I would subsequently discover, go down well in the French camp. For the reverse fixture, in Paris, the pre-match build-up in the French press had focused on how their enforcer Raymond Domenech was going to sort me out. I had no idea whether or not these were Domenech's intentions but I was not taking any chances. Within five minutes I left my calling card. I went in hard on the French midfielder and did not see him again for the rest of the game.

Although, under Liam, Ireland now had seasoned, strong players like Mick Martin, Ray Treacy, Don Givens, Alan Kelly, Terry Conroy, Paddy Mulligan, Joe Kinnear and John Giles, it was not often that new international-class, up-and-coming Irish players surfaced. Every now and then, when the squad got new blood it was a welcome event. With such a small pool of players, we needed all the help we could get. One such player, who joined up with us in May 1973 for our World Cup qualifying match against France in Paris, was Gerry Daly. Gerry, a skilful, goal-scoring midfielder had just signed for Tommy Docherty's Manchester United for £18,000 and was a highly promising player. However, at nineteen years of age, with his new club deal and a first Ireland call-up tucked into his back pocket, Gerry had more than a touch of youthful cockiness about him. He was ripe for the kind of baptism of fire that new initiates usually received in the camp.

In the team hotel in Paris, Ray Treacy, Don Givens, Joe Kinnear and myself laid the trap for the unsuspecting Daly. With the four of us headquartered in Ray's room, Gerry was contacted 'long distance' in his own room. Ray, who was a master at impersonations and generally the joker in the pack, took the lead. With his best Manchester accent in full flow, he told a keyed-up Daly that he was the renowned Manchester journalist David Meek, calling to talk to Gerry about the exciting new chapter in the player's career. First off, there were a few standard questions: Was he enjoying being an international footballer? What did he think of the team's prospects against the French? Then, with Gerry increasingly warming to his sudden moment in the spotlight, Ray upped the ante. 'Do you think that, in time, you might even perhaps be as a big a household name as John Giles?' 'Yes, absolutely,' Gerry enthusiastically responded. 'In fact, I will be even bigger and better than John Giles eventually.' Ray then asked Daly if any practical jokes had been played on him by the rest of the squad. 'No', Gerry replied confidently, he was 'far too sharp' to get caught out like that. With Gerry falling for the set-up, hook, line and sinker, it was decided to take it to the next level.

'Meek' then told Gerry that it would be great if he might be willing to pose for some photos in the hotel lobby in an Ireland jersey, because the top French sports magazine *L'Équipe*, no less, was eager to do a full spread on Ireland's new wonder kid. A French photographer would be in the lobby at 10 p.m. Gerry eagerly assented and the shoot was on. After the call was over, we went downstairs to find an animated Gerry already telling some of the squad about his sensational publicity opportunity. After enquiring about the fee involved, we convinced Gerry that he was not being paid nearly enough for the gig and persuaded him to ask for a much higher amount. He was, after all, 'a top player now' and deserving of far more money than had been offered.

In the meantime, armed with one of our cameras, we managed to persuade one of the hotel's English-speaking waiters to pose as the all-important 'French photographer'. Sure enough, right on cue at 10 p.m., the lift door opened and Gerry walked out into the lobby, resplendent in the full regalia of football boots, shorts and Ireland jersey, to meet the photographer. The camera got to work. Gerry started throwing shapes, and the camera loved him so much that we all chipped in with a few extra suggestions for different poses that he might strike.

Eventually, the photographer shook hands with Gerry and left. That was a wrap but there was still that thorny matter of the renegotiated fee to be thrashed out. Once things had settled down again and with Gerry back in his room, David Meek was on the blower again. 'Did the photographer arrive?' a concerned voice asked. Yes, he had, but Gerry was now not at all sure about the money on offer. He wanted more. Ray, doing a superb job of staying in character, feigned exasperation and reluctantly agreed a new improved fee for Gerry. Again, we assembled downstairs to be greeted by a triumphant Gerry informing us of his new deal with David Meek and of how much he was looking forward to the article.

Gerry, who was rooming with Nottingham Forest's Miah Dennehy, was still talking about his 'big deal' into the late hours of the night, when Miah, unable to get a wink of sleep, snapped and told all. It had been a set-up. Gerry had been conned. There was no deal, no article, nothing.

It was quite some time before the four of us got back into Gerry's good books.

In 1973, after only eleven games in charge, Liam Tuohy resigned from the position of national manager. In his time, as would be the case with John Giles and then myself, the Ireland job was a low-paid, low-glamour, part-time position. Liam had only so much time to give to the job: he was the manager of Shamrock Rovers, the father of a family of six, and an area manager with the HB ice-cream company in Dublin. We were all shocked when the news was announced. Liam had been extremely popular with the players. He loved the game and it was never about personal gain for him. Everything he had was given for the Ireland cause. As a token of gratitude, the players bought him a brand new pram for his youngest child.

Although, under Liam, Ireland failed to qualify for the 1974 World Cup, results improved markedly on previous eras. The hugely impressive 2-1 win over France at Dalymount Park in 1972 and the 1-1 draw away to the French the following May clearly showed the progress we had made.

On 21 October 1973, in a 1-0 home friendly-win over Poland, John Giles began his long reign as Ireland's player-manager. John was the Republic of Ireland's first recognised world-class player and was, at that time, the linchpin of Don Revie's great Leeds United side of the 1970s. John had an aura of confidence, a self-belief that encouraged us to think that we could succeed in international football. When we faced big players, John was not scared; when we faced great sides, he was not intimidated. That rubbed off on us. The past was forgotten; there would be no more notching-up of moral victories. John meant business.

Under John, I would primarily play as a holding midfielder. He was our midfield-playmaker so my job was generally to win back the ball and give it to him. Like all great players, he could receive the ball under any amount of pressure and still make space. It was as if space found him. You did not to have to worry about John looking after himself. Give him the ball and he would do the rest. His range of passing, off both feet, was also exceptional. I count myself lucky to have played alongside John in an Ireland jersey.

If John's style of play was measured, his approach to management was no different. His team talks, in particular, were something that I always found of interest. His dissection of the game – what was going right, what was wrong and why – was invariably spot on and his ability to quickly provide each player with precise tactical instructions no less so. No matter how the wind was blowing and whether we were scintillating or downright dreadful, John was unfailingly clear-headed and dispassionate in his analysis. He saw what needed to be changed and put it right.

John's first campaign was the 1976 European Championships qualifiers, but before that, in May 1974, he took the squad to South America for a close-season tour. We were scheduled to play Brazil in Rio de Janeiro's Maracaná Stadium, Uruguay in Montevideo, and Chile in Santiago.

Facing Brazil, on 5 May, in the legendary Maracaná was undoubtedly the highlight of the tour. The Maracaná, built in 1950 for the World Cup, was, for us, the spiritual home of Brazilian football. The Brazilians were the reigning world champions, having famously won the World Cup in Mexico in 1970 with what many consider to be the greatest team in history. Although the great Pelé had retired from international duty by 1974, there were still a number of players from their World Cup winning side on show, including the winger Jairzinho and the attacking midfielder Rivellino. Rivellino, with his deadly left foot and dazzling dribbling skills, was the major threat.

Before the match, John primed us on what to expect and warned us of the dangers of freezing. He reminded us that whatever about the noise from the huge home crowd, this was still only a game of football. The rules had not changed and we should play our football as we would in any venue. It was an enormous stadium with a world-record capacity of nearly 180,000. Owing to its oval shape, it had the effect of enveloping the players.

The match was Brazil's send-off for the 1974 World Cup in Germany and, understandably, the stadium was in a celebratory mood. When we walked out onto the pitch, with the vast crowd of Brazilian supporters surrounding us, we were like ants in a sea of yellow.

In the pre-match ceremonies we had a large banner unfurled, saying, in Portuguese: 'The Republic of Ireland wishes Brazil well in the World Cup.' It was a public relations master stroke. The crowd, clearly appreciating our thoughtful gesture, applauded when they read the message. We now had the crowd a little on our side: not a bad start when you are about to face the best football team on the planet.

I was assigned to marking Rivellino, a huge challenge for sure, but one I relished. As a professional footballer, you want to pit yourself against the best. It is the only way to find out what you have in you as a player. Giles, whom the Brazilian players held in great esteem, played alongside me in midfield and had a magnificent game. He was both the engine and the engineer behind everything positive we did.

The game would be another milestone for us. We lost 2-1 but put on a fine performance. I mostly managed to contain Rivellino. I stuck to him like an overcoat but I could not stop him from scoring what would prove to be the winning goal. In the fifty-sixth minute, he sold me a dummy that sent me flying in the wrong direction while he went the other way and spectacularly smashed the ball home. At the final whistle, when I swapped jerseys with him, he kept repeating animatedly, pointing at me: 'Loco, loco, loco.' Evidently my man-marking had been a bit too vigorous for Rivellino's liking, and during the game he had been booked for kicking out at me. From a player of his calibre, I'll take that as a compliment.

Off the pitch, news of our stay in Rio had spread beyond football circles. One evening when we were in our hotel, having heard that the Ireland team was in Brazil, an Irish Catholic missionary priest came to see us. He greeted us warmly and wished us luck in our forthcoming games. Then in a more serious atmosphere, the priest blessed the entire squad. Finally, he asked us to gather around. There was one last message: 'Listen, lads. A word of advice: if you are heading out on the town, there is a cracking place down by the sea called the Sunset Bar. The ladies there are wonderful.' We looked at each other, stunned. Moments earlier we were being solemnly absolved of all our worldly sins by God's representative, now the padre was giving us top tips on the Rio nightlife!

The next day we travelled to Montevideo and played Uruguay on 8 May. The Uruguayans beat us 2-0. Again, we put in a good account of ourselves but the Uruguayans were good for their win.

The most controversial game of our tour was on 12 May against Chile in Santiago. The country was in the grip of General Augusto Pinochet's repressive dictatorship and the signs were evident everywhere you looked in the capital city. Soldiers and military vehicles were stationed on most street corners and a strict midnight curfew applied. Although we were relatively safe inside our hotel rooms, we could not fully escape the stark reality of life in the city. Not long after midnight, when we had turned in for the night, gunshots crackled outside our windows on the street below. Joe Kinnear and Eamon Dunphy, who were rooming together, were up quickest and from their window saw soldiers dragging a man's body from a car. After that, no one felt safe.

Our venue for the game was Santiago's ghastly Estadio Nacional where, some eight months earlier, during Pincochet's bloody coup, thousands of opponents of the new regime had been lined up on the pitch and summarily executed at gunpoint. This was a stadium with a dreadful story to tell.

When we got into the dressing rooms, the recent events were all too apparent. The walls were pockmarked with bullet holes and freshly whitewashed to conceal the bloodstains. When we went out onto the pitch, we saw armed soldiers lining the perimeter, their guns pointed towards the crowd for the entire game. In a macabre atmosphere we, at least, ended the football side of our tour on a high with a 2-1 win. I scored our first goal with a header from a corner kick and Jimmy Conway scored the winner.

By 1974, I was beginning to realise that my place in the Ireland first eleven was no longer a given. New players were arriving on the scene to displace me. I found out the hard way during one pre-match meeting. The players were gathered at our Dublin training base at Blackrock College in preparation for our opening game in the 1976 European Championship qualifiers. We were due to play the Soviet Union the next day, 30 October 1974, at Dalymount Park. After John had finished discussing our game plan and set-piece routines, I piped up with a question. Given that in our last game, against Chile in the summer, I had scored from a corner kick delivered by John himself, I enquired if I should employ the same tactic against the Soviets.

'Do you want me to go up under the bar, John?' I innocently asked. Silence! John said nothing. I said nothing. Things moved on. I wondered why he did not answer me. It then hit home: John was dropping me and here I was casually assuming that I would be in the starting eleven. I had royally put my foot in it.

John spoke with me in private after the meeting and confirmed that I would not start against the Soviet Union. Afterwards, the players could not stop laughing and, although I can also laugh at it now, it certainly taught me a good lesson! The bright side was that I was dropped for a young, long-haired Liam Brady who was beginning his fantastic journey in an Irish shirt.

The match itself could not have gone better for us. With Don Givens scoring a hat-trick, Ireland recorded a landmark 3-0 win over the Soviet Union. After the game, as elated as I was, I had no time to hang around for the celebrations and neither did Don Givens. Both of us had to get back to England that night for club duty. Portsmouth was due to play Bristol City on 2 November and I was required to report for training on 31 October. Don, a Queens Park Rangers player, had his own appointment to make.

We did not even shower. Instead, we hastily did what we called 'the hand-and-face wash', threw on our tracksuits and ran out of Dalymount Park. There was no transport lined on for us, not even a taxi, so we started thumbing at the side of the road in the middle of Phibsboro. Don, the hat-trick hero, had the match ball under his arm. We got lucky: after only a few minutes' wait, a car pulled over. When the passenger door was pushed open a disbelieving face leaned over and peered out at us. 'Is that Don Givens and Eoin Hand?' We assented sheepishly and realised that this was actually an Ireland fan that had left the stadium minutes earlier. He turned to Don. 'Don Givens! You just scored a hat-trick for Ireland. What are you doing here?' The amazed and kind Ireland fan drove us all the way to Dublin Airport himself and we made our flight.

In our next game we drew 1-1 away to Turkey on 20 November 1974 and then defeated Switzerland 2-1 on 10 May 1975. I had regained my place in the team after the win over the Soviets due to the fact that Terry Mancini had been sent off in that game. Terry had first been selected in October 1973 after his QPR teammate Don Givens had told him, by chance, that his half-Irish parentage qualified him to play for the Republic of Ireland.

Although these results kept us in contention in the group, defeats in our next two games, in 1975, would see Ireland yet again losing out on qualification for an international tournament. We lost 2-1 to the Soviet Union in Kiev on 18 May in front of 100,000 fans, with our only goal being scored by myself. Three days later we went down by a single goal to Switzerland in Berne.

On these trips, practical jokes at the expense of FAI delegates were a staple diversion. With a contingent of often unworldly-wise officials travelling with us, there was plenty of material to work with. When we travelled from the Soviet Union to Switzerland in May 1975, one unfortunate delegate from Athlone got the treatment. This official had bought a doll in Moscow, a purchase he was particularly pleased with and, boy, did the rest of us need to know about it. On the flight to Berne, we had a pain in the head from listening to him. 'Would you look at my doll? Isn't it lovely? It's got the Athlone colours and everything. Look at it there.'

An unknown prankster waited for the official to fall asleep and stealthily crept down the gangway and managed to get the doll. A few minutes later, when the official had woken up again, a severed doll's head went tumbling down the centre of the plane, then legs and arms, followed by a lonely torso. The official was furious with the sight of his once 'lovely doll' now lying all over the place. He jumped from his seat and made straight for the manager's seat. 'This is an absolute disgrace,' he told a shocked John Giles. 'I want an investigation into this and I want to know who broke my doll.' Of course, the culprit was never found.

My final appearance for the Republic of Ireland came on 29 October 1975 against Turkey at Dalymount Park. Although we managed a resounding 4-0 win, with the exceptional Don Givens scoring all four, the match ended another disappointing campaign for us. We lost out on qualification to the Soviet Union. The Soviets topped the group, on eight points, with Ireland in second place, on seven. However, compared to the recent dark days of Irish football, it represented huge progress. The commanding victory over the Soviet Union at home, in particular, had shown that Ireland could now mix it with the heavyweights of international football. As John Giles put it, in his assessment of the campaign, we were no longer 'the Cinderellas of Europe'.

As already stated, at club level by this time things were rapidly turning sour for me. Having endured two unhappy seasons under Ian St John, it

Standing for the national anthem. My last game for Ireland, against Turkey at Dalymount Park on 29 October 1975. In all, I received twenty caps for Ireland and played under four managers: Charlie Hurley, Mick Meagan, Liam Tuohy and John Giles. Behind me are (*l–r*): Noel Campbell, Liam Brady, Mick Martin, Paddy Mulligan, Ray Treacy, Terry Conroy, Tony Dunne, Mick Walsh, David O'Leary, Jimmy Conway, Joe Kinnear, Mick Kearns, Don Givens and Jimmy Holmes. (Sportsfile)

was in January 1976 that I signed full-time for Arcadia Shepherds in South Africa. I knew the country well from the many guest appearances I had made there. My brother Eamonn was living in Durban, so the move was not a huge stretch for me. I would spend two seasons with the Shepherds under the Danish player-manager Kai Johansen. I was glad to get a new club after the experience of playing under St John, but the downside was that I knew well that the move would spell the end of my international career.

I rang John Giles and told him of my plans. He wished me well but also made it clear that he could no longer select me for the national side given the relatively poor level of the South African game. He did not need to explain himself; I was well aware what the cost of the move would mean for my Ireland career.

I had been honoured to play for Ireland and could, perhaps, have earned more caps had I remained in the game in England. The feeling I got when I lined up for the national anthem with Ireland will always stay with me. When the crowd went silent and the band struck up 'Amhrán na bhFiann' I was filled with emotion. There are few spine-tingling moments in life; that was one of them.

Looking back on my international playing career, some odd things stand out. For one, the sheer number of times we played against Poland. Of my twenty games for Ireland, four of them were friendly matches against the Poles, but this was not something peculiar to my own era. The fixture had vintage. The longer-serving players had been going through this routine throughout the 1960s. Ray Treacy, for example, whose Ireland career was longer than my own, would face the Poles nine times.

Why did we play them so often? From the late 1950s onwards, and throughout the 1960s, '70s and '80s, there were seventeen friendly matches organised between ourselves and Poland. 'Poland, again?' was the bemused feeling amongst the squad when yet another of these fixtures was announced. When it came to travelling abroad with a squad of international footballers, Poland, and, particularly the nightlife of its cities, was very much to the FAI's liking. Compared to the price of goods in Ireland, beer and luxury gifts could be picked up for a song in Poland, and on the country's busy black market, dollars could be exchanged for *złoty* at up to ten times their value. If you were a visitor looking for a good time in a foreign city, there was no downside to this. And for the more enterprising officials, spotting the opportunity to turn a buck, there was even business to be done there. One FAI delegate started buying women's underwear wholesale in Poland for resale back in Ireland.

Often, on arrival in the country, if the game was to be played in one of the less glamorous cities – like Katowice, Wrocław or Kraków – the officials would not even bother to travel with us. Instead, booked into the plushest hotels on offer, they would hang on in Warsaw and enjoy themselves while we played an international match on the other side of the country. It was another example of the parallel worlds that coexisted in Irish football.

With my international career at an end, my family and I moved to South Africa in early 1976 and I began my stint with Arcadia Shepherds. In 1977, our second child, Warren, was born in Pretoria.

South Africa opened up a new world to me and brought me into close contact with the country's controversial racial laws. With the apartheid system deeply entrenched, not even football was safe from discrimination. In general, there was no racial intermingling: a league had either white players or black players. Arcadia Shepherds, however, showing pioneering bravery, had signed its first black player, Vincent Julius, in 1976. Vincent, until then, had played only in the so-called non-white leagues in Soweto. He was adored in the Soweto townships, something I witnessed at first hand when I accompanied him into some of those vast settlements. As soon as we appeared on the street, Vincent was surrounded by throngs of excited children.

Essentially, by signing Vincent, Arcadia Shepherds was openly flouting the country's racial laws and was, effectively, daring the regime to act. The story had already spread beyond South Africa with the American network ABC even coming to Pretoria to interview Vincent for a special televised feature. Fearing a backlash in the international press, the ruling elite did precisely nothing about the situation.

When Vincent made his debut against the Johannesburg club Highlands Park, there was palpable tension in the ground. Instead of noise, there was a pregnant silence. The opposition protested against Vincent's presence, but to no avail. Vincent played. During the match he was the subject of typical racist taunts from the Highlands Park players. After one player called him 'kaffir', Vincent had the perfect riposte. Some minutes later he scored a goal, and, when passing his persecutor, he asked him: 'So, what do you think of the goal the kaffir just scored, eh?' From then on, thanks to Vincent's and Arcadia Shepherds' courage, mixed teams became a commonplace.

At the club's end-of-year dinner, Vincent was present along with everyone but all was not well. Before the player-of-the-year awards ceremony began, the club chairman, Saul Sachs, took me aside for a word. 'Eoin, as captain, you will have to tell Vincent that he must leave before the ceremony and the dancing starts.' I objected and said that I would do no such thing. We, a team, were celebrating together. Vincent was a very important player and now I was being asked to send him packing while the white folk lived it up for the rest of the night. 'What if Vincent wins player-of-the-year?' I said.

Sachs was unmoved. 'It is the law, Eoin. He *must* go.' 'Fine', I responded, 'if Vincent goes, we all go.' And we did. I rounded up a large group of players, including Vincent, and, in solidarity, we left to continue the night in a nearby restaurant owned by a good friend, Werner Weinbeck.

I was glad for the chance to introduce Vincent to Werner, and to be able to point out an unusual picture on the wall. It was a grainy black-and-white shot of yours truly awkwardly squaring up to Franz Beckenbauer in the Olympic Stadium in 1970. To Werner, an ardent devotee of all things Beckenbauer, my actions were little short of sacrilege – and he could not help poking fun at me. Underneath the framed photograph were the words: 'The Cheek of the Century.'

The pay I received from Arcadia Shepherds was not great, so, in addition to the football, a part-time job was needed. The club fixed me up with a Ford car dealership in Pretoria where I worked as a salesman. It was not really a proper job. I could not speak Afrikaans, so selling cars was going to be a tough assignment. Whatever about the lack of cars that I was shipping (I might have sold two in six months), I got on well with my boss, Chris Mitchell.

The people of Pretoria were rugby-mad and Chris was no exception. One day we were arguing about how much skill was required to be a rugby penalty taker. I argued that rugby players, compared to footballers, kicked the ball in the completely wrong way and, moreover, that it was not all that difficult to score penalties in the game. Chris told me to put my money where my mouth was and prove that I could kick penalties as well as professional rugby players. With a bet laid, he took me to the city's Loftus Versfeld stadium and asked me to demonstrate my alleged prowess. This was where my GAA past came in handy. In general, I was able to put the ball over the bar from various angles.

I took my winnings from Chris and afterwards thought that there might be an opportunity in this. I suggested to Chris that before major rugby matches, such as Curry Cup games, a kicking competition could take place between a rugby player and a footballer. Chris liked the idea and took it to Ford, which was a major sponsor of rugby in the city, and the company went for it.

A date was set for me to take on a renowned rugby penalty-taker before an upcoming Curry Cup match. It would be a televised event and a golden boot was even created as a prize for the winner. Unfortunately, as the game

In South Africa (*from left*): manager Kai Johansen, Bobby Charlton and me, after a game for Arcadia Shepherds in 1976. I played with the Pretoria-based club for two seasons between 1976 and 1977. Here Charlton is guesting for us.

came closer, the rugby authorities ruled out the prospect of a footballer taking part in it. I was out. Instead, only rugby players would contest the competition. It was disappointing not to be able to participate, but the competition itself became a success and ran for many years afterwards.

After my second season in South African football, I decided to come home and I made enquiries for the 1977/78 season. I put the word out and quickly got a lucky break when John Giles asked me to sign for Shamrock Rovers. John was back in Ireland managing Rovers after having spent a season playing in the United States with Philadelphia Fury. He had exciting plans for Shamrock Rovers and hoped to turn the team into a fully professional outfit that could, perhaps, one day seriously compete in European football. After a short, enjoyable spell with Rovers, which lasted for just seven games, I was unexpectedly contacted by Portsmouth in December 1977.

The club asked me to help out as a player-coach and also offered me a year that would culminate in a testimonial match. I still had my house in Portsmouth, so it made sense to move back. John understood my position and did not stand in my way. It was my first coaching assignment and one that I was eager to make the most of. The end of my playing days was approaching, so I knew I had to think about a fallback position. Ian St John had now gone, having been let go at the close of the 1976/77 season, and Portsmouth was playing in the Third Division.

The new manager for the 1977/78 season was Portsmouth and England legend Jimmy Dickinson. Jimmy had been promoted from the job of club secretary and, although he had sworn that he would never become a manager, he did not let the club down when it called on him. In a two-decades-long playing career, Jimmy had amassed 822 appearances for Pompey – still (at the time of writing) the record number of appearances for the club. He also played for his country, at left half, forty-eight times. Jimmy commanded great respect in the club and in the wider game. He was a huge figure but, as I soon found out, he was not quite the right material for football management. 'Gentleman Jim', as he was known, was simply too nice a man for the cut and thrust of management. He could not give a rollicking for love or money. Jimmy was the kind of manager who would nearly ask you for permission to drop you.

At the end of Dickinson's first season, what Portsmouth had eluded for so long finally caught up with the club: the drop into the Fourth Division! It was regrettable that it should come under Jimmy's stewardship. In attempting to revive the fortunes of an ailing Portsmouth, the club legend had inherited a sinking ship and his was a thankless task. A club on the slide is notoriously difficult to turn around and the strain of it all was too much for Dickinson. In the 1978/79 season, with his team lying in eighth place in Division Four, Dickinson's managerial career ended abruptly. In March 1979, after a dramatic 1-1 draw with Barnsley, Jimmy, on reaching the dressing room, collapsed with a heart attack. He was rushed to intensive care and, although he survived, he could no longer take control of the team. His assistant, Frank Burrows, took charge for the remainder of the season. Promotion was not achieved but, opting for continuity, the board would appoint Burrows as permanent manager in the summer of 1979.

I knew that the 1978/79 season would be my last playing in England. Portsmouth had always been good to me and, sure enough, they gave me permission to arrange a testimonial match at Fratton Park, to be played in April 1979. John Giles, as helpful as ever, provided the opposition in the form of the Republic of Ireland international side. With my family and friends in the crowd, it was the send-off that I'd hoped for. I was particularly delighted that Werner Weinbeck came all the way from South Africa to be there on the night.

I was glad to have had a second spell at Portsmouth. After my acrimonious exit in 1976, I was given the chance to heal the rift and say a proper goodbye to the fans and to everyone at the club. The committee established to organise my testimonial match was exceptional and put a huge amount of work into making that final year such a memorable one. I look back with happiness on my years at Portsmouth. I made great friends there, including my neighbours Mike and Ann Lister, and also Dave Rees, a fanatical supporter of Pompey. On the social side, like many footballers, in order to wind down I played golf. I spent many happy hours at Waterlooville Golf Club with its members and, especially, my sadly departed friend Terry Manns.

With the recognition from Portsmouth, this final season ensured that I finished my football career on a high.

Looking back on my playing career, I have enough self-awareness to know that, as a player, I was not a world-beater. What I may have lacked in talent, though, I made up for in commitment. I was reliable: managers knew what they were going to get from me. I was a tough tackler, a good reader of the game, strong in the air and possessed pace. And, although I had enough composure to sometimes play as a holding midfielder, my ability on the ball was limited. In possession, I kept it simple, and satisfied myself with finding teammates who were more creative than me.

In the Second and Third Divisions, there were old-fashioned, tough-as-teak centre halves, but, equally, on the other side of the divide, were imposing, stand-up centre forwards as well: big target men who were not afraid to bring the fight to you. With no quarter asked and none given, I endured some genuinely bruising encounters but, when the final whistle went, you shook hands with your foe and walked off the pitch together. That's how it was. Although I gradually developed a bit of a reputation for being a 'hard man', I always played within the rules and would never have gone out to hurt anyone intentionally. I did not plan it this way, but having a reputation that preceded me sometimes had its advantages. If it gave you any advantage over an opposing forward, you were already winning the mental battle.

During my time at Portsmouth, I began to get tired of all the argy-bargy with opposing players. We were playing Watford in one bad-tempered encounter and, when I was being marked by their defender Tom Walley, at a corner, instead of pushing and shoving, I decided to try a new strategy. I began to tickle Walley and did it rile him! 'What the hell are you up to?' he shouted. This unorthodox method was proving just as effective as the usual physical jostling, so I kept going with it. Walley was certainly distracted. When the final whistle went he ran over to a group of Portsmouth players and, in a confused tone, asked: 'Is he queer or what?'

Portsmouth may not have been a high-achieving club in those years but it was a close-knit one and one that did not forget the community it came from. Each December the players would hold a Christmas show and donate the proceeds to charity. One Christmas, with my burly centre-half image parked, I was even persuaded to dress up as a woman and perform on stage!

Like every lower-league player, a lingering regret I have is that I did not play in the First Division. I would have loved that. I discovered, subsequently, that there were a number of transfer requests for me from Division One clubs while I was a Portsmouth player. In one case, apparently Newcastle United had made serious enquiries about signing me.

Of course, as a player, I knew nothing about these background manoeuvrings. Those were the days before player power existed. As was the case with the vast majority of professional players of that era, the clubs held all the aces. If another club came in and made a bid for you and your own club said, 'No. We're not happy with your offer. Come back with another one', you would never hear about it. You were the club's property to do with almost as they wished, so you were certainly never consulted if another club expressed interest. There were no agents who might be able to set a fire under the club every now and then and secure you a better deal or force through a lucrative transfer. The way the contracts were set up meant that you were essentially dependent on the club's favour. You generally took what you were given. You might try to squeeze an extra £10 from the club every few years, if your contract was under discussion, but, if you even got that, you were doing very well.

Centre halves' night off: Me (*left*), at a Portsmouth players' Christmas concert in 1970, dressed as the damsel in distress, with my defensive partner Harry Harris. (*The News*, Portsmouth)

With Portsmouth behind me and before taking my next step in football, the summer of 1979 brought a few last guest appearances in South Africa. In a number of specially arranged exhibition matches, a selection of mainly English and Scottish internationals, including Bobby Charlton, played three games, including one against Orlando Pirates, then the biggest club in South Africa. I was on board with the visiting side because of my familiarity with the South African game and so I lined up with a stellar cast from the British game.

Bobby was our manager for the tour, and, true to his competitive nature, he took it very seriously. Bobby Moore, however, who was also taking part, was not so excited about the last game against the Pirates. At half-time Charlton began to give a talk to the players. I looked over to Moore; he was dozing off on the bench! The match was an exhibition game and Bobby, like many of the players, had not been too bothered to get an early night. Charlton couldn't believe his eyes and called out, 'Bobby, come on. Wake up and pay attention.' Moore responded nonchalantly: 'Relax, Bobby. Don't be so uptight. We're here to enjoy the tour, aren't we?'

Whatever about the lackadaisical attitude on that occasion, on the pitch Moore was coolness personified. Partnering him at centre half, I had the privilege to see him at close quarters. He read the game expertly and his vision and passing were exceptional. He made it all look so easy. Towards the end of the game he turned to me and said, 'I'm going off'. And he did. He strolled off, walking straight past a bemused Charlton. I didn't know if he was coming back. He didn't. I ended up playing centre half alone for the remainder of the game.

Once the excitement of the South Africa tour had faded, I was left with the insecurity that all ageing footballers from my generation had to face: finding an answer to the looming 'what next?' question. That summer I received offers to play for clubs in South Africa and the United States. Football was on the rise in the US at the time, with the newly formed North American Soccer League, so it was a tempting option. On the other hand, I was now seriously considering football management. I weighed up the possibilities and decided that I would try to make the move into football management, come what may. After playing under numerous managers and observing what I felt were their strengths and weaknesses, and absorbing those lessons, I was keen to do it my way. It was time to put theory into practice.

3

'It wouldn't happen to Ron Greenwood'

Limerick United and the 1982 World Cup Qualifiers: 1979–1981

As I was preparing to leave Portsmouth at the end of the 1978/79 season, Limerick United contacted me about their vacant manager's position. At the time, I was considering offers from a Greek and a Cypriot club, both of which were player-manager roles. The Limerick option, however, definitely interested me more. It would take my family and me back to Ireland and it looked to me to be an ideal club in which to learn my trade. I met the club chairman, Michael Webb, and board member Harry Gibson-Steele in London and soon afterwards accepted the job as player/manager.

When I arrived at the club at the end of the summer in 1979, I was not sure what to expect. The club was not a renowned heavyweight in the League of Ireland. Its last and, at that time, only league success had come twenty years earlier in the 1959/60 season.

As a young manager in his first job, I was keen to win the players' trust. At our first squad meeting I was direct with the players. I told them that if they behaved like adults, they would be treated like adults, that we were going to work hard on our fitness but we would also have some fun. If there were any past problems, I was not interested; as far as I was concerned, everyone started with a clean slate.

Before I took the post, Dave Mahedy had been caretaker manager. One of my first acts was to sit down with Dave. I was impressed with what he had to say and, eager to keep continuity, I decided it was right that he should be my assistant. I trusted Dave and wanted him to look after the players' fitness training. That was his speciality and so it would prove.

I did not have to wait long to see what the squad were made of. They adapted to our methods immediately and were willing to train as hard as they were pushed. As player/manager, I joined in training with them, so they saw that anything they were asked to do, their manager was willing to do too. In the pre-season fitness work, Dave put us all through our paces. I wanted to make it clear that we were in this together. There was going to be no special treatment for the boss.

Dave added a weights programme to the players' fitness schedule, a practice that was unusual in the League of Ireland at that time. So thorough were his methods that the players quickly nicknamed him Hitler, but our efforts were paying off and we became an extremely fit bunch of players.

Because I was chiefly a centre half, everyone assumed that one of either Brendan Storan or Joe O'Mahony, the club's preferred centre-half pairing, would be dropped to make way for me. However, once I'd watched Joe and Brendan in our pre-season games, I realised that it would be folly to break up what was an excellent defensive partnership. Instead, I picked myself in a midfield holding role. I also kept Joe O'Mahony as club captain.

To an already excellent squad, I added four signings who would prove to be important additions as the season unfolded: Johnny Matthews on the left wing, and three strikers: Des Kennedy, John Delamere and Gary Hulmes.

Des Kennedy had recently been released by Galway United but I liked him as a player. I invited him to train with us and, in a pre-season friendly match, I decided to try him out. Des was asked to play up front for the opposition while I lined up at centre half for Limerick. In order to test his mettle, I marked Des myself. I went in hard on him a few times early on but I got back every bit as good as I gave. I knew then that I wanted him. He would be ideal as the powerful battering ram required to spearhead our attack.

I was also conscious that Des would complement his strike partner, Tony Morris, very well. Tony was the rapier, the fox-in-the-box; he was light, quick on his feet and a prolific scorer of goals – Tony would net nineteen times in the 1979/80 season.

Meanwhile, Gary Hulmes, with his pace, gave us options over the top, and the left-footed John Delamere, also a strong target man, provided a genuine alternative to Des Kennedy. Finally, Johnny Matthews gave us the width to stretch teams when needed.

Going into the 1979/80 season I felt quietly positive, but did not expect what was to come: we went unbeaten in our first eight games, winning seven and drawing one, scoring nineteen goals along the way.

When, on 18 November, we confidently defeated the reigning league champions, Dundalk, 2-0 in Limerick, I looked around and for the first time thought, 'something special is happening here'. I could feel it. Even though there was some way to go in the season, we had the togetherness and self-belief of winners. And the Limerick public thought so too: our attendances went up game by game.

We were a happy crew and, throughout my managerial career, that is the way I have always wanted my squads to be. At Limerick, once our match was over, the dressing-room door would remain shut for maybe a half an hour, and if I had some tough words to say, I would say them. Once that was dealt with, if it was an away match, we would stop on the way back for a pint or two. Everyone had to sing regardless of whether or not they had a note in their head. That was all part of the bonding.

There was a system of fines in place, but it was not something I had to resort to very often. On the rare occasion that a player stepped out of line, however, I did not hesitate to deduct some money from his wages. To take the edge off the punishment, the money was always put into a kitty that would eventually help to pay for the squad's end-of-season night out. In one instance – we were on an away trip to Donegal to play Finn Harps – when we arrived at the team hotel, I had told the players that if they wanted to have a relaxing drink, then it should only be a couple of half-pints. Content that the message was received and that all the squad would prepare properly for the match the next day, I went for a stroll around Bundoran with Dave Mahedy. As we passed one pub, I happened to glance in the window and caught a glimpse of some very familiar faces: a couple of our boys enjoying a sneaky pint. I walked in and said, 'Hello, lads.' Both turned white. 'Enjoy that pint now,' I continued. 'Make sure you finish it and get your money's worth because it's going to be the most expensive pint you'll ever drink. You are both fined a week's wages.'

As the season developed, the holding role in midfield was suiting me perfectly. Having played professionally in England, I had that bit of extra positional awareness and composure on the ball compared to many midfielders in the league. I was also generally able to read things fairly well. My job was winning the ball and giving it to Johnny Walsh, our creator-in-chief, just as I had when I played for Ireland in midfield. He would be my John Giles. When we had possession, he and Pat Nolan, an excellent overlapping right-back, had to make sure they were available. I scored twelve goals in the course of the season. Mostly I netted from a few set pieces or from sneaking into the box late from open play. A personal high was the four goals I scored in a 4-1 rout of Cork Hibernian.

At Limerick I began a pre- and post-match routine that I was to observe throughout my management career. As a general rule, the club's officials were asked not to come into the dressing room for at least half an hour before and after the game. This sometimes led to friction between myself and a few of the Limerick directors and later, when I managed Ireland, with FAI officials. I was willing to put up with the hassle, however, because, for me, the dressing room had to be protected as the one sacrosanct space where everyone could express themselves in private. My attitude was that the players and playing staff would not stride into the boardroom while the directors did their work, so why should they have the right to walk into what was *our* workplace?

In April 1980, with Limerick United still going strong in the league, John Giles resigned as Irish international manager. Former Irish international goalkeeper Alan Kelly was appointed to replace John, and Alan asked me to be his assistant. He knew me well from our days playing together for the Republic of Ireland and, living in England himself, he wanted someone based in Ireland. I was delighted to get the chance to work with the international team but, with Limerick United now having a realistic chance of winning the league, my main focus was on securing that for the club.

On 20 April, the final day of the season, the prize was won. At St Mel's Park in Athlone, in a 1-1 draw with Athlone Town, we got the point that crowned us League of Ireland champions. Dundalk, in second place, had pushed us all the way and we won the league by a solitary point.

The scenes after the match were truly memorable. Thousands of Limerick fans spontaneously flooded the pitch and lifted us off our feet. Joe O'Mahony and goalkeeper Kevin Fitzpatrick, with thirty-five years' service between them – neither of them had ever played for any other club – were in tears. I could not have been happier for this group of players. I had arrived as a stranger to them less than a year earlier but they had adapted to new methods with little or no complaint and had grown stronger and stronger as the season went on. The challenge had been thrown down to them and they had risen to it spectacularly. They were a spirited, hard-working and talented group of players.

Before the season had begun, critics had suggested that the squad was past its best, but really they were only approaching their peak when I took over. I was, in a way, the last piece of the jigsaw. So-called part-time players, they had been as professional in their approach that season as any full-time players I had come across in my career. It was Limerick United's second ever League of Ireland title.

We also reached the semi-final of the FAI Cup that season but narrowly lost to the eventual cup winners, Waterford United, in a thrilling replay.

Things were now moving very fast for me. Less than two weeks later I joined up with the Irish international squad as Alan Kelly's assistant. Our first game was a friendly against Switzerland on 30 April. A weakened Ireland won 2-0, with first-half goals from Don Givens and Gerry Daly.

Alan's reign would prove very short. There was not much money in being the Ireland manager in those days so, to make ends meet, Alan was holding down several jobs. Aside from leading the Republic of Ireland team, he was the Preston North End manager, as well as the owner of a sports business in Preston. Preston North End put pressure on him to drop the international gig and focus on club matters alone and he did. Ireland was again manager-less.

A few days later, in early May, I was voted the Irish soccer writers' Soccer Personality of the Year. At the awards reception, the president of the FAI, Charles Cahill, took me to one side. He said that the FAI wanted me to become caretaker manager of the national team for the friendly match with Argentina on 16 May. Cahill then added that the full-time manager's job would be advertised shortly and that I would be well advised to apply for it. I was stunned. When I arrived at Limerick United in August 1979, I did not imagine that a year later I would be in contention for the biggest job in Irish football. I knew then that, as the man in situ, I stood a great chance of landing the role, providing the team and I acquitted ourselves well against Argentina.

I also had to attend to practical matters. With success coming on the pitch at Limerick, I now felt comfortable enough to settle properly in the city. I bought a house in Limerick and brought my wife Pat, and our two

Receiving the Irish soccer writers' Soccer Personality of the Year award in May 1980 from Jimmy Magee (*left*) and FAI president Charles Cahill. It was at this event that Cahill asked me to become caretaker-manager of the Irish international side. (*The Irish Times*)

sons, Gary and Warren, over from Portsmouth to join me. For the previous few months, whenever possible, I had been travelling back and forth from Britain to see them. It was not ideal but, as in so many cases with football, juggling family and work commitments can prove very difficult.

With my family settled, I turned my attention to the Argentina match. The Argentinians were the world champions so to have them play in Dublin was a huge event. I carried out detailed research on their players and set up our team to contain their threats, yet to trouble them when we had the ball. Our right back, Dave Langan, was under specific orders to stay close to a young Diego Maradona. Although Maradona's exceptional ability was obvious from the first whistle, Dave succeeded where most failed: he shackled and frustrated the South American playmaker. We lost the match by the only goal but put in a very strong performance against one of the best sides in the world.

When I became manager of the Republic of Ireland football team in 1980, at thirty-four years of age, I was one of the youngest managers in international football. The appointment was an honour and a wonderful challenge for me. (Sportsfile)

In July I formally applied for the Ireland job. The applications were apparently confidential but the inevitable leaks reached the press. Aside from myself, the candidates were Pat Crerand, Liam Tuohy, Theo Foley, Ray Treacy and Paddy Mulligan. After giving what I believed was a positive interview for the job, and with my recent successes to point to, I left reasonably hopeful of landing the role. That night, at eleven o'clock, the FAI's general secretary, Peadar O'Driscoll, rang to say that I was successful. Although some very testing years were ahead of me, when I took that call in the summer of 1980 it was a wonderful feeling. I was the manager of the national side with a World Cup qualification campaign to look forward to, Limerick United had just won the league and, as a result, had been drawn against Real Madrid in the European Cup.

On my appointment, at the age of thirty-four, I was, according to members of the press corps, the youngest international manager in the world. The challenge ahead was going to be daunting, for sure, but my overriding feeling was one of great excitement. The position was a part-time one and I would continue as full-time player/manager of Limerick United. I did not even bother to negotiate my salary with the FAI. I was so engrossed in the prospect of leading the country's national side that I agreed to the terms without a second thought. The starting salary was £12,500 but, for me, money was not the main consideration.

Now that I was in charge, I had decisions to make. As an assistant, I opted for the former Stoke City and Republic of Ireland international winger Terry Conroy. Terry and I had become friends when we played together for Ireland and we had even debuted for the national side together, against Czechoslovakia in October 1969. I trusted him and felt that he would be very good with the players. The fact that Terry was based in England was also important – I needed someone there permanently who could watch our players in action.

For my captain, I chose Liam Brady and, although I believe the significance of the captain's role is overestimated, I still considered it carefully. It is a misconception to think that a captain must be the player who bawls everyone out of it for ninety minutes. It takes a lot more than a good set of lungs to lead men. Brady was not the most vocal of players on the pitch, but he led by his courage and ability and so commanded the respect of the entire squad. When players saw that he was unfailingly willing to receive the ball, no matter how late in the game, and no matter how much pressure he was under, he inspired them. In later campaigns, I would alternate the captain's role, with Tony Grealish taking the armband in the 1984 European Championship qualification campaign, while Frank Stapleton led the team for the 1986 World Cup qualification matches.

We operated with a skeleton crew. Aside from the playing squad, there was me, Terry Conroy, a physiotherapist – Mick Byrne, whom I had inherited from John Giles and who doubled up as our kit man – and a doctor, who was in attendance only at games. That was it! And Terry Conroy was only a casual employee of the FAI. He received a match fee, like the players, and no more. There was no army of scouts, performance analysts, masseurs and handlers to smooth out every bump we encountered. We got on with it as best we could.

The Football Association of Ireland (FAI) general secretary, Peadar O'Driscoll, congratulates my assistant Terry Conroy and me at the final whistle, c.1981. (Sportsfile)

Because I became the Republic of Ireland manager at such a young age, it meant that I was walking into a dressing room to manage players who, only five years earlier, I had played alongside in an Irish shirt. Liam Brady, Mick Martin and Gerry Daly, for example, had been teammates of mine under John Giles' management. In a relatively short time, I had gone from being one of the lads to becoming the boss. I had been their buddy; now I was the gaffer. In football, as in any job, this abrupt step-up in rank can be fraught with difficulties. At Portsmouth I had witnessed at first hand how not to manage this transition. When, in 1973, my former teammate Ron Tindall became elevated to the position of club general manager, one of his first moves was to side with the board when its members had controversially aired the notion of reducing the players' bonuses. It may have been naivety; it may have been ambition, but that did not matter. Any respect that the players might have held for Ron vanished in a heartbeat. Players' attitudes can be unforgiving: you are either one of them in the dressing room, or you are one of those yes-men in the boardroom. Ron had nailed his colours to the mast and there was no turning back.

I was not going to make that same mistake. The only way to deal with such a sudden promotion is to wear your authority lightly. If you do as Tindall did, and rashly overshoot the mark, any respect you might hope to command goes out the window.

Some of these Irish players still saw me as their former teammate so, given those circumstances, it would have been ridiculous for me to waltz into the Ireland set-up and start barking orders like a parade-ground sergeant major. I made it clear that I would respect them. They were international players. They could handle themselves. 'Call me Eoin', I said, 'not boss.' And that is the rapport that the players and I maintained throughout my tenure as Ireland manager. My philosophy was that respect should be earned, not demanded.

My preferred tactical formation was a 4-3-3 system. For me, 4-3-3 gave us the desired balance and it generally suited the available personnel. I was always an attack-minded coach who went out to be as positive as possible. Having three upfront gave us numerous options for relieving pressure, by either playing the ball into the channels or to the feet of the central striker. It also gave us the width to trouble teams. With four at the back, however, bolstered by a holding player in midfield, we still maintained the defensive solidity upon which good performances could be built.

I generally stuck to this approach with Ireland and there were sound reasons for my choice. I had so little time with the squad that there was never a chance to practise new formations with them. Invariably, I had them for a single day of training before an international. This meant that any message I would give them had to be simple and consistent. I would have liked to try out various tactical approaches but, on the whole, it was not realistic to expect reliable results from such a limited amount of time on the training ground.

The vast majority of the squad played in either a 4-4-2 or a 4-3-3 formation with their clubs. This was what they were accustomed to and I could really only piggyback off that familiarity. Although I would occasionally adopt, say, a 5-3-2 line-up, I was loath to do so – you ran the risk of players being unable to adjust to the new positions they were placed in. The risk was sometimes reduced, especially when you had versatile players to draw on who could play in multiple positions, but not so when you were calling on specialist players who, generally, excelled in only one area of the pitch.

John Giles' tenure as Ireland's player-manager became known for its strong focus on possession football. John, being a world-class player himself, firmly believed in ball-retention and he was right. His insistence on this approach helped to develop Irish football. John's approach also brought some landmark victories for Irish football and a second-place finish in the 1976 European Championship qualifiers. Coming after me, Jack Charlton's devotion to an ultra-pragmatic long-ball game could be seen as the polar opposite to John's passing game.

Between these contrasting visions there is a large middle ground and my own preference was for a style somewhere between the two. I did not want to overcomplicate matters. Ultimately, you are trying to score more goals than the opposition in ninety minutes of football. I always remembered the words of former Scotland manager Jock Stein. When I attended a coaching conference in Split in the former Yugoslavia in the early 1980s one coach was enthusiastically presenting his thoughts on the minutiae of various tactical formations. Jock, a member of the group, had heard enough. In his thick Scottish accent he bellowed, 'Ach, you can either play or you can't play, for God's sake. You can talk all day but, before your tactics, you've got to have players who can either play or can't play.' Jock was certainly oversimplifying matters, but the spirit of his message stayed with me.

For sure, as I learned from Giles, I wanted us playing possession football, but, equally, the ball should go forward early, where possible. Possession is risk-free: you have the ball; the opposition does not. Your opponent cannot score, but, unless you force the issue, neither can you. At some point, you have to take the risk and look for that final ball that may lead to the breakthrough but may also lead to you losing possession. Penetration is the ultimate objective in football and, so, if there is an opportunity to achieve that, it has to be taken, as early as possible. The desire to keep the ball should never override the need to seize on an opening. The first ball, if it was on, should be forward; the next should be diagonal; if that was not on, then sideways; and, finally, if there is no other choice, backwards. My thinking was always that our players should be looking to play the ball forward first, but *only* if the ball was on. For example, if Frank Stapleton was free, then we needed to find him. I knew that, usually, when Frank got the ball, it stuck and our play could build with support from midfield.

All this did not mean long-ball football, however. That's why the last option was to go backwards; if nothing was on, we kept the ball, until an opening came again, and so on. A long ball is, by definition, essentially an aimless, hopeful pass; I, by contrast, advocated constructive passing, whether it be short, medium or long range. We sometimes hit long balls, but only if it was to exploit an identified weakness in the opposition's defence.

Extreme long-ball philosophies merely trade on percentages. The basic idea is that if the ball is going forward enough times into sufficiently dangerous areas of the pitch, then the law of averages says that, somewhere along the line, a flick on, a deflection or maybe just a bounce of the ball will go your way, and lead to a chance to score. It is based on a curious logic: fundamentally, you are committing to giving the ball away in order to get it back again. If penetration is the point of the game, then, in my book, a constant long-ball style is not a very efficient means of achieving that. Its hit-and-miss nature means that you will spend an awful lot of wasted energy chasing hopeful balls, energy that could be spent doing something more useful with the ball.

Once he succeeded me as Ireland manager, in February 1986, Jack Charlton's long-ball tactics, whatever about the success they brought, also, frankly, wasted the talents of Liam Brady – probably the most skilful player this country has ever produced. In Charlton's preferred approach, Liam was reduced to being like the net in the game of tennis, with the ball being launched from back to front, right over his head.

During my own tenure, I was determined to use Liam properly. He was our most creative player and so I was always conscious of making sure that our set-up enabled him to get on the ball as much as possible, and in the right areas of the field. Liam had the capacity to make things happen, to fashion openings that others could neither see nor execute. He had magic in his left boot and, although he was mostly one-footed, his balance was such that he invariably had little trouble shifting the ball back onto his favoured foot. Like many great players, with his pinpoint-accurate passes and trademark composure on the ball, he made the difficult look easy. I had known Liam since he was a promising young boy playing on the streets of Dublin, so I needed little convincing of his importance to our plans. I had first met him in Dublin in 1964, when he was only about eight years old, and a few months after I had signed for Swindon Town. Accompanied by two of his older brothers, who were also professional footballers, Liam was introduced to me in a Drumcondra bar. He politely shook my hand. His brothers were obviously proud of Liam and fully believed that whatever ability they had, it was soon going to be eclipsed by their much younger sibling. 'See this boy here,' they said. 'He is going to be a great player and go all the way to the top.'

In 1980, having just signed for Italian giants Juventus in the close season, Liam was also now our highest-profile player. He was a specialist No. 10 who was at his best getting on the ball in the space behind the forwards and creating the openings on which others could capitalise. Without sacrificing the defensive structure of the team, during my term Liam was given licence to roam for Ireland. However, he was not entirely exempt from defensive duties. In international football, when the occasion calls for it, you need eleven players getting goalside.

As a player, and certainly towards the end of my career, I was always trying to learn from the managers under whom I'd worked – Liam Tuohy and John Giles, for example, were great teachers of the game. They instilled great self-belief in you and had you wanting to play for them. For me, as a manager, placing such emphasis on motivating players was crucial.

Some might argue that, at international level, players should already be motivated and that it is not the manager's job to do that. My belief, however, is that, no matter how much you rationalise it, as a manager you are dealing with fallible creatures who each respond very differently to the ebb and flow of matches. In international football, many so-called 'confident' club players meet their Waterloo when they come up against the very best opposition. A centre half, for example, who is usually commanding and authoritative at club level, can get torn to shreds when he faces off against the pace, strength and movement of a world-class striker. The rules suddenly change and your player finds himself with a situation he has never faced before: now, the none-shall-pass cocksure stopper of club renown is getting a fearful runaround. This is a player who needs encouragement and, as the manager, looking at the player's individual psychology, you have to decide whether to be reassuring or if strong words are needed.

You try whatever works. Sometimes the crude old-fashioned rollicking has its place, although it is not something to over-employ: use it too often and you lose credibility.

When it came to pointing out players' weaknesses, something which would mainly occur at club level, I was mindful to word my advice in such a way that the message would get home. If there was a good player inside struggling beneath brittle self-esteem, then browbeating him into submission until he did what he was told would not work. It had to be constructive: I wanted to make sure that he went away understanding what was required of him but with his confidence still intact.

Although I knew that I was presiding over probably the strongest Irish international squad in the country's history, I was also acutely aware of our limitations. Compared to larger football nations, Ireland did not have a deep pool of players from which to select. This meant that the search for new players never stopped and, to find them, the net had to be cast as wide as possible. Even though my selecting British-born Irish players, or players who qualified to play for us through their Irish grandmothers, sometimes jarred with nationalist sentiment in Ireland, I had no difficulty with picking such players. I needed international-level footballers wherever I could find them. Even had I been a dyed-in-the-wool nationalist, I would still have picked non-Irish-born players. There are some beliefs that football managers do not have the luxury of holding. This was one of them. You are a pragmatist; you want to win football matches.

Throughout my tenure I trawled through lists of possible players and, wherever possible, worked with contacts to establish who might, in fact, be eligible for the Republic. Although the accent that the player spoke with, or the country he happened to be born in, made no odds to me, his desire to represent Ireland very much did. When I found a player with an Irish background but who, say, might also have been eligible to play for England, when I contacted them, they had to show that keenness to play for Ireland, and Ireland only. I discovered the importance of this when, in my first year in charge, I made an approach to Steve McMahon. McMahon, then a young player at Everton, and later of Liverpool fame, told me that he was interested but he would prefer to wait and see if he might get capped for England. That was Steve's decision, and I respected it, but once I heard those words, I was not going to expend another drop of energy trying to convince him otherwise. It was nothing to do with patriotism, and this was no 'Are you Irish?' litmus test; it was simply that, just like at club level, I needed players who had the desire to play for Ireland. They had to supply that ingredient; I couldn't give it to them. If it's not there, you are wasting your time.

My experience with Seamus McDonagh was quite the opposite and his was exactly the kind of response an international manager hopes to get from a player. Seamus may have been born and raised in England but he was green inside, as I was soon to find out. Seamus was playing in the First Division with Everton at this stage, and at twenty-eight, was already a highly experienced goalkeeper. I liked him and wanted him for Ireland. When I first went to England in 1980 to sound him out, I wasn't sure where Seamus's allegiances lay. He put that confusion to bed pretty quickly. Wondering if he identified more with England than with Ireland, I thought it best to play it safe and address him as 'Jim'. He didn't take much persuading. 'Eoin, I would swim across the Irish Sea to play for Ireland, and don't call me Jim: it's "Seamus".' Before we could get into any more details, he abruptly began reciting from memory the 1916 Proclamation of Independence. I was not quite sure how to react to this impromptu performance but, either way, I took it as a good sign. I would cap McDonagh in a 3-1 friendly defeat to Wales in February 1981. After that, he would go on to be my usual first-choice goalkeeper for the rest of my term as Ireland manager.

Another of our English-born contingent was Tony Grealish. Tony, although first capped by John Giles, would become a key player for me. Much like McDonagh, he was 'more Irish than the Irish themselves' and knew the words to countless Irish rebel songs, of which the Irish-born players knew little or nothing. With his dynamic, combative style in the midfield engine room, Tony, with tousled hair and Viking beard, was the kind of guy you were happy to go into battle alongside. He was a natural leader, and although known for his ceaseless industry, he was no mere artisan. Grealish could play as well and conjure up the odd vital goal from deep positions. Some players find a new level when they pull on the colours of their country. Tony, who had a nomadic career at club level, always upped his game for Ireland. He was, invariably, a consistent name on my team sheet.

In the 1982 World Cup qualification phase, Ireland was drawn in Group Two with France, Belgium, the Netherlands and Cyprus. It was an exceptionally difficult group and it was clear that we would have to be at our very best to stand a chance of making it to the World Cup in Spain. Two would qualify from the group. With France, Belgium and the Netherlands all world-class sides, easy games in Group Two would be few and far between. Under John

Giles, in what was his final game as Ireland manager, we had already defeated Cyprus 3-2 away on 26 March of that year, so I began my first campaign with two points already secure.

The first competitive game of my tenure came on 10 September 1980 against the Netherlands at Lansdowne Road. The Dutch game was my first experience of the Lansdowne Road pitch and I was not impressed. It was bumpy and the grass was disgracefully long. This was, after all, the home of Irish rugby; the FAI was merely renting the stadium from the Irish Rugby Football Union (IRFU). During the rugby season, the IRFU was not all that interested in cutting the grass to the length that was needed for a football game, so, more often than not, Irish football put up and shut up.

Trying to play on this surface once was enough for me. For our subsequent games, although I was not always successful, I would request from the groundsman that the grass be cut and that the surface be improved as much as possible. I know that in later years, when Jack Charlton was in charge of the Irish team, the IRFU's orders were just the opposite: Jack, preferring a long-ball game, did not mind if the grass was left long. The extra length helped to hold up balls that had been launched into the corners. For us, however, it was far from an ideal surface for keeping the ball on the carpet – the way we generally wanted to play.

On the evening of the Dutch game, a gale blew up and made conditions difficult for both sides. For my first game in charge, I played Gerry Peyton in goal. In defence, I opted for Dave Langan at right back, brothers David and Pierce O'Leary as central defenders and Chris Hughton at left back. In midfield, Mark Lawrenson was my holding player, with Gerry Daly to his right and Tony Grealish to his left. Up front, I selected Frank Stapleton and Don Givens with Liam Brady playing in a roving role to their left.

We opened the game aggressively, and we needed to, because we were playing into a very strong wind. It was obvious to me quite early that the Dutch were not comfortable with the conditions. They were not settling on the ball and it was clear that they were struggling to play with any composure. Most of the early exchanges were played in midfield, with neither side finding decisive openings in behind the defence. Dave Langan was making headway down the right wing throughout the half. Mark Lawrenson was looking composed and creative in midfield. Mark, although a defender by trade, was versatile enough to perform in the centre of the park and this game was proving it.

The Netherlands were coming to life only on the break, and, even though we dominated the first forty-five minutes, the visitors very nearly scored from two quick-fire counter-attacks. For the majority of the half they had been going nowhere, but when the chance came, they pounced. We had only the agility of Gerry Peyton to thank for the game remaining scoreless. Those flashes of brilliance from the Dutch were a warning sign, but we didn't heed it. Early in the second half, despite us being on top again, in the fifty-seventh minute another rapid breakaway put us behind. Peyton failed to collect after colliding with the Dutch right winger and Simon Tahamata was on hand to slot the ball into an empty net. It was a body blow. For all our good play, we were behind and the crowd were now silenced.

Once settled, we continued to attack and established control once more. The goal, however, was not coming and the minutes were slipping away. I wondered if we were going to be the victims of a Dutch smash-and-grab. With twelve minutes to go, however, we finally drew level. After a beautifully worked four-pass move, involving Liam Brady and Tony Grealish, Gerry Daly side-footed home from ten yards. Now the big push came and we went in search of the winner. It arrived in the eighty-fifth minute. From a rehearsed set piece, Brady delivered the ball into the box where an unmarked Mark Lawrenson acrobatically scored with a diving header. We held out for a hugely important victory.

It was a major confidence boost to beat the Netherlands. Our win, earned by coming from behind against one of the top nations in world football, proved to me that we were no longer the just likeable underdogs. Despite the difficulty of the group in which we found ourselves, I felt that this game established us as realistic contenders for qualification. We now had maximum points from our first two games and with another home game to come, against Belgium, we were very well placed to make decisive strides in the group.

After the high of beating the Netherlands, my attention turned back to my full-time position at Limerick United. On 17 September we faced the Spanish champions Real Madrid in the first round of the European Cup. The Limerick board had decided to play the game at Lansdowne Road in order to avail of the ground's larger capacity and so bring in higher gate receipts. The move backfired. It was optimistically suggested that over 30,000 might attend but fewer than 6,000 did – apparently, at that point, the worst-attended competitive fixture in Real Madrid's history. Most Limerick fans simply could not afford to make the trip. The crowd numbers, however, were the only dampener on what would turn out to be an exceptional Limerick performance.

Six-time winners of the European Cup at that time, Real Madrid were giants of European football and utterly dominant in the Spanish domestic game. In the previous six seasons they had won five league titles and three Spanish cups. They were also in red-hot form. A week earlier Athletic Bilbao had been thrashed 7-1 by the Madrid club. The Real side was packed with Spanish internationals, including Juanito, Isidro, José Antonio Camacho and Gregorio Benito, and complemented by West Germany's Uli Stielike and England's Laurie Cunningham. As if that were not enough, buttressing this supremely talented team was a famously parsimonious defence.

In the days before the game, Madrid's manager, Vujadin Boškov – a former 57-times capped Yugoslav international – confidently noted: 'We have respect for every side we meet, but I believe we will proceed to the next round.' The David-and-Goliath pre-match narrative wrote itself. The magnitude of our task could not have been clearer.

My advice to the players was to show no fear. We were the champions of Ireland and had earned the right to test ourselves against the best sides in Europe. My one demand was that, whatever might unfold, we would do ourselves and the people of Limerick proud. This was not about standing back and admiring the opposition; we aimed to win the match. If we were going to do damage to Madrid, it had to be now, in the home leg, because travelling to the Bernabéu, their famous home stadium, in the second leg in search of a good result would be an enormous challenge.

Once the match kicked off, any fears that I may have had vanished. We were playing superbly and, as the game progressed, it would become increasingly difficult to tell which team were the part-timers from Limerick and which were the aristocrats from Madrid. Our passing was crisper than ever and, even though the quality of Madrid was evident from the off, we were coping. I had assigned myself the task of keeping Stielike quiet in midfield. In the first few minutes, I went in hard on him with a crunching tackle. I had to let him know that I was there and get the message home quickly that Limerick United meant business.

Gerry Duggan and Johnny Walsh, meanwhile, were combining excellently in midfield while, up front, Des Kennedy and Tony Morris were forcing untypical errors from the Madrid back four. Des, in particular, was having such a good game that, across the ninety minutes, the Spaniards would assign three different men to him. In the twenty-sixth minute our forward, Johnny Matthews, had the ball in the net but, in a marginal decision, it was called offside. The half ended scoreless.

When the second half got under way, I expected a backlash from Real Madrid. It came but, again, we dealt with it and continued to look dangerous on the ball. There was no denying it now: whatever about the huge discrepancy between the two sides on paper, we were matching one of the best clubs sides in Europe and slowly beginning to realise that we might be on the cusp of something extraordinary.

In the fifty-first minute we stunned the Spaniards. A Jimmy Nodwell free from the left was flicked onto Kennedy. Suddenly, Des, who had shaken off the close attentions of his marker, was in space six yards from the Spanish goal. He controlled the ball and slotted it past Miguel Ángel in the Madrid goal. A disgusted Ángel picked the ball out of the net and booted it downfield. The Spaniards were in shock and Limerick United was in uncharted territory. The club was looking at the greatest result in its 42-year history and one of the finest results in the history of the League of Ireland.

Now our opponents were rattled and, predictably, went up a gear in search of a way back into the game. Forward Francisco Pineda came on to add fresh legs to their attack. The game passed the seventieth minute and still we were ahead. Then, after some swift interplay in midfield, Pineda was released. Although he made it as far as the left-hand corner of the eighteen-yard box he was running away from goal when our keeper Kevin Fitzpatrick dived at the Spaniard's feet. Pineda, conscious that he was heading down a blind alley, made the very most of any contact and went flying across the turf. The Danish referee, Amundsen, pointed to the spot. Juanito duly scored the penalty and our focus now shifted to holding what we had. Madrid pressed again and squeezed us into our own half. With only six minutes to go, the heartbreaker came. A Juanito free kick was met by Pineda. Fitzpatrick saved his first effort but the forward scored from the rebound. Real went home with a 2-1 win.

Although to have such a historic result snatched from us so late in the game was a bitter pill to swallow, we knew that we had performed magnificently and, crucially, because of this, we had belief and something to take to Spain.

We travelled to Madrid at the end of September and, on the day before the match, got a reminder of just how a huge a club we were about to face. Our Spanish hosts gave us a tour of the Bernabéu and when we got to their trophy room we were suitably impressed. It was heaving with silverware. Our guide, however, noticing our surprise, quickly interrupted and told us that we were mistaken. This was only the entrance hall. He then led us into the real trophy room. It was four times bigger than the last one.

On 1 October, in front of 60,000 Real Madrid fans, we lined up at the Bernabéu for the second leg. I told the players that this was a once-in-a-life-time opportunity and that they should go out, play their own style of football, enjoy themselves and forget about the opposition's reputation. They were human and fallible; the first leg had proven that.

Once again, in the early play, we were living with Real Madrid and were not overawed. However, their class began to tell and they sliced us open twice in the first half, with Santillana and Juanito scoring. Our resistance did not collapse, however, and in the forty-third minute we were back in the game. A Pat Nolan free kick was headed on and there was Des Kennedy again to volley home for us.

A minute later we were inches from drawing level. The Spaniards, to my surprise, fell for a set-piece routine that we had been practising in the build-up to the game. I found myself completely free in front of goal but dragged my shot wide.

You get precious few handouts at this level of football and, sure enough, that miss would prove to be our last realistic chance. In the second half, Madrid scored three more times, with Ángel, Laurie Cunningham and Pineda netting. It finished 5-1 on the night and 7-2 on aggregate.

Real Madrid would concede only two more goals in the tournament and go all the way to the final where a single Alan Kennedy goal saw them go down 1-0 to Liverpool. Limerick United was out of the European Cup in the first round but we could take only positives from the experience.

On 15 October, Belgium came to Lansdowne Road for the next World Cup qualifying fixture. By 1980 Belgium had one of the strongest teams in Europe. In June of that year they had gone all the way to the final of Euro 1980 where they narrowly lost 2-1 to West Germany. With world-class players like Jan Ceulemans, Erwin Vandenbergh, Wilfried van Moer, Eric Gerets and Jean-Marie Pfaff in their ranks, I knew that we were in for a battle. Even though the Belgians had an array of attacking talent to draw

Limerick United at the Bernabéu Stadium. In the 1979/80 season, my first season in management, Limerick United won the League of Ireland title. Our reward was a first-round tie against Real Madrid in the 1980 European Cup. Pictured are, *back row (l–r)*: Pat Nolan, Gerry Duggan, Des Kennedy, Brendan Storan, Kevin Fitzpatrick, me, Tony Meaney, Mick O'Donnell, Gary Hulmes; *front row (l–r)*: Francis Brosnan, Johnny Matthews, Joe O'Mahoney, Tony Morris, Jimmy Nodwell, Mick Ryan and Johnny Walsh.

upon, their style was to set up with an extremely tight, defensive unit. They gave very little away, so what few chances you got against this disciplined side you had to take. The visitors, marshalled expertly by Gerets at the back, were also masters of the offside trap, so I emphasised to our front men that they needed to concentrate and look across the line at all times.

In order to stretch the highly compact Belgian defence, I decided to pick the Liverpool winger Steve Heighway on the left of our front three. Steve was a direct and speedy winger who, once in possession, ran straight at defences. You could rely on him to hug the touchline and to give the opposing full back plenty to worry about.

Belgium, playing with almost the confidence of a home side, opened the match very strongly, with Ceulemans, in particular, proving a handful for us. In the twelfth minute we were trailing. A long, looping header into the path of Belgian forward Albert Cluytens caught our defence square. Then Cluytens flew past Mark Lawrenson and Chris Hughton before coolly skipping around Gerry Peyton and passing into an empty net. At this point in the game I was very concerned. Belgium had their lead but showed no signs of sitting back and settling for it. In fact, they pushed harder and, had they taken their chances, we could easily have been 3-0 down at the break. Instead, thankfully, we held out and even grabbed an equaliser in the forty-first minute. After a defence-splitting through ball from Brady, Gerry Daly rounded Jean-Marie Pfaff in the Belgium goal and played it into Grealish, who applied the finishing touch. We now at least had the chance to regroup and show our mettle in the second half.

The next forty-five minutes would, however, prove tense, with little or no room for expansive play and very few chances created. Belgium began to hold what they had – a valuable away point – and, naturally, proved difficult to break down now that they had shut up shop. It finished one apiece and, although it was a point dropped at home, I considered ourselves fortunate to have held Belgium to the draw.

After three games played, we had five points and led the group. France was in second place with two points, Belgium, third, on one point, and the Netherlands and Cyprus in fourth and fifth respectively, with neither having had yet secured a point.

Our next match, away to France on 28 October, was going to be our toughest test. The French had numerous top-class players, such as Jean Tigana, Alain Giresse, Maxime Bossis, Didier Six and Dominique Rocheteau, but the magnificent Michel Platini was clearly the ace in the pack, and, at that time, one of the greatest players in the world. Platini, although renowned for his attacking prowess, was, in fact, the complete midfielder. He did not just score goals prolifically: with his vision and passing ability he also made them and, all like great players, he always managed to have time and space on the ball. If the French had possession on the left or the right, then we had to make sure that we knew exactly where Platini was. With his uncanny knack for ghosting into dangerous positions in the opposition box, tracking him was a huge challenge. Despite the threat, weighing up the situation, I opted not to man-mark Platini. I felt that it would have taken one of our players out of the game, but not necessarily have stopped France's talisman.

The game represented a milestone for the FAI because it was the first time that the Association invoked a UEFA ruling that forced clubs to

The Ireland team line up before the World Cup qualifying match away to France, 28 October 1980. The Irish players are (l–r): Liam Brady, Gerry Peyton, Michael Robinson, Steve Heighway, Chris Hughton, Tony Grealish, Mick Martin, Dave Langan, Frank Stapleton, Mark Lawrenson and Kevin Moran. (Sportsfile)

release players for competitive international duty. Arsenal and Spurs were due to contest a Milk Cup tie and we had been refused the release of Chris Hughton, Frank Stapleton, David O'Leary and John Devine. We won our case and, in the end, the Milk Cup game was rescheduled to accommodate us. The game was also notable for being Michael Robinson's debut.

As anticipated, France began the game on the front foot. They were attacking aggressively down the wings, with Platini and Tigana running the show in midfield. Tigana, in particular, was making powerful runs through the middle. It was also evident after the early exchanges that he was under orders to manacle Liam Brady. The French midfielder shadowed Liam everywhere and managed to keep him quiet while still having the ability to trouble us in attack. Our defence was heaving under the French pressure and, after twelve minutes, it cracked. A cross from the left was too high for Chris Hughton and the elusive Platini was on hand at the back post to chest down the ball and calmly fire home from close range. We were under the cosh for the remainder of the half, and although we came close through efforts from Grealish and Robinson, we were not doing enough to draw level.

In the second half that changed. The impetus went out of the French play and we gradually made inroads. The decisive moment in the game came early in the second half when Michael Robinson 'scored' an excellent goal. I thought that Michael had netted a goal on his debut, but he hadn't. It was disallowed. The reason given by the referee was that Kevin Moran had handled the ball while heading it down to Robinson. I am not sure what kind of view the official had of the incident but the video footage afterwards clearly showed that Moran had *not* handled it. The Irish people watching at home, however, could not commiserate with us because transmission of the match had been down when Robinson scored.

Had Michael's goal stood, an already frustrated-looking France might have crumbled under the expectations of a home crowd that demanded victory. Instead, they were emboldened to go on and put the game beyond us. In the seventy-seventh minute, they did just that when Jacques Zimako broke from deep and lofted the ball over the onrushing Gerry Peyton to make it 2-0.

I felt that the score line flattered the French, and, even though I was not pleased to leave Paris empty-handed, I knew that we were still in contention in the group. The French had yet to come to Lansdowne Road.

Our last game in 1980 was at home to Cyprus on 19 November. In what was a straightforward victory, we won 6-0, with goals from Gerry Daly (2), Tony Grealish, Michael Robinson, Frank Stapleton and Chris Hughton. We obviously needed the win, but, equally, we needed the goals because it was becoming increasingly likely that goal difference might determine the outcome in the group.

We ended 1980 on seven points from five games. Our first assignment in 1981 was the return fixture against Belgium, played at Brussels' Heysel Stadium on 25 March. We were without the injured Mark Lawrenson and David O'Leary. The first half went as well as we could have hoped. We dealt very well with the Belgians' pressure and their only real threat was coming from set pieces. Then, on the cusp of half-time, we had the ball in the Belgian net, but, for reasons that still remain a mystery to me, it was disallowed by the Portuguese referee Fernandes Nazaré. It had been a goal minted in north London with the Arsenal teammates Liam Brady and Frank Stapleton combining beautifully. Brady lofted a free kick into

The goal that never was, against Belgium in the 1982 World Cup qualifiers on 25 March 1981. Here the Irish players are protesting against referee Fernandes Nazaré's inexplicable decision to disallow Frank Stapleton's goal. We lost 1-0 to Belgium, a result which saw us finishing third in the group and so failing to qualify. (Sportsfile)

the near-post area, where Stapleton, who had peeled away from his marker expertly, slotted home. Frank was three or four feet onside and neither he nor anyone else so much as touched a Belgian player. A perfectly good goal now counted for nothing. With half-time so near, it would have been the ideal moment to take the lead but it wasn't to be.

The first half had been played in constant rain and in the second half the conditions worsened. The Brussels sky opened and the rain became torrential. A thunder-and-lightning storm soon followed and for a few minutes it even seemed that the game might be stopped. Inevitably, the pitch tore up and gradually transformed itself into a muddy quagmire. Both sides found it increasingly challenging to play football, and the game soon descended into an exhausting dogfight, with neither side looking like scoring.

The Belgians, in particular, needing the win, were extremely frustrated. The stalemate, however, suited us, because a draw would have kept us in a commanding position in the group. Then, with only three minutes remaining, Eric Gerets took an operatic dive, which the referee duly bought. Belgium was awarded a free kick on the very edge of the eighteen-yard box, on the right. A direct free kick from René Vandereycken looped into the box and ricocheted off the crossbar with the ball going almost vertically up into the air. With bodies everywhere jostling for position, Jan Ceulemans muscled his way towards the dropping ball, illegally held down McDonagh and headed home powerfully from three yards. It should have been a free kick out but, instead, the goal gave Belgium a 1-0 win.

As soon as the final whistle went, the players and I surrounded the referee to voice our disgust. Mickey Walsh, who played for Porto in the Portuguese league and so spoke some Portuguese, led the protests. He repeatedly labelled Nazaré a cheat but got no response, not even a ticking-off. Liam Brady then asked Mickey Walsh for the Portuguese word for 'thief'. Armed with his new word, Liam then ran back to Nazaré and called him just that and, ultimately, had to be physically held back he was so enraged.

I also could not contain myself. The sense of injustice cut deep. I joined the chorus and accused the referee of being corrupt and a robber and, in a moment of genuine indiscretion, I went further than that and said, 'You are a disgrace. You have taken money. You have taken a bribe.' Now that is the most serious thing I have ever said to a match official and I should have been reported to UEFA, but nothing came of it. Nazaré simply stood there motionless as I laid into him. He offered neither defence nor explanation. Even if I had been reported, that is one complaints process that UEFA would not have enjoyed sitting through: the undisputable video evidence would have made for very uncomfortable viewing.

In our dressing room afterwards there was a collective sense of disbelief that the game should have ended so abjectly. We could have come away with a draw, maybe a win, but now, nothing. The players' eyes were fixed on the floor. We might yet emerge from this group, but we had been robbed of two vital points.

As a rule, in football management, I have never been in the habit of laying the blame for defeat at the door of the referee. Yes, you are sometimes on the receiving end of poor refereeing decisions but, over the course of a season or an international campaign, you can usually be stoical about ill fortune and console yourself with the thought that the luck will even itself out eventually. But I could not apply that logic to the game against Belgium. We had been done by an unaccountable, shocking display of refereeing and with such costly consequences. A draw in Brussels would have kept our fate in our own hands but, instead, the defeat meant that we were now up against it in the group. With the Netherlands away and France at home to come, our final two games were going to push us to the very limit.

Our return match with the Netherlands came on 9 September 1981 in Rotterdam. The Dutch, who themselves still harboured hopes of qualifying, began with an attacking formation, and threw everything at us. The great Ruud Krol, a key component of the Dutch Total Football sides of the 1970s, was expertly controlling the Netherlands defence from his sweeper role. We managed to survive the early onslaught and countered a number of times. In the eleventh minute, however, we were the architects of our own downfall. Steve Heighway, dropping far too deep and collecting the ball from McDonagh in the left back position, tried to find Mick Martin. Frans Thijssen intercepted and, after a one-two with Cees van Kooten, he received the ball again and beat McDonagh from close range.

We rode our luck for the next thirty minutes or so, with the skilful Dutch forward Johnny Rep causing us particular problems. We drew level in the fortieth minute when Heighway, making amends for his earlier error, floated in an inviting cross from the right. Michael Robinson pulled away from his marker and scored with a tremendous volley from the edge of the box.

In the second half, we were once more pushed back by persistent Dutch pressure. Rep, again, was the thorn in our side. In the sixty-fourth minute, he flew past Dave Langan on the left wing and drove into the box where Langan, in chase, rear-ended him. Arnold Mühren converted the resulting penalty. At 2-1 down, and just when it looked as if we might cave in, we found renewed strength and began to dominate the home side. Seven minutes later, Frank Stapleton got the equaliser that secured us a crucial away point. The goal came from a powerful break forward from Mark Lawrenson, who showed both tenacity and skill to reach the touchline and pull back for Stapleton to head home.

We went into our final game, against France, on eight points and with our hopes of going to Spain still alive.

On 14 October a supremely confident French team arrived in Dublin. For us, the task was crystal clear: we had to beat the French. France still had two home games to come against Cyprus and the Netherlands. If we defeated them, they would have to win both those games to draw level with us on ten points. Then second spot, and the final qualifying berth, would be decided on goal difference.

The tension in Dublin had been building all morning. When we travelled to the ground with a police escort, I knew something exciting was unfolding. The streets were lined with scarves and green shirts. People kept spilling out of pubs and houses to cheer us on as the team bus rolled by. It was wonderful and the kind of following that I had never seen an Irish football side receive. We may have had only an outside chance of qualifying but the fans had bought into it and now their support was going to be vital.

The atmosphere inside Lansdowne Road was the most electric I have ever witnessed. With a bumper attendance of 54,000, it was the biggest crowd up to then to watch the international side playing in Ireland. Our performances in the group so far had convinced the public that Ireland could achieve what we had never achieved before: to qualify for an international tournament. We had earned their backing; now we needed to deliver on that. In the dressing room beforehand, I heard the deafening noise coming from the stands above us. It felt like all of Ireland had been crammed into Lansdowne Road to inspire us to victory.

Our plan was to keep the play at a high tempo because we knew France could hurt you if given time on the ball. We could not afford to sit back and let them have the freedom of the park to knock the ball around at their leisure. Instead, we were going to see how they liked playing under intense pressure. The instructions were to get tackles in early and to squeeze the play by defending the halfway line. I wanted to hit them early and get the crowd firmly behind us.

The Lansdowne crowd could be fickle. To get them going, you needed to give them something to shout about. I was determined that, today, we would. In the tunnel, moments before running out for the kick-off, our players were pumping up one another. I knew they were up for this and so did the French. Our opponents seemed taken aback at our unbridled display of passion.

When we walked out onto the pitch, the wall of sound hit us. A huge tricolour hung over the wall at the gasworks end emblazoned with the words: 'The French eat frogs; we eat the French.'

When the game kicked off, the roar from the stands set the tone for what would prove to be a riveting contest, played at an incredible level of intensity. Our tactics were working. We pinned the French back from the first whistle and took the lead after five minutes. Ronnie Whelan, not giving Gérard Janvion a moment on the ball, robbed the French defender with an aggressive tackle and fed Michael Robinson. Robinson, who was playing like a man possessed, drove at the French down their right side, jinked around a flailing French defender and broke into the eighteen-yard box. The whole ground was on its feet. Robinson delivered a low, powerful cross into the six-yard area where, under severe pressure from the arriving Frank Stapleton, the off-balance Philippe Mahut hammered the ball into his own net. The noise around the ground went up another a few notches as the fans now sensed that we could win this game.

As usual, however, we did not do things the easy way. Only four minutes later the French were back in it. In a sensational, sweeping move involving Alain Couriol and Bruno Bellone, France carved us open. Bellone, completing the move, turned on a sixpence past Kevin Moran and Dave Langan, and shot home from twenty yards. It was an exquisite goal and a harsh reminder of the talent in the French ranks.

We, however, resumed exactly where we had left off. Stapleton and Robinson were troubling the French defence and Dave Langan was marauding down our right flank. The French goalkeeper, Jean Castaneda, was earning his keep. He touched a powerful Stapleton shot around the post before dramatically saving from a Kevin Moran overhead kick.

In the twenty-fifth minute, the French cracked and we went ahead once more. A Mick Martin cross from the left sowed havoc in the French box with three defenders and the goalkeeper being drawn towards Stapleton. Everyone missed the ball and it fell to David O'Leary at the back post. David kept his head and pulled it back to the penalty spot where Stapleton side-footed it into the top-left corner. Frank was having the game of his life in green.

Minutes later Ronnie Whelan stepped out of midfield and cannoned a long-range effort off the French crossbar. The French were still in the game but were now visibly creaking under the pressure. We were thirty minutes in and, their single goal aside, they had barely had a touch.

I would have settled for a 2-1 lead at half-time, but when, in the fortieth minute, we scored a third, we were in dreamland. We were putting one of the best sides in the world to the sword. The goal came through the direct route. A long goal kick from Seamus McDonagh was flicked on by

Robinson to the feet of the French midfielder Jean-François Larios. Larios, normally a picture of serenity on the ball, panicked and attempted a rushed back pass. The ball ran straight back into the path of Robinson, who hit it first time past Castaneda. At 3-1, the French, pointing the finger of blame at one another, were in disarray. Seamus McDonagh was targeting the French defence with high balls because we knew they were vulnerable to the tactic. The goal proved the point to a tee. We went in at the break 3-1 up and filled with self-belief.

In the dressing room, the players were on a high but we still had another forty-five minutes to play and needed to gather ourselves. As fearful a pounding as we had given the French, it was clear to me that they would not take this lying down. They, too, had pride and the self-assuredness to come back out fighting. The players were told to forget the first half: it was gone. They needed to play the second half as if it were 0-0.

The second half was another seesaw affair. We managed to maintain our two-goal advantage until, in the eighty-third minute, Platini, after a beautiful reverse pass from Didier Six, popped up at the opportune moment to fire home from close range. The scene was set for a seven-minute siege, with Platini moved up front. France now bombarded our goal and, with only two minutes to go, it looked as if they might finally draw level. A rifled cross found Six free at the back post and he shot goalwards. Seamus McDonagh stepped up to deliver his best and most important save in an Ireland jersey. He flashed to his right and touched the ball around the post. McDonagh's miraculous save convinced me that we were going to do it. Minutes later, the referee blew the final whistle, the crowd spilled onto the pitch and we celebrated one of the great days of Irish football.

Belgium had already qualified as group leaders, so it was France or Ireland that would join them in Spain. We had done our part and sent the French away with a job to do: win their final two home games. Because France's goal difference was already significantly better than ours, realistically they would have to drop points for us to progress. We could only watch and wait. We did not expect them to slip up against the Cypriots, so our hopes lay with the Netherlands.

To gather myself after a rollercoaster day, I needed some quiet. Terry Conroy and I, having left the city, decided that a remote pub in Leixlip, The Hitching Post, would do the trick nicely. Some hope! When we entered the bar, a crowd of merry fans rushed us and lifted me off my feet.

Dave Langan evades the opposition with Ronnie Whelan looking on. Here, on 14 October 1981, in what was the finest victory of my time as Ireland manager, Ireland defeated Michel Platini's France 3-2 in a thrilling 1982 World Cup qualifier at Lansdowne Road. (Sportsfile)

'Hip-hip-hooray', they roared, as my 15-stone frame was hurled into the air three times like a rag doll. I was actually a bit worried that I might get hurt. What if one of these guys missed his catch? On the final shout, they dropped me to the ground like a sack of spuds and dispersed. Terry walked over, and in a one-liner spawned from countless trips slumming it with Ireland in below-par conditions, helped me to my feet and, in a nod to my English counterpart, said: 'Eoin, it wouldn't happen to Ron Greenwood.'

Unfortunately for us, France, in their final two games, did the necessary. They defeated the Dutch 2-0 at the Parc des Princes on 18 November, a game I travelled to Paris to watch. A demoralised Netherlands side, already out of contention in the group and rent by internal disputes between players and management, put in a lacklustre performance. On 5 December our campaign was over when France comfortably overcame Cyprus 4-0 in Paris and beat us to the final qualifying spot on goal difference. In the final standings, Belgium topped the group with eleven points, France and ourselves had ten apiece, while the Netherlands finished with nine points. Cyprus propped up the group on zero points. The gnawing sore was the fact that if Fernandes Nazaré's truly shocking refereeing display had not intervened, and we had held onto a point in Brussels, we, and not the Belgians, would have travelled to the 1982 World Cup. A wonderful group of Irish players were denied the opportunity to compete in football's greatest showcase.

It was the closest the Republic had ever come to qualifying for a major tournament. The French would go on to star at the World Cup where, after a thrilling 3-3 draw with West Germany in the semi-finals, they were ultimately eliminated by the Germans 5-4 on penalties. For many observers, France was the team of the tournament.

Northern Ireland, led by Billy Bingham, had qualified for the World Cup, as runners-up in their group. Throughout my term I had to become accustomed to unfavourable comparisons being made between the Republic and Northern Ireland. Although Northern Ireland was the first of the two to qualify for a World Cup (in 1958), by the 1980s the Republic were easily on a par with our neighbour. Some critics pointed out that, on paper, the Republic actually had much the stronger squad and questioned why Northern Ireland was travelling to Spain and we were not. There is merit to the argument, but only superficially. Northern Ireland – although their achievement had to be commended – qualified from a significantly weaker group than ours. Aside from Scotland, who topped that group, Northern Ireland faced Portugal, Israel and Sweden, none of whom were footballing forces in 1981. Added to that, Northern Ireland qualified on nine points and scored only six goals, while we garnered ten points and scored seventeen goals in what was most certainly the group of death. Billy Bingham and his squad deserved to go to the World Cup: they played what was in front of them and succeeded, but I am not going to accept the idea that our qualification paths were comparable.

Nonetheless, to see Northern Ireland qualifying and performing excellently in the summer of 1982 while we went on our summer holidays was, frankly, difficult to accept. Allied to that was the fact that 1982 was a great year for Irish sport generally. In Rugby Union, Ireland, led by Ciaran Fitzgerald, had won the Triple Crown for the first time since 1949. It would have been wonderful if we could have added a first World Cup appearance to that list of achievements.

Shortly before the 2002 World Cup, in a fascinating sequel to the controversy around Fernandes Nazaré, Paul Howard, writing for the *Sunday Tribune*, called to where I was living in Rathmines. He asked if I might still have video footage of Ireland's fateful encounter with Belgium in 1981. After rummaging through the house, I found an old VCR tape of the match and handed it over.

Paul's idea was to travel to Portugal, track down Nazaré, and confront the former referee with the video evidence. He managed to corner his man in Lisbon. A few weeks later, the results of Howard's investigation appeared in the *Sunday Tribune*. It did not make for comfortable reading, especially if you were Fernandes Nazaré.

Howard brings up the matter of Frank Stapleton's first-half disallowed goal. Immediately Nazaré jumps in and confidently proclaims that Stapleton was offside and that his linesman had made the call. Howard hits play, the footage rolls and Stapleton is shown so far onside as to render any debate on the matter irrelevant. Nazaré quickly revises his memory. 'I think I made a mistake when I told you it was offside. Yes, now I remember. I awarded an indirect free kick. My hand is up to say indirect. And Liam Brady shoots direct. That is why the goal was disallowed. Nobody touches the ball before it goes in the goal.' Howard presses Nazaré, reminding him of how Stapleton actually volleyed the ball into the net after Brady's delivery. Snookered again, but undeterred, Nazaré finds a new escape route, and claims that, in fact, the ball deflects off himself before flying past Michel Preud'homme in the Belgian goal. 'The ball hits off my back and goes in the goal. I remember that is why I disallowed the goal.' Once more, the video footage is played and the four feet between the ball and Nazaré is highlighted for him.

This time, however, finally, there is no explanation forthcoming. Nazaré has nothing further to add.

4

South American Lessons

1982 Summer Tour

While the pain of failing to qualify for the 1982 World Cup was still raw, the FAI came to me with a genuinely intriguing proposal. As a reward for the progress we had made, the general secretary, Peadar O'Driscoll, told me that the FAI had arranged a tour of South America for that summer. I was listening. 'Who will our opposition be?' I asked. 'Chile, Brazil and Argentina,' he replied proudly. I couldn't believe it! Playing Chile was good. Playing Brazil was even better, but playing Argentina in the summer of 1982 was frankly ludicrous. It was early May and an increasingly bitter Falklands War had been raging for more than a month. I knew that there was no way on earth that English clubs would release our players while their own country was at war with Argentina.

I was becoming weary of the FAI's eccentric travel plans. Only weeks earlier we had played Algeria, in Algiers, in what was the Republic's first match on African soil. The logistics of this trip made me begin to realise that nobody was joining up the dots at Merrion Square. The game was played on 28 April, on another continent, just as the English club season was reaching its climax. Naturally, it was very difficult to convince clubs to release players for such a long journey and at such a vital time of the season. Liverpool denied permission for Mark Lawrenson, Ronnie Whelan and Kevin Sheedy to travel because the club was on the run-in to clinching the First Division league title. Spurs said no to my request for Chris Hughton and Tony Galvin because they were due to play Birmingham City on the same night as our game with Algeria. Aside from these players, I missed out on ten other squad regulars because of the fixture's bad timing. We subsequently lost a frustrating match 2-0. Whatever about not being able to get players, the impracticality of these arrangements meant that we had travelled from London to Algiers at the end of April, returned to London in early May, and were due to fly out from London again, this time to South America, on 19 May. Three continents in three weeks!

In any other circumstances, I would have been delighted at the thought of playing Argentina. After all, they were the reigning World Champions and, in Maradona, they had a player who was obviously on the way to being the world's greatest. In footballing terms, it is fair to say that the FAI had done very well to arrange such a fixture, but it was simply the wrong time to play this game. The belief that we could just gather our players from Britain, land in Buenos Aires and play a harmless game of football, regardless of the political reality, was ridiculous. We would be making a major mistake if we went ahead with the fixture and I felt compelled to speak up. I met Peadar O'Driscoll in the lounge area of Shelbourne's Tolka Park in Dublin and immediately aired my concerns. I was firmly put back in my box. '*You* are not a politician. *You* are a football manager,' O'Driscoll told me. Fair enough, I *wasn't* a politician, but did I really need to be one to know how untenable the FAI's proposition was? And, in any case, I was not taking a political stance but making a blunt football point: I was just worried that we would have no players.

Furthermore, the planned tour was putting a strain on the relations between the Irish and English football associations. In those days there was no compulsion on clubs to release players for friendly internationals. So, as a small nation, nourishing any goodwill that existed between Ireland and the English FA was essential for our continued survival in international football. Opting to jeopardise this relationship was highly risky and I feared that the fallout would make it even harder for me in the future to get players released from English clubs and I made this point to the FAI.

The FAI, however, stridently declared that the Falklands conflict had nothing to do with us. 'Ireland is neutral,' some officials proclaimed. The FAI was also, I believe, under pressure from the Irish government, which did not want to be seen to be bowing to British demands. The neutrality argument may have been perfectly logical on a political level, but such a simple-minded view made little sense in a football context. With the exception of Liam Brady, who, as mentioned, then played in Italy's Serie A, the vast majority of our players earned their living in England, with English clubs. Their families depended on that continued employment. These players regarded it as no trivial dilemma. In fact, tensions were running so high in England that some commentators suggested that if the Irish players took part in the Argentina game, their very future in English football would be put in question. The harsh treatment that Spurs players and Argentinian internationals Ossie Ardiles and Ricky Villa were receiving from sections of the British public proved just what sustained abuse we could have been exposing our players to. In Ardiles' case, in order to weather the storm, he was compelled to go out on loan to French club Paris Saint-Germain for the 1982/83 season.

In spite of this issue hanging over my head, the prospect of going to South America and, in particular, to be playing Brazil in the Maracaná was exciting, both to me and to the players. As someone who had played against Brazil in the same stadium in 1974, I was well aware of what a special venue it was. This historic stadium was a footballing mecca, and to play Brazil there was no less than the ultimate test of where you stood in the world game. One way or another, this tour would tell us just how good we were – provided, of course, that I had a full-strength squad on which to draw.

Considering the sensitive nature of the Argentina fixture, I was surprised that the FAI did not seem to share my concerns. They were enchanted with the prospect of the game and did not want the feel-good atmosphere to be punctured. One spokesperson suggested that it would be no less than 'the greatest tour the Republic has ever had'. Understandably, for an organisation that was invariably short of cash, money played an important part in the decision. The FAI hoped to make at least £50,000 from the tour – a sum of money they could not easily put at risk.

Unfortunately, I was now going to have to try to sell the Argentina game to the English clubs. Although I felt deeply uncomfortable going to the clubs' managers with such a strange request, I officially had to make the approaches. In truth, my heart was not in it. I resolved to make token overtures to various clubs, knowing that I would be rebuffed, and thereby prove to the FAI that the Argentina fixture should not go ahead. Owing to the sensitive nature of the topic, I travelled to England to talk to the managers face to face.

Manchester United's Ron Atkinson was first up. We met at Old Trafford. I was not looking forward to the inevitably prickly exchange. I knew Ron from my playing days and we had often faced off against each other when Portsmouth played Oxford United. Ron was Ron: what you saw was what you got. Mr Bojangles, as he was known (he was fond of his jewellery), was flash and charismatic, but he was always likeable and a genuine leader. He was also not one to mince his words or suffer fools gladly. Ordinarily Ron was accommodating but these were, by any standards, extraordinary circumstances. I began gingerly. 'Ron, I need my players released for a South American tour. 'Sure, Eoin,' he replied, clearly not sensing where this was going. 'Who are you playing against?' Pause, before the impending eruption. Here we go, I thought. 'Brazil and Chile and Argentina, Ron.' 'What?' he exclaimed. 'You can tell the FAI that Ron Atkinson says "Fuck off".' Under a barrage of indignation I quietly replied: 'Yes, but I still need your official response, Ron.' 'That is my official response, Eoin: tell them to *fuck off*.' No ambiguity there, then. That was Kevin Moran, Frank Stapleton and Ashley Grimes scratched from my plans – all important players.

I continued on my dubious errand. Next up was Tottenham Hotspurs' manager Keith Burkinshaw. I wanted Chris Hughton, my first-choice left back, and the as-yet-uncapped Tony Galvin. Galvin's impressive performances on the left wing for Spurs had persuaded me that he was ready to step up to international level. His pace and directness were qualities generally lacking in our squad. And he was not just a head-down speed merchant either, as some had suggested; he was also capable of getting his head up and picking out the right option. I travelled to White Hart Lane to put my case to Keith.

Burkinshaw had been nothing less than a gentleman in his dealings with me in the past, but even his patience was stretched by the request being put to him. 'That's comical,' he told me and politely refused.

What had been clear to me from the start was quickly becoming a reality. The English clubs were not going to release their players and now the word was out: Ireland is thinking of playing Argentina. Everyone in the English game was asking: 'What has got into you people?'

I decided to go back to Ireland and try the other managers by telephone. I got in touch with Arsenal's manager Terry Neill to enquire about David O'Leary's availability, but he too showed scant enthusiasm for the idea. Arsenal then announced that they did not want O'Leary or John Devine to travel. Anyhow, O'Leary had shown little interest in the tour and I had found it very difficult to make contact with him on the topic. It was no

With the current Brighton and Hove Albion manager and former Irish international footballer, Chris Hughton, at the Brighton club's Amex stadium in 2016. Chris was a regular in the Ireland set-up during my term as national manager.

surprise to me when he subsequently publicly admitted that he did not want to go on the tour, regardless of his club's position.

Meanwhile my chances of having a strong squad were worsening by the day. The bad news would not stop coming. Liverpool quickly followed Arsenal's example and made it clear that Ronnie Whelan, Mark Lawrenson and Kevin Sheedy would not be released. Birmingham City manager Ron Saunders confirmed that Dave Langan would not be allowed to join us, and Brighton and Hove Albion ruled out the prospect of Tony Grealish, Michael Robinson or Gerry Ryan being made available. As for Mick Martin at Newcastle United, it was not looking good at all. When I made enquiries, the club chairman cryptically replied 'Put an extra sixpence on his insurance and he'll be ok,' and then declined to state the club's position. Although my options were limited in most departments, defence was of particular concern. Who was I going to play at centre half in the absence of Mark Lawrenson, David O'Leary, Kevin Moran and Mick Martin? Myself?

I went back to the FAI and pleaded with Peadar O'Driscoll to cancel the Argentina game. I reasoned that was the only course of action open to the FAI if there was to be any hope of salvaging at least the Brazil and Chile games. O'Driscoll would not budge. I was told to get on with it.

The Argentinian football officials, hearing the reports from Ireland, were now getting anxious and sought confirmation from the FAI that the Irish team would honour the fixture. They also stressed that they wanted recognisable names in our squad. It was now that one of the odder moments of the whole episode occurred. Someone in the FAI thought that a good way of appeasing the Argentinians would be to include Tony Ward on the tour. Tony, who has always been a great friend of mine, was certainly recognisable. Having won the European Player of the Year in 1979, by 1982 Tony was a genuine international rugby star and so it was felt that his presence would increase the publicity value of the tour, both for us and for the Argentinians. Although Tony was an accomplished footballer – he had played for my Limerick United side en route to winning the FAI Cup in 1982 – capping him for Ireland was never a serious possibility. Tony's first commitment was always to rugby.

At this point, in mid-May, the situation was dire. There were serious doubts over whether we could actually commit to this tour. I was determined that, if we went, it should be with the strongest squad possible. Professional and national pride was at stake.

With political pressure mounting and cold reality beginning to seep into the FAI's reckoning, the Argentina game was finally, and suddenly, axed from the schedule with only four days to go before our departure. I should add that the Association changed course only when I told them that I definitely could not get a team together. Now with only days remaining, the FAI officials were hurriedly trying to find replacement opposition for Argentina. They feared that they would make a loss from the tour and were getting desperate. If only they had listened to sense weeks earlier and cancelled the Argentina match at that point, we might have actually had time to find a decent alternative opposition and balance the accounts into the bargain. The South American nations were generally strong, so I would have been happy with most possible opponents.

Again, however, the FAI proved frustratingly unreliable in its efforts to organise this additional fixture. First they announced that everything had been solved – an agreement had been made to play Peru instead of Argentina. Great, I thought. But then, almost immediately, the Peruvian FA denied that any such arrangement existed. We were back at square one and running out of potential countries to play. If there was to be another opponent, for obvious practical reasons it would have to be on the South American continent. The FAI, however, cast the net much farther afield: all the way to Central America where they made contact with the Honduran FA. Nothing doing: the Hondurans were not interested. Apparently, the FAI, now with a sizeable financial hole to plug, had pushed it too far by demanding a fee of £36,000 for the fixture.

Now that the Argentina game had been wiped from the itinerary, at least the political situation had been dealt with. I began frantically ringing around to see if some of the English clubs would relent, given that the Argentina game had been scrubbed. On 12 May alone, I made fifty calls and, over the next few days, it would become hundreds.

I now faced new problems, however. Some clubs, such as Manchester United, had by this stage included their Irish players in their plans for post-season tours. United made it clear that Stapleton, Moran and Grimes were booked on their North American tour and would fly out on the same day that we planned to travel to South America.

A further complication was the fact that that season's FA Cup Final, between Tottenham Hotspur and QPR, was going to be played on 22 May – three days after our departure. This affected my plans to involve Gary Waddock, then a midfielder with QPR, as well as Spurs players Chris Hughton and Tony Galvin.

I now looked to the League of Ireland for players. I knew the League's players very well because I was still player-manager at Limerick United. However, I had yet another setback because the League's better players had already gone on tour to New Zealand as part of a League of Ireland selection. Even with these restrictions, I was still able to call on Dundalk striker Mick Fairclough and Limerick United's Johnny Walsh. Fairclough was getting his first call-up to the national squad and Walsh his second. Aside from the two League of Ireland players, I also selected the Aston Villa left back, Eamonn Deacy. I had first called up Eamonn a few weeks earlier for the Algeria game.

It was a relief to know that we would not play Argentina, but the decision had come too late. The upshot of it all was that the squad for South America would consist of only seventeen players, some of whom were not regular squad members.

In some cases I was compelled to pick players who were highly inexperienced at international level. It was not an ideal time to be blooding new talent, given the pedigree of opposition we would be facing.

Despite the challenges, however, my opinion was that I had a group of players who could compete on the tour. There were a few positive late inclusions who had made me form this opinion. Mark Lawrenson and Mick Martin were in. That would take care of some of my defensive concerns at least. Likewise, Brighton and Hove Albion relented and gave permission for Grealish, Robinson and Ryan to take part.

On the day on which we were to travel, 19 May 1982, the problems showed no signs of abating. Players and officials gathered in London's Heathrow Airport as arranged, but Mark Lawrenson, for reasons then unknown to me, failed to show up. With options (and time!) running out fast, I had to find a solution quickly. I rang Fulham. To my immense relief, they gave me their blessing for Seán O'Driscoll to join us. Full marks to Seán: he did not need to be asked twice and he made it to the airport at the shortest possible notice. He was also a new cap.

The absence of Lawrenson was a major blow. What was already a heavily depleted squad was now going to be shorn of one of its best players. I discovered only in later years that the FAI had, in fact, known that Mark was not going to show up on that day but, of course, had not let me know. It seems that the removal of the Argentinian fixture was not enough to convince the Liverpool manager, Bob Paisley. He told his Irish international players that the club was still not in favour of them travelling and backed this up by ringing O'Driscoll at the FAI to formally deny permission.

The squad that flew from Heathrow was: Seamus McDonagh (goalkeeper), Eamonn Deacy (defender), John Anderson (defender), Mick Martin (defender), Mike Walsh (defender), Liam Brady (midfield), Tony Grealish (midfield), Gerry Daly (midfield), Kevin O'Callaghan (midfield), Seán O'Driscoll (midfield), Johnny Walsh (midfield), Gerry Ryan (forward), Mick Fairclough (forward) and Michael Robinson (forward). We left with fourteen players but, in addition to this, I was assured by the FAI officials that Stoke City's Brendan O'Callaghan would fly out in time for the tour's second match, as would Chris Hughton and Tony Galvin.

On the flipside, the players I missed out on were: Mark Lawrenson, Ronnie Whelan, Kevin Sheedy, Frank Stapleton, Ashley Grimes, Kevin Moran, David O'Leary, John Devine, Mickey Walsh, Dave Langan, Gary Waddock, Mick McCarthy, Gerry Peyton, Packie Bonner, Joe Waters, Terry Donovan, Pat Nolan, Paul McGee, Don O'Riordan, Ray O'Brien, Paul Gorman and Gary O'Reilly. Twenty-two in all!

When we left London, the only seasoned internationals I could call on were Liam Brady, Mick Martin, Gerry Ryan, Gerry Daly, Seamus McDonagh and Tony Grealish.

We were now leaving Heathrow without even knowing the country we would play in the final game of our tour! This was highly unsatisfactory, to say the least. I began to wonder how an alternative friendly was going to be arranged against an international side at such short notice. I was also concerned about the quality of opposition we might get in the circumstances.

I did not dwell long on the issue, however, as a much more serious issue reared its head in mid-air. After we had changed flights in Madrid to begin the long journey to South America, O'Driscoll dropped the bomb. Although the FAI had abandoned the idea of facing the Argentinians, it had not changed the travel itinerary: we would still fly to Argentina before proceeding to Santiago, Chile. It was down to economics. Maintaining the current itinerary was obviously cheaper than booking new flights. This meant that, with the continuing Falklands War, we were bound for Buenos Aires' Ezeiza International Airport with half our players holding British passports – and for a ten-hour stopover! Although clearly nothing could be done at this stage (we were airborne, after all), I still let O'Driscoll know how I felt. I told him that flying into Buenos Aires with so many British passport-holders on board was reckless. I tried to explain that they could be arrested but, as was so often the case, the general secretary did not see the problem.

Flying south on our long journey, we had plenty of time to mull over our worst fears. What would happen when we landed? No one knew for sure how bad the situation was inside Argentina. Some of the squad were getting very worried. Michael Robinson, however unrealistic his fear, was particularly concerned that the Argentine authorities might detain him as a British spy. These players (while on Argentinian soil) would effectively be treated as citizens of an enemy state, so I could certainly see Michael's point.

And, as we all knew, the military junta, which had been ruling Argentina as a brutal dictatorship since 1976, had a terrible reputation. A number of British journalists had already been jailed for the crime of simply finding themselves on Argentinian territory.

Seamus McDonagh took a sleeping pill after leaving Madrid and expected to wake up in Santiago. Instead, he came to with the lights of Buenos Aires airport unfolding in the night sky below. He, like the rest us, had been kept in the dark on a crucial matter.

Just as we landed, however, comedy intervened to briefly puncture the heavy atmosphere. As we were gathering our baggage and filing out of the plane, I did a double-take when I noticed one FAI official getting ready to disembark. It was three o'clock in the morning, pitch dark outside and he was wearing sunglasses. I asked him why he had the sunglasses on. 'This is South America, Eoin. Everyone wears sunglasses here; the sun is always shining, isn't it?' Sure enough, looking unfazed, he walked off into the night air with his brand-new shades on.

Once we got off the plane and made our way to the airport arrivals area, events took a bad turn. Questions followed. Who were we? What was our business in Argentina? Minutes turned into hours and still we did not know if we would be allowed to leave the country. It was genuinely scary. The FAI officials were negotiating with the Argentinian officials and trying to explain that we were what we said we were: an international football team on tour. After plenty of nail-biting on our part, they relented and allowed us to board our plane to Santiago. There was genuine relief when we took off and the atmosphere on board became palpably more relaxed. With the politics finally out of the way, we could focus on the forthcoming tour.

We landed in Santiago on 20 May and were due to play the Chileans the next day. Santiago was grim. At this time, it was still under the military dictatorship of General Augusto Pinochet and it showed. From what we witnessed, it was clear that this was no ordinary place. Attesting to the oppressive nature of the regime, there were soldiers everywhere you went on the city's streets. The venue of our match would be the same infamous national stadium where I had played for Ireland in 1974. On the morning of the match there was yet more bad news: FAI treasurer Charlie Walsh rang from Dublin to inform me at the training ground that Tony Galvin would not be travelling after all. Despite the assurances I had received before leaving for South America, Walsh now told me that Galvin, because of a passport issue, could not be cleared to represent the Republic in time for the forthcoming games. This was disappointing, but, with our first game only hours away, I turned to the immediate task ahead. To be honest, given how poor the scheduling had been, and the general lack of support coming from the FAI, I was unsure how the contest would unfold.

In front of a crowd of 16,000 at Santiago's Estadio Nacional, we did not start well. After forty-five seconds Chile took the lead through their centre forward Miguel Ángel Gamboa. The goal came in controversial circumstances. Our first attack was repelled and then, taking us by surprise, a second ball was suddenly thrown onto the pitch. The Chileans proceeded to counter-attack quickly and, with our defence caught square, found the net. Chile was a highly defensive side, preferring to soak up pressure and then play on the breakaway. For this reason, the early lead suited their game plan well: they could sit back and try to protect what they had. For the remainder of the first half, we gradually grew into the game, with Liam Brady, in particular, constantly probing and seeking the decisive pass. On the left of our front three, Kevin O'Callaghan was causing problems for the Chilean rearguard. He played one excellent cross into the box but Michael Robinson failed to get on the end of it. On the whole, we were guilty of taking too many touches when in positive positions.

In the second half, the Chileans employed the same defensive strategy and we slowly began to lose penetration. We resorted to more optimistic long balls. It wasn't working. We became dangerous again only in the final fifteen minutes, when we managed to stretch the play by bringing O'Callaghan into the game more often.

The game, however, would produce no more goals, and so the Chileans hung on to take victory. Considering that we had played the match on the day after a long-haul flight and with a far from full-strength side, a 1-0 defeat on the South American continent was, I believed, not a disastrous result. It was clear to me, however, that there was a lack of familiarity among the players, some of whom were playing together for the first time.

With the result barely digested, more complications arose the next day. I got news from England that the Cup Final had ended in a 1-1 draw and the replay was scheduled for 27 May – the same day that we were due to face Brazil. This meant that both Gary Waddock and Chris Hughton would be able to make it out only for the tour's final fixture, whoever that was going to be against.

We flew to Rio de Janeiro on 22 May to prepare for the match with Brazil and, once we settled into our hotel base, I was quickly reminded of just what it was like to travel with FAI officials. While doing my best to wrestle with the numerous football issues piling up in my in tray, I was also trying to deal with the FAI. Many of the officials were drawn from local football in Ireland and were effectively travelling with us as a reward for their work in the local Irish game. Although the players, management and support staff, as on any tour, were in South America to work, our officials, with the exception of O'Driscoll, were essentially on holiday. This meant that they were on an entirely different wavelength from the rest of us. In ordinary circumstances, these people would not have found themselves in exotic South American locations. When they did, the consequences could be quite humorous.

Late one night, at our Rio hotel, I was getting ready to turn in for the night when I met an animated John Farrell, the president of the FAI, in the hotel lobby. He had spent the evening at a formal dinner arranged by the Brazilian Football Association. Farrell had been a guest of honour and, as was the norm, he had been given a gift by his generous hosts. He was brandishing a broken and battered-looking statue of a swan. With the severed neck in one hand and the body in the other, he shouted: 'Look at the shit fucking present they gave me, Eoin!' In a fit of pique, Farrell had actually broken it in two. I had a closer look and quickly realised that it was worth substantially more than the crestfallen Farrell had estimated. 'Hold on a second, John. This is valuable. This is onyx', I told him. 'Oryx, what the fuck is Oryx?' he snapped back at me. '*Onyx*, John. *Onyx*. That's an expensive present.'

His face dropped and the former scowl was rapidly replaced with an oh-no-what-have-I-done type-expression. He quickly turned on his heels to find the Brazilian delegate, calling out 'I need a new one. I need a new one. This one's broken.' Whatever flaws he may have had, I liked John Farrell. He was an honest, straight-up guy.

After the Chile match, unfortunately, it was obvious that Michael Robinson was not fit to face Brazil and that his tour was over. Michael flew home with injured knee ligaments. On 24 May, Brendan O'Callaghan flew out to replace him.

Now, with a few days to go before the Brazil game, there was time to train and also to let the players relax a little. The squad were keen to experience the Rio atmosphere, so one day we went for a stroll on Copacabana Beach. From my time in Brazil in 1974, I knew all about the hazards of Rio and warned the players to look after their money. With unsuspecting tourists everywhere, the busy beach was a pickpocket's heaven. After my stern warning to the squad, I did not think that I would, in fact, be the first to fall foul of the local fraudsters.

It happened all so casually. When I was walking along the beach a young woman came up to me and started becoming all touchy-feely, effectively offering sex. I ignored her and moved on. A few minutes later, however, an agitated Brendan O'Callaghan came to me to say that a woman had just groped him with one hand and tried to rob his wallet with the other. I asked him if she had red hair and a purple top. 'Yes. That's exactly the one', he told me. I felt my back pocket. There was no wallet there!

In the days before the game, the Brazilian FA made a very unwelcome surprise move. Unaccountably, they had switched the match venue, at short notice, from Rio de Janeiro's Maracaná Stadium to the Parque do Sabiá Stadium in the provincial Brazilian city of Uberlândia. This was a big disappointment for many of the players, who were understandably keen to play in Rio's historic stadium. I know Liam Brady, for one, cited the magnetic draw of the Maracaná as one of the reasons he had come on the tour in the first place. From a preparation perspective, it also added yet more arduous air miles to our itinerary. Yes, the Brazilians would also have to make the flight, but they would not have been halfway around the world in the previous week, as we had. Although I enquired, I never managed to discover the real reason for the change of venue. From as much as I understood, it was a politically motivated decision to take the national team to provincial Brazil and away from the traditional footballing bases of Rio and São Paulo.

On 26 May, the day before the Brazil match and the FA Cup Final replay, I rang the Spurs' secretary to make sure that Chris Hughton would still be travelling. After all the mishaps that had already occurred, I was not leaving anything to chance. I was told that all was in order. I then checked Chris's travel arrangements with his wife in their London home at approximately 6 p.m. that day and she told me that Chris would fly from Heathrow on 28 May.

I was happy to get this confirmation at least but, very quickly, I had a fresh set of problems to deal with. The players had been promised a fee of £1,080 each by the FAI, but it still had not been paid. Aside from the £180 that they had received at the outset, the players had no other cash and now, after a week in South America, many of them were running out of money. In addition, they were becoming increasingly frustrated with the fact that the tour's final game had not yet been decided upon. The FAI still could not confirm a part of the itinerary that should have been nailed down long before our plane took off from Heathrow seven days earlier. Instead, like an aimless touring comedy troupe, we were travelling around another continent with no clue of our final destination. You cannot treat professional players like this and not expect a backlash and so, predictably, I now had a budding mutiny on my hands. Morale was on the floor and several players threatened to walk out of the tour if the money was not paid and clarity immediately given on our final game.

I needed to act. I went in search of O'Driscoll but he was nowhere to be found in the hotel. I walked outside and eventually discovered him relaxing in the early morning heat of Rio with Farrell. I told them of my deep unhappiness with how the tour was going. 'Don't worry, Eoin. We'll get it sorted. We'll get it sorted,' O'Driscoll kept repeating. I was coming close to breaking point. I would have needed ten feet of paper to itemise everything that had already gone wrong on this tour and now they were telling me not to worry. I snapped: 'Well then, get it sorted.' But they just did not get it. 'What's wrong with you, Eoin? This is the greatest tour we've ever been on. We are in Rio. This is brilliant,' O'Driscoll told me. That said an awful lot. I began to realise that being there at all was the measure of success for the FAI. The Association and I couldn't have been further apart.

I would have to up the ante. I told them that I would resign on the spot if they did not pay the players immediately and tell us where our final game would be played. This was as far I could push it and, certainly, I was ready to walk but still they did not look particularly fazed. Mercifully, though, they relented and promised to pay the players in full within days. Problem number one solved. Good. But, problem number two – the issue of our last game – was only beginning. I was informed that it would be against Trinidad and Tobago *in* Trinidad, a mere 4,000-odd kilometres, and at least a six-hour flight away, by the quickest route.

Whatever about the immense travel distance, though, it was the choice of route that beggared belief. Once more, with the FAI's false economies to the fore, the organisation had gone shopping for flights in the bargain basement. Amazingly, I was told that we would fly from Rio to the Colombian capital,

Bogotá, then change flights and board a connecting plane to Caracas in Venezuela before changing once more en route to Port of Spain in Trinidad. As well as involving three separate flights, this was clearly the long way around – a glance at an atlas would have told you that. So far, so bad, but the punchline was yet to come. We would board the flight to Bogotá at 7 a.m., only two hours after returning from Uberlândia at 5 a.m. I protested vehemently, but Farrell and O'Driscoll were not for turning. As always with the FAI, the organisation knew the price of everything but the value of nothing.

Rather than waste my time arguing, I decided to do my own research. Finally, after some phone calls, I discovered an alternative route. There was, in fact, a direct flight from Rio to Miami in the United States, where a connecting flight would take us on to Port of Spain. This was a much shorter journey and it cut out the laughable early-morning, two-hour turnaround between flights. Unable to deny the merits of the proposal, the FAI officials caved in and agreed to this option.

With the practicalities looked after, there was now only the small matter of facing one of the top international sides in the world. I had the best players I could assemble, but, ultimately, this was not the same squad who had just recently taken the Republic of Ireland so close to World Cup qualification.

You do not arrive to play Brazil without having your house in order but, with all the disarray of our tour, that is exactly what we were doing. We were going into the lion's den seriously weakened. If we'd had our first-choice eleven, we would not necessarily have won – I realise that – but we would certainly have pushed Brazil a lot more and, at least, forced the best out of them. Unfortunately, many of our best players were back in Europe, and there was not a limitless pool of first-rank backup players from which to choose.

There is no transfer market in international football. Splashing the cash on new signings, like a club manager might do, is a luxury that is just not available to you. You cannot go out and buy a player if you are lacking cover for a certain position. You can only bide your time, keep your eyes open, and hope that another gem will present itself somewhere along the way. For this reason, international management is a case of the loaves and the fishes: you are always trying to extract the maximum from available resources.

Looking back now, the build-up to the Brazil game was very odd. In a move that could never happen in today's incredibly controlled international camps, we actually shared a chartered flight with the Brazilian squad to take us to the match venue in Uberlândia. This created the surreal experience of finding ourselves at close quarters with our opponents for a couple of hours.

I got talking with the Brazilian manager, Telê Santana, and many of the players. Despite their footballing prowess and their undoubted star quality, it struck me how humble and polite they all were. There were no pampered egos in that squad, just down-to-earth men honoured to wear the yellow-and-blue of Brazil. Liam Brady was mixing with some of the Brazilian players whom he knew from playing in Italy, Falcão, in particular, who at that time played for Serie A's AS Roma. Santana even took a Brazil tracksuit top, passed it around the plane for every player to sign and then offered it to me as a gift. It was a kind gesture. Finding the Brazilians so approachable almost lulled you into a false sense of comfort, but I knew that once they crossed the white line, the smiling would be over.

Coming into the match, Brazil, for all their brilliance, were not exactly in scintillating form, as was evident from two recent unimpressive home draws against Czechoslovakia and Switzerland. However, with an attack boasting the likes of Zico, Sócrates, Éder, Careca and Falcão, they were unquestionably the best offensive side on the planet and favourites to lift that summer's World Cup. The occasion had a celebratory feel to it. The 72,000 jubilant home fans, packed into the stadium, were there to see off a side that, only days later, would travel to Spain for the World Cup.

Despite everything, we started the game well. The inevitable early onslaught came but we held back the storm and even began to look comfortable. Éder, on the left wing, however, was beginning to trouble us. On the half-hour mark, he played yet another dangerous cross into the box which we managed to clear, but only into the path of the onrushing Falcão. Known for his long-range strikes, he did not need an invitation to shoot. He hit an instant snap shot which looped in over a caught-off-guard Seamus McDonagh. I was disappointed that we had conceded a goal, but we remained solid for the rest of the half. When we went in only 1-0 down at half-time, I was happy enough. We had kept our shape and largely frustrated our hosts. We were still in this game.

The second half, however, was a very different story. Éder murdered us from dead-ball situations. He was known for having one of the most powerful left boots in the game and, as we soon found out, it was pretty accurate also. In the fifty-fifth minute, he delivered a vicious corner to the back post where Sócrates rose highest to nod the ball home. Our heads dropped and the sluice gates were flung open. With our players now tiring, some of whom were not fully accustomed to the rigours of international football, and concentration levels plummeting, we were no longer able to provide meaningful resistance.

Ten minutes later it was déjà vu: Éder again unerringly hit the back post with an unstoppable in-swinging corner and Serginho headed in Brazil's third. In the sixty-ninth minute, Éder sent in his third well-placed corner. McDonagh came for it and caught the ball but then spilled it as he fell to the ground. Luizinho was on hand to hammer the ball in from three yards: 4-0. I was now worried about how many goals we might ship. The game was gone, I knew that, but it would get worse – a lot worse. In the seventy-third minute a short corner from Éder was dummied by Sócrates on the edge of the eighteen-yard box. It fell to Falcão whose deflected shot found its way to Sócrates once more. The Brazilian captain fired the ball into the roof of the net to make it five. Two minutes later Serginho added a sixth on the break. And then, in the seventy-ninth minute came the final indignity. A low, driven corner by Éder curled towards our goal where the great Zico turned sharply and hit the net from close range, to give his country a 7-0 win.

When the final whistle went, our players were crushed. They were so shocked and dejected, they made straight for the tunnel without swapping jerseys with their opponents. After what they had just been through, that was the last thing on their minds, even if a Brazilian jersey is a prized possession in international football.

The Brazilian players, in all fairness, did not gloat. They were, in fact, almost apologetic about the ruthless manner in which they had put us to the sword. To get back to Rio, we had again to share the flight with the Brazilian squad but this time with our heads in our hands as our opposite numbers sang their way through the night sky with the chain-smoking Sócrates orchestrating the whole concert. We could have done with some privacy at that stage, but at least it was a chance for a few of our players to finally swap shirts with their counterparts.

In the days after the Brazil result, I thought about the game incessantly. Any manager earns his corn by dissecting a result with a dispassionate eye. Win, lose or draw, you are looking for signs of progress, positives that can be applied in future matches. Where the media, in a knee-jerk response, might often view defeat as an unqualified disaster, as a manager you are paid to cast a more analytical eye over proceedings. You may have, in fact, seen plenty to convince you that your team is making real progress. With the Brazil result, however, there was nothing to take from it. It was a pointless hammering, nothing more. At the time of writing, it is still the Republic's record defeat. A woefully under-strength and tired squad got the footballing lesson it deserved.

Lack of preparation puts you on the back foot. When nothing has been properly planned, you are stuck in a reactive pattern, with each new setback coming as an unwelcome surprise. This was the exhausting rigmarole that the tour had trapped me in: chasing my tail in constant firefighting mode.

Back in Rio, before we left for Trinidad, the tour's next drama erupted. Naturally, everyone was extremely unhappy with the Brazil result, but it hit Liam Brady particularly hard. He decided that he wanted to quit the tour and fly back to his wife in Turin on the next available flight. Liam was determined: he insisted he would cover the cost of the fare himself, no matter what the expense. He was deeply depressed over the way Brazil had routed us. It had been his dream to play against the Brazilians, but he had never thought that, when it finally came true, it would be such a nightmare. None of us had ever been on the receiving end of such a hiding. And Liam had his professional pride: he knew some of the Brazilian players and had been eager to put in a good account of himself on Brazilian soil. It hadn't happened.

Although, looking in from the outside, Liam's behaviour may have seemed difficult to understand, he was, in fact, under a lot of pressure, and I knew that. It was his first wedding anniversary and he had just learned that his wife was pregnant with their first child, and, say what you like about professional footballers leading a privileged existence, it never gets easy being away from one's family. Furthermore, Liam was in protracted negotiations with the Genoese club Sampdoria. He had just finished his second season at Juventus and, although his time there had been a success, the talent that the Turin club could draw on was pushing Liam down the pecking order. Midfielders Michel Platini and Zbigniew Boniek had just arrived that summer from Saint-Étienne and Widzew Łódź respectively, so suddenly Liam was looking for a new club. Serie A was the best, and richest, league in the world in the 1980s; it was no shame to lose your place in that league's premier side.

Whatever about the reasons for Liam's stance, though, I had to try and persuade him that the only sensible option was to finish the tour. The press, with headlines that would have written themselves, would have torn him to shreds. Liam would have been unfairly portrayed as a deserter who had abandoned his fellow countrymen at their lowest ebb. The press would not have given a thought for the extenuating circumstances. They would have crucified Liam. I knew that Liam was devoted to playing for his country and, in the case of the South American tour, he had been one of the first players to confirm his intention to travel, while many other big names had stalled over the invitation.

I urged Liam to consider the impact this decision would have on his career, but he would not listen. This was serious. I then approached his close friend Mick Martin in the hope that he could talk Liam around. As for the rest of the squad, I felt they did not need to know what was taking place. I had to contain the situation and change Liam's mind. We were on a very tight schedule and were due to leave for Miami the following morning. Brady, to have any hope of boarding the plane, needing convincing that night. Unfortunately, even Mick got short shrift and could not get his good friend to change his mind.

As a final throw of the dice, I told my assistant, Terry Conroy, to stay back with Liam in Rio, while I, with the rest of the squad, travelled to Miami. Fortunately, the next day, 28 May, the situation calmed down. Brady was unable to get a flight to Italy at such short notice and Terry was able to impress upon him that he would be far better off playing football in Trinidad than hanging around Rio at a loose end. The two took a later flight and joined us in Trinidad two days later.

We were exhausted from our exertions and in no condition to play another game, but there would be no let-up. The players were like zombies at this stage and I could see no value in playing further matches, but onwards we marched. What the FAI had buoyantly termed 'the greatest tour the Republic has ever had' was quickly becoming more about hoovering up air miles than playing football matches. It was back to the airport for a draining long-haul flight to Miami and the Caribbean to fulfil the tour's schedule.

At this point, I also knew that Gary Waddock would not be part of the tour. Along with Chris Hughton, he was one of two players I had hoped would make it for our final game. However, given that the FA Cup replay had been played only on 27 May, I did not expect either player to come. It was just a bonus that Chris had indicated his desire to travel. Chris's attitude was never less than excellent and his willingness to join up with us in such circumstances proved the point.

On the day we were leaving for Trinidad, I took a phone call from Charlie Walsh in Dublin. To my disbelief, he was now telling me that there actually was no flight from London to Trinidad that day, so Chris Hughton would not be joining the squad. This just made no sense. The FAI had booked a flight ticket for that day, so surely there was a flight? I wanted to get to the bottom of it. I phoned the Hughton household to find Chris livid on the end of the line. He had gone to White Hart Lane to collect his plane ticket, as planned, and had even travelled to Heathrow Airport. However, just as he was about to check in, his name was called over the tannoy, informing him that there was an urgent phone call for him to take. It was his wife telling him not to travel. A mystery woman had phoned her to say simply that Chris should not travel because he was no longer needed. I have never found out the identity of this caller nor just what the true explanation of it all was. I could only agree with Chris when he made it clear how unhappy he was. It was the day after an exhausting FA Cup Final replay (which Spurs had won), yet he had made every effort to get to South America to play for his country. The worst part, though, as I subsequently found out, is that there *was* actually a flight to Port of Spain that day. This was all just a money-saving exercise. Someone with a tight hand on the purse strings (presumably the treasurer Charlie Walsh) had made a football decision without consulting me.

On arriving in Trinidad, our first assignment was not to play the national side, but to play a warm-up game against the island's best club side, ASL. Our demoralised and jet-lagged players were not in any state to contest a football match and it was not a great surprise when we lost 2-1. Liam scored our only goal, despite coming straight from the airport and making it to the ground with minutes to spare. The game was an ordeal for us. I remember one player being so disorientated that he ended up playing with his shorts on backwards. The same player would thank me for taking him off at half-time. It is the only time in my memory that a player actually thanked me for substituting him.

On 30 May, with the players rested, we played the Trinidad and Tobago national side and comfortably won 3-0. However, although we managed to win this one game – in a tour where everything that could have gone wrong did – even this result was now bizarrely snatched from our hands. The record books say that Trinidad and Tobago won 2-1, but we actually won the game 3-0. We had, in fact, as already mentioned, lost 2-1 to the club side ASL a few days before. There was no press pack at the game, so Trinidad and Tobago, with the help of one local journalist, slyly reversed the results of the two matches. Bear in mind that this was the pre-Internet age. There were no videos of the matches that could have been uploaded to YouTube to expose the deception. It was unfair, but what could I do? We had just been thrashed 7-0 by Brazil. I wasn't going to come home and boast about having slain the mighty Trinidad and Tobago.

The South America tour revealed a lot to me. There was such a fundamental disconnection between the FAI officials and the players and management staff. We were trying to win football matches but, to give ourselves every chance, the off-pitch arrangements should have been much better. The FAI, although perhaps well-meaning in its efforts, proved on this trip, however, that its officials did not understand how vital these aspects of preparation were. Obviously there had been issues with the travel agent who had booked the trip, but ultimately the buck stopped with the FAI officials. It was their responsibility to make sure that everything was in tip-top order *before* our plane left the tarmac at Heathrow.

It was shocking to see the reality because I knew how high the stakes were. After our performances in the 1982 World Cup qualifiers, Ireland's reputation had soared. It was the country's best-ever qualifying campaign. Finally, other leading nations were taking us seriously. But now, with our calamitous summer tour lurching from one scene of mayhem to another, whatever respect we had commanded was dwindling by the day. It takes a long time and a lot of work to earn kudos in international football, but, regrettably, not long at all to lose it. The FAI had initially shown great ambition in lining up the South American tour but they simply lacked the know-how and experience to organise it in a proper and professional manner.

No matter what way you dressed it up, the tour was a disaster. I was already trying to forget that it had ever happened and, most importantly, I wanted to try and get it out of the players' systems as quickly as possible.

Coming into the summer of 1982, we had made significant progress on the pitch and with that came genuine self-belief. What I needed from the South American trip was an opportunity to build on that confidence by putting our best foot forward and facing some of the world's strongest teams. Everything about this tour, from its conception to its execution, was a shambles.

During the South American tour, I found out the hard way just how amateurish the FAI was. The tour was not pleasant to live through. From now on I decided that I would try personally to ensure that travel and accommodation arrangements were better organised. Mundane operational tasks should not be left with the manager; however, with the FAI you had to accept them as part of your duties.

Now, though, my attention turned to the next big challenge: qualifying for the 1984 European Championships.

5

Alligators and Six-Inch Nails

1984 European Championship Qualifiers

After our near-miss World Cup campaign, and with expectations set higher than ever for an Irish national team, we were drawn alongside Spain, the Netherlands, Iceland and Malta in Group Seven of the 1984 European Championship qualifiers. We were well aware that the margin between success and failure in this group was going to be paper thin: of the five teams, only one would qualify for the tournament in France. Spain and the Netherlands were clearly the favourites in the group. I hoped that there would be no hangover from our doomed summer tour.

On the organisational side of matters, I finally managed to improve our accommodation arrangements for home games. Up to then, the FAI had always billeted the squad at the Green Isle Hotel in Clondalkin, on the west of Dublin, with our training camp being located at the Maccabi Grounds in Crumlin. The logistics did not add up: the players were flying into Dublin Airport, then travelling across the city to stay in Clondalkin, followed by training back towards the city in Crumlin. Without consulting the FAI, I decided to do some digging. I enquired from the Dublin Airport Hotel if they would be willing to give a good group rate for the Irish squad. They offered us accommodation at the bargain price of £15 a head. For the hotel, it was a publicity coup to have the national side quartered there. After that, I contacted the managers of the Aer Lingus Social and Athletic Association (ALSAA) grounds on the Old Airport Road, a training ground situated on the very doorstep of Dublin Airport. They, too, jumped at the suggestion. I ran the idea by Charlie Walsh and he was delighted. 'Let's do it', he said.

The Republic of Ireland line-up in 1982: I had the good fortune of managing one of the greatest generations of Irish football. *Back row* (*l–r*): Kevin Moran, Seamus McDonagh, Mark Lawrenson, Ronnie Whelan, David O'Leary. *Front row* (*l–r*): Dave Langan, Liam Brady (captain), Frank Stapleton, Chris Hughton, Michael Robinson and Mick Martin. (Sportsfile)

Everyone was happy: the FAI saved some money and we could now train and stay in the one location.

We opened our Euro '84 campaign with a demanding assignment, away to the Netherlands, in Rotterdam on 22 September 1982. The Dutch were steadily returning to being a force in world football. After finishing runners-up at the 1978 World Cup, the Johan Cruyff-led golden generation had moved aside, leading to a number of relatively fallow years on the pitch. By 1982, however, a new group of players was ready to fill the void. The core of the team that would go on to win Euro '88, in style, was already in place: Ruud Gullit, Marco van Basten, Ronald Koeman, Frank Rijkaard, Adri van Tiggelen and Hans van Breukelen, all up-and-coming players during this campaign.

On our side, we had three late withdrawals to contend with: Ronnie Whelan, Gerry Peyton and Kevin Moran were all out injured. The Dutch had adopted an entirely new formation and took a much more expansive approach than I had anticipated. A number of weeks earlier, when I watched them draw 1-1 away to Iceland in the group, they had conservatively strung five players across midfield with one up front. However, with home advantage, they began in Rotterdam with an offensive-minded 4-3-3 line-up. I knew what the change meant: they were intent on knocking us out early, and, unfortunately, that is just how the early exchanges would play out.

The Dutch applied the pressure from the first whistle and with less than a minute gone, a poor headed clearance by David O'Leary landed at the feet of forward René van der Gijp, who crossed for Dutch midfielder Dick Schoenaker. From close range McDonagh had almost no chance and, predictably, Schoenaker hammered it home. A dream start for the Dutch; a nightmare one for us: 1-0 down after only thirty seconds!

We were finding it very difficult to come to terms with the Dutch players' movement off the ball. Our opponents' front six were interchanging positions with each other fluidly and at will, so we repeatedly ended up being outnumbered in defence, with Mick Martin left on his own as the last man. I was disgusted at the casual cynicism of the streetwise Dutch midfield and defence. They were content to concede free kicks against Robinson, Daly and Stapleton whenever necessary and then routinely line up behind the ball to defend the ensuing set piece.

Conceding an early goal away from home, before you have established any rhythm in a match, can cast your best-laid plans to the wind but, thankfully, we had enough about us to retain our shape and not crumble. Eventually we gained a toehold in the game and worked our way back into what was turning out to be a very nasty first half. Daly, Robinson and Grealish, in particular, tested van Breukelen.

In the second half we continued to match the Dutch, with Liam Brady orchestrating our best moments from deep. However, we lacked variety in our game and in this respect we badly missed Ronnie Whelan. His intelligent off-the-ball runs could have caught the Dutch on their blind side.

In the sixty-fourth minute we fell to a piece of individual brilliance from Gullit. Owing to his height and physicality, he came off the better in a tussle with Chris Hughton on the left wing. He then turned instantly and rifled home from over twenty yards, across McDonagh's body. The speed of Gullit's vision and execution caught us off guard. It was a goal fashioned out of nothing. We were 2-0 down and facing an uphill battle. Despite the odds, I was pleased that we continued to probe and to seek the opening that might get us back into this contest. Brady was having a superb game and so in the seventy-fifth minute I replaced Tony Galvin with Gary Waddock. My reasoning was that the extra defensive ballast that Gary would bring to midfield would allow Brady to take a completely free role in attack. The change paid dividends. A few minutes later, Brady wrong-footed one Dutch defender with an exquisite dummy and brought an excellent flying save out of van Breukelen from twenty-five yards. In the seventy-ninth minute, Brady again showed great tenacity and ability to get down the Netherlands' left flank to square for Gerry Daly who slid the ball home from close range.

We pinned the Dutch back in the final ten minutes but could not find the equaliser. Narrowly losing away to the Netherlands was, on paper, not a bad result, but we were very disappointed. We had gone to Rotterdam to win and we had high ambitions in this group. With so few games to contest in the campaign, we now had a must-win match coming up at home to Iceland on 13 October 1982.

Iceland was an organised and highly defensive side. As mentioned, the previous month they had held the Dutch to a draw in Reykjavík and this game proved that they liked to soak up pressure and then spring attacks on the break. We would need to build attacks steadily and overcome the Icelandic resistance without losing our shape. To deal with Iceland's counter-attacking threat, I employed two holding players, Grealish and Waddock, to anchor the midfield. Whelan and Brady were given licence to get forward as much as possible to give support to our front two. When the game got under way, Iceland stuck to form with their four defenders staying at home and paying close attention to Robinson and Stapleton. We were being stifled and were not making enough positive runs from deep. On occasion we also looked nervous at the back. The main threat from the visitors came from high balls into the box but Seamus McDonagh was dealing with them comfortably.

In the thirty-sixth minute we got the goal that calmed our nerves. With his back to goal, Robinson passed back for Whelan who played an inch-perfect ball into Stapleton's path. Frank turned and shot expertly across the Icelandic keeper. It was an excellent, composed goal.

In the second half Iceland offered nothing going forward and it only became a question of whether or not we could finish them off. Mark Lawrenson, at right back, was having one of his best games for Ireland and was breaking forward almost at will. Aside from his obvious ability on the ball, Lawrenson was an exceptionally versatile player. I had been criticised for using him at right back but Mark had it in him to play in a number of positions. I variously deployed him at centre half, full back and in central midfield. In defence he was masterful. With his timing, pace and positional sense, he rarely had to resort to the last-ditch tackle. Mark didn't clobber forwards, he coaxed and guided them away from the danger area until eventually there was no longer any threat. He also had a great attitude: whatever you asked of him, he would just say 'Yeah. Sure, Eoin. No problem.' I think if I had asked him to go in between the sticks, he would have asked, 'Where are the gloves?'

In the seventy-fifth minute a powerful run and a stabbed finish from Grealish brought our second goal and the daylight we needed between us and our opponents.

With our campaign up and running, I now turned to the prospect of facing Spain at home in November. From our perspective, this was the key game. The Spanish were the strongest side in our pool and so we had to do the damage now that we had them at home; it would be a tall order to get anything from the reverse fixture in Zaragoza. We had an inauspicious start to our preparations. With Kevin Sheedy, Gary Waddock, Ronnie Whelan, David O'Leary, Dave Langan, Kevin Moran and Gerry Daly all withdrawing owing to injuries, we were far from full strength. The Spaniards had a number of danger men whom we would have to watch closely. Particular threats were the Real Madrid centre forward Santillana, the Real Zaragoza midfielder Señor, and the powerful Barcelona midfielder Víctor. Spain also, of course, had the excellent Luis Arconada in goal.

Regardless of the minuses we had to contend with, we had to take the game to the Spanish. In the early exchanges I was delighted to see us doing just that. Despite very tight man-marking by the Spanish defence, our front three of Robinson, Stapleton and Kevin O'Callaghan were creating problems with their movement. In the second minute, when a Michael Robinson shot was deflected, Ashley Grimes came onto the ball and, without breaking stride, lashed a left-foot shot into the top corner of the Spanish net from all of twenty yards. It was the perfect start: the Spanish were rattled and the Lansdowne crowd were in full voice. That said, we had not delivered a knockout blow. The Spanish had numerous talented and experienced players. They would come back into this game, we knew, and when they did, we would have to be ready to batten down the hatches.

Sure enough, the Spaniards lived up to their vaunted reputation and started making inroads. Spain's midfield and front three were constantly interchanging positions, with sometimes the strikers dropping back, only to launch surprise attacks from deep. On top of this, the two wingers, Pedraza and Marcos, were not behaving like conventional wide men. Instead of hugging the touchline and keeping width in the Spanish line-up, they were making unexpected runs across the pitch. Their movement was at times bewildering and we were in danger of being dragged all around the park. It took all our concentration and discipline to keep our shape but, largely, we did.

For the next thirty minutes or so we matched the Spaniards in all departments and looked good for our lead. The only concern I had was that we were being occasionally outnumbered on the break. Although Grimes was important to us in attack, today from the left side of a midfield three, his decision-making was proving to be a bit too cavalier. Some of his sallies forward were a touch reckless, leaving Brady and Grealish badly exposed when the Spaniards broke from deep positions.

In the thirty-second minute, however, a well-executed set piece brought Spain back into the contest. Brady conceded a free kick on the left wing and the subsequent delivery was volleyed home emphatically by the Spanish sweeper Antonio Maceda. Disappointingly, in a costly lapse of discipline on our part, Maceda, unmarked and in acres of space at the back post, had ample time to score. Half-time came with the score still at a goal apiece.

At the start of the second half we again looked sharp, and with a full house behind us at Lansdowne I was confident we could push on. Within two minutes, I was revising my optimism. Señor was released on our right side by a beautiful pinpoint-accurate pass from Víctor. He shot powerfully across our goalmouth where Mick Martin, in order to thwart the arriving Santillana, had no choice but to stick out a leg to block the delivery. The result was an own goal. I felt sorry for Mick. He, of all the players, least deserved to put into his own net in an Ireland jersey. Mick had never let us down.

Suddenly, the mood dropped around the old stadium. The Spaniards had succeeded in silencing the home crowd; now they would up the ante. In the sixtieth minute we were 3-1 down. With full back John Devine caught too far forward, Marcos cut in from the left and split our centre halves with a through ball. A deflection carried the ball past Lawrenson and Víctor came onto the pass and coolly rounded McDonagh to score. To be two goals down to world-class opposition with only thirty minutes to play was, by any standards, a very bad position to find ourselves in. However, when we might so easily have folded, we rallied, and, showing great character, pushed back the Spanish again. There was a surge from the crowd as they sensed that this game was far from done. Four minutes later we had a breakthrough. After a Liam Brady free kick from the left, Stapleton, in a trademark manoeuvre, lost his marker, Maceda, by checking his run and headed home powerfully at the near post. In what was turning into a thrilling end-to-end match for the neutrals, the pendulum had swung again, and now the Spanish were the ones on the run.

Our opponents' weakness was down the flanks, in particular, on their left side. I decided to switch O'Callaghan from the left to the right in the hope that he could put further pressure on the struggling Camacho. The rewards were almost instant. In the seventy-sixth minute, O'Callaghan beat two Spaniards with superb skill, including a drag-back that left Camacho floundering, before crossing with the outside of his left boot for Stapleton to head in at the back post.

We were now piling on the pressure, with a reeling Spain doing all they could to keep out whatever we threw at them. The crowd was willing us forward and even though we had to go on the offensive, and we were showing great self-belief in seizing the advantage, we did not quite go about it in the right way. Whatever the circumstances are in a match, no matter how intense the white-hot heat of battle might be, success calls for a cold-blooded temperament. Fortunes may fluctuate but temperament should not: when you are down in a game, you shouldn't panic; when you are ahead, you shouldn't panic; when you are level, you shouldn't panic. Chasing a game is precisely one of those high-pressure times when a team must stay on an even keel. You have to build attacks in a composed fashion, and continue to pass, move and probe the opposition with a final ball at the right time and with the right pace. Throwing caution to the wind is not the answer: it lulls you into a cavalier style with the ball going forward far too early. In our enthusiasm, we were guilty of adopting this overeager approach. If we could have stayed level-headed, we could have killed off a Spanish side that was, by the end of the game, very much on the ropes. We had displayed great fighting spirit but one crucial home point had been dropped in a critical game.

The year ended with us having secured three points from a possible six. The Netherlands lead the group on five points while Spain and Ireland were next, both on three.

The next year, 1983, began with upheaval for me. I was still managing Limerick United full-time at this stage as well as managing Ireland. In the previous year, at the age of thirty-six, I had finally retired from playing. I was slowing down, losing my sharpness and missing tackles; I felt that if I continued, either I or someone else would be seriously hurt. However, on the managerial side I now had extra duties. As part of my international role I had attended a managers' conference in the former Yugoslavia. On my return I was surprised to receive a letter full of foul language from the Limerick chairman, Pat Grace. He was unhappy that I had made the trip and strongly suggested I was failing in my obligations to Limerick United. Results had dipped at the club in recent weeks but, still, I was furious with Grace's attitude. Aside from the fact that his letter was abusive, I could not see that his sudden change of mood was justified. He had always been more than happy to bask in the glory of having the Ireland manager in his employ when times were good.

Furthermore, I wondered why we were suddenly communicating by letter. Could he not talk to me face to face or even just ring me? If Grace had been open with me and addressed his concerns in a dignified and reasonable manner, I would not have taken issue. I might have disagreed with his position but I would have respected it. I rang Grace and said that we needed to meet. He suggested that I come into his office in Limerick.

I said no and told him I would see him in the Jurys Inn in Limerick. This meeting had to be on neutral ground. It didn't take long. I walked in, gave Grace his letter back and told him: 'You can shove that letter up your arse,' then walked out. Although I did not quit there and then, it was the beginning of the end. I stayed at Limerick United for the remainder of the 1982/83 season and formally announced my departure that summer.

It was certainly not the way I wanted my time with Limerick to end. I have only the best memories of the players, the fans and the city, but the trust between me and the chairman was gone and that was fatal to any working relationship. In management, stability is essential and I no longer had that at Limerick. I had to resign. It may have been an acrimonious ending but there was no shortage of positives to look back on. From a position as genuine outsiders in the League of Ireland, we had won a League of Ireland title, an FAI Cup in 1982 and played in Europe for three successive seasons. Aside from our encounter with Real Madrid in 1980, we had also earned creditable draws in Europe: 1-1 away to English First Division side Southampton in

(*L–r*): Tony Ward, the singer Paddy Reilly, myself, Moss Keane, the Munster and Ireland rugby player, and balladeer Luke Kelly, on the opening of our sports shop in Firhouse, Dublin in 1983. (Sportsfile)

At the opening of the sports shop in 1983: (*l–r*) Kevin Moran, Karen Reeves (manager), me, Frank Stapleton and England international Ray Wilkins.

the 1982 UEFA Cup and 1-1 at home to Dutch side AZ Alkmaar in the 1983 Cup Winners' Cup.

I will always be grateful for the opportunity the club gave me as a young manager. There is no doubt that, in my own career, Limerick was a huge turning point. The success I enjoyed there played a major part in me being offered the Ireland job.

After Limerick I investigated making a living outside the game to supplement my Ireland income. Tony Ward was opening a sports shop in Firhouse in Dublin and we decided to go into partnership together. Although I did not have business experience, I was keen to try and achieve some financial stability for my family. In football management, things change rapidly and you are rarely looking beyond the next season. That takes its toll on your family, especially when you have, as I did, young children whose futures you have to cater for.

I still have a close bond with the players of Limerick United who won that famous League of Ireland title all those years ago. Every player from that title-winning squad are now legends of Limerick football folklore and rightly so. We still get together twice a year to honour what we achieved in 1980. I began as their manager and became their friend.

Ireland's first game in 1983 took place on 30 March against Malta at the island's new Ta'Qali Stadium in Attard. The opposition were not strong. In football terms, they could not match us but I had heard rumours that the pitch was in poor condition, and that was a worry. After plenty of back and forth between our associations, I was finally allowed to inspect the surface a couple of days before the match. I understood immediately why the Maltese officials had been reluctant to permit the inspection: the state of the pitch was shocking and actually dangerous. To this day, I still cannot recall seeing anything as bad, at any level of football. Any amateur club, even, would have turned up their noses at this excuse for a playing surface. Aside from the bumps and divots peppered across the pitch, a cursory survey turned up shards of glass, bricks, broken bottles and a selection of six-inch nails – one of which I kept as evidence. The pitch, the stadium – none of it was actually finished, as I soon discovered. Ta'Qali was a construction site, yet UEFA expected us to contest an international fixture there. Ordinarily, you do not grumble too much about the condition of pitches or the facilities that are laid on by smaller clubs or nations. You accept that they do not necessarily have the resources to provide top-level infrastructure. This pitch, however, was a genuine health risk for the players. This was proven when we tried to train on the surface. David O'Leary went over on his ankle and was not fit to play.

I asked John Farrell and Peadar O'Driscoll to contact UEFA and lodge a formal complaint about the state of the pitch. They duly did and UEFA determined that the Austrian referee, Adolf Mathias, would inspect the pitch the day before the match. The referee agreed that the surface was poor, but, with perhaps a nod to diplomatic sensitivities, still declared it 'just playable'.

The debacle of the pitch had also caused a minor political kerfuffle. Some papers had rounded on John Farrell, suggesting that by lodging a complaint with UEFA, Farrell had been fishing for excuses should Ireland fail to beat the lowly Maltese. John was livid. Now, when John Farrell worked himself up, he did not always have the greatest command of the English language. At a busy press conference on the island, he let loose: 'I am well aware that certain allegations are being made against me in the press and, listen to me now, you can rest assured, I will not stop until I catch those alligators.'

Malta's inability to provide international-level facilities had been an issue throughout the qualification campaign. UEFA had previously suspended the country from playing at home, forcing them to play instead at neutral venues abroad. The Netherlands had already been the beneficiaries of this suspension when they had thrashed the Maltese 6-0 in Aachen, Germany, on 19 December 1982. Although, technically, the Dutch were playing away from home on this occasion, the fact that it took place barely over their border meant that, in fact, the venue was more like a home away from home.

After seeing the lamentable playing surface in Malta, I knew immediately that the conditions were ripe for a giant-killing. This was going to be akin to a hard-fought FA Cup third-round tie with the bigger First Division side being forced to deal with the inhospitable conditions of a lower-league ground – with all things made equal just for one day. The only sound approach to these encounters is to front up, make sure you win the physical battles, and hope that your greater ability and fitness will ultimately produce the breakthrough. In all, these are not enjoyable games. We were going to have to adjust our game to suit the conditions. The desperately uneven surface obviously would not favour any kind of passing game, so we had to be more pragmatic in our approach and to take the direct route when it presented itself. We were being forced to employ Fourth Division-style tactics. We had to avoid playing through the middle and, instead, go wide and get balls into the box.

Just to add spice to an already heady brew, gale-force winds began to sweep across the open stadium as the game kicked off. In the early stages the players struggled to adjust to the conditions because the strong wind was causing the ball to swerve wildly. A few eccentric bounces very nearly caught out our defence. It was like chasing a jittery beach ball on a breezy day at the seaside. With about twenty minutes on the clock, however, we settled down and began to find our rhythm. Unfortunately for us, and in the true fighting spirit of the underdog, the Maltese goalkeeper had chosen that day to have the game of his life. He pulled off a succession of acrobatic saves from Chris Hughton, Michael Robinson and Frank Stapleton.

There was no score at half-time and as the minutes ticked away in the second half, I was becoming increasingly anxious. Whatever about the mitigating factors, we all knew that anything other than a win against Malta would have been catastrophic for both our qualification chances and our reputation. Offering excuses for failing to beat a tiny football nation does not wash when you can call on a squad packed with English First Division players.

We continued to probe but I was not sure where the goal was going to come from. Then, when Ronnie Whelan gave away possession late in the game, while trying to back-heel the ball in the middle of the park, I was furious and jumped from the bench to give him an earful. Ronnie had great ability and, in different circumstances, a cute back heel might well have been the right thing to try but with the divots, the debris and an increasingly hostile, gale-force sandstorm whipping in off the Mediterranean, Ronnie's move was ill-advised.

It was then with some irony that I sat and watched our winning goal in the eighty-ninth minute. How was it scored? Well, from a back heel, of course. In a crowded box, with no obvious opening presenting itself, Stapleton had the presence of mind to back-heel the ball past a stationary Maltese goalkeeper. Job done! We said farewell to the Ta'Qali and went home, relieved with our two points.

Our narrow win, while hardly anything to cheer about, was an acceptable one when you consider that Spain would later trail 2-1 on the same pitch before escaping with a 2-3 victory, courtesy of another late winner.

Our return fixture with Spain came on 27 April in Zaragoza. Both Kevin Moran and Michael Robinson withdrew from the original squad with injuries but, more importantly, we could not call on Liam Brady because he was serving a one-match suspension for a booking he had picked up in the game against Malta. That was a significant minus for us because with Liam in the side we stood a better chance of retaining possession – something that was vital for us to stay in contention in this, the most difficult away fixture.

The Spanish Football Association was putting everything into winning this game. They had even taken the dramatic measure of clearing the Spanish domestic schedule by cancelling all La Liga matches for the two previous weeks. That gave Spain's manager, Miguel Muñoz, a two-week training camp to get his players in optimal shape. It was a highly progressive move and one that would never have happened in the British game. In addition, in the run-up Spain had played a number of friendlies against Spanish club sides that favoured a style similar to ours.

For us, the tactic was to get at Spain's Achilles heel, which the Dublin game had shown us to be in their full-back positions. My plan was to approach the early part of the match with a defensive mindset and then open up and try to hurt them out wide as the game wore on. Even though a draw would have kept us in contention in the group, I wanted us to have a chance of going home with a win. To counteract the threat of Víctor, I played Ashley Grimes on the left of midfield to provide extra cover for Chris Hughton at left back. Gary Waddock was the holding player in midfield and, alongside him, I had asked Grealish and Whelan to get forward when possible.

Although we managed to slow down a highly mobile and motivated Spanish side in the first half, our tactics were generally not working. The set-up was wrong. Neither Whelan nor Grealish were supporting our front two and the tactic of playing Grimes at left wing had backfired. On the other side of the pitch, however, Lawrenson was attacking the Spaniards with some success from right back. This told me a lot. Mark was used to playing this way at Liverpool and so, for us, he adapted to this dual role with ease. It underlined for me, once more, how difficult it was to get players to adapt to new tactics with so little time to spend on the international training ground.

In the second half the game ran away from us. Early in the half, and just when the Spaniards were showing signs of frustration, a breakdown in communication between McDonagh and O'Leary at a high cross led to a tangle and the grateful Santillana headed into an empty net. From then on, Spain played with great confidence and, although the introduction of O'Callaghan on the left troubled Juan José at right back, the Spaniards were good for their lead. We created some positive chances but showed an unfortunate hesitancy when it came to taking them. When, in the eighty-ninth minute, Hipólito Rincón headed in at the back post, our fate was sealed.

Our hopes of qualifying were now in ashes. With Spain and the Netherlands having highly winnable games to come against Iceland and Malta, only an unlikely full-scale collapse from both nations, and a clean bill of wins for us, would have brought us into the reckoning once more.

On my arrival back at Dublin Airport, I took personal abuse from the public for the first time. It's not as if there was an organised band of protestors waiting for me with banners. It was just a case of random punters recognising me and lobbing a few off-the-cuff insults at me as I made my way through the airport. The tide of public opinion (baited to some extent by minority sections of the press) was turning against me, and although there would be more great days ahead, the tone had definitely shifted.

On 21 September 1983 we flew to Reykjavík for our return fixture with Iceland. The game was notable for being the first time in the competition that I had the entire squad to draw on as Ireland manager and not a single withdrawal to contend with. I was delighted to stand at Heathrow Airport with a full complement of players.

The only concern going into the game was the history that existed between the sides. In our first meeting in the group, at Lansdowne Road, tempers had become frayed and some of the tackling had got too feisty. The Everton defender Mike Walsh had gone in late on an Icelandic forward, Pétur Ormslev, and the injured party ended up in a Dublin hospital. The player had not forgotten and had certainly not forgiven. At a managers' conference in the former Yugoslavia, Iceland's manager, Jóhannes Atlason, warned me that the sense of animosity was still very much alive in his squad. And, although Mike Walsh was not playing this time, we could not afford to lose any players to suspensions, so everyone was reminded to keep the head and not to get dragged into silly tit-for-tat exchanges.

The Icelandic players were semi-professional and for this reason the country had typically struggled to get all its best talent available for international fixtures. For this game, however, the Icelandic FA had pulled out all the stops and made sure that their strongest eleven would be fielded. Even so, and despite the Icelandic team enjoying home advantage, I expected us to come away with a victory. At this juncture in the group, we were on five points while Iceland was on three.

We began the match confidently and our superior ability became evident very quickly. Brady, in particular, was having an exceptional game. Although I was happy with the early pressure we were exerting, we were caught napping badly when, after only ten minutes, one of the Icelandic forwards found himself in space behind our back four. Seamus McDonagh, thankfully, saved his centre halves' blushes, with a courageous, last-ditch save at the feet of the forward.

In the sixteenth minute our lively start paid off. Liam Brady picked up the ball on the halfway line, hit the accelerator and danced past four defenders with ease. His driving run took him right into the Icelandic box where he pulled back a pinpoint-accurate pass for the arriving Gary Waddock to hit home from eighteen yards. The goal typified Brady. He had the rare ability to beat men at will. With a sudden injection of pace over five yards, Brady, almost gliding across the surface, would ghost past opposing players as if they were not there. Gary Waddock was also, by this stage, a valuable player for us. A product of the QPR youth academy, Gary was a tigerish tackler with a strong engine. He always provided cover from his holding midfield role for the more attacking players in our team and, as this strike illustrated, he had the odd important goal in him also.

Five minutes later it got even better for us. Stapleton toyed and teased with two defenders on the right-hand side before turning and delivering an inviting cross into Iceland's box. Robinson met it with an arrow-like diving header that flew into the Icelandic net. It remained 2-0 at the break.

In the second half, by sitting back too much, we gave ourselves a nervy twenty minutes or so. The Icelandic players, buoyed up by a noisy home crowd, took advantage of our hesitancy to create a number of good opportunities. Seamus McDonagh, however, as was so often the case, was on song and made numerous telling saves to protect our two-goal lead. We survived the push and came back into our own again, with Brady once more acting as creator-in-chief. In the eighty-first minute we killed the game as a contest. Chris Hughton attacked down the left wing and crossed to find Mickey Walsh in space. Walsh's header sailed past the Icelandic keeper, Bjarnason, squeezing in at the near post. Even though our qualification hopes were over at this point, the thoroughly professional 3-0 win away from home had pleased me. It was also, up to that time, Ireland's record away win.

Once on board the return flight from Iceland, with everyone in good humour, I struck up a conversation with the flight captain and, in a move that would definitely not be replicated in our modern security-conscious times, he invited me into the cockpit to have a look around. We were getting on so well that I ended up staying there for take-off – and then for another hour of the journey! I had no idea what was unfolding on the other side of the door in the passenger seats. Our physio, Mick Byrne, was having a bad time. He had been late boarding. By the time he had got on the plane, I was in the cockpit. The players jumped on the opportunity. 'Mick,' they shouted, 'Eoin's not here. We don't know where he is and the plane is about to leave. What are we going to do?'

Now Mick was as earnest as the day was long. He was panicking and wondering out loud what had become of me. The players, for their part, ably assisted in the articulation of Mick's worst fears by outlining an array of terrible scenarios that might have befallen their manager. Mick was flummoxed. The plane started to gather speed on the runway, as Mick grappled with the crisis. In the midst of the chaos, Terry Conroy, looking out of the window, abruptly shouted: 'Look, look! It's Eoin. He's running after the plane.' In a flash, Mick looked out his window and strained every sinew to catch a glimpse of Ireland's beleaguered manager, puffing and panting, leading by example and heroically chasing down a Boeing jet. But no … I was just out of sight. The plane took off into the Icelandic sky and a thoroughly dejected Mick slumped into his chair for what promised to be a very long journey indeed. When, an hour later, I strolled out of the cockpit, full of the joys of spring, Mick immediately realised he had been stitched up like a kipper. He leapt from his chair and fired a torrent of abuse at his tormentors, who responded with tears of laughter.

Our penultimate game in Group Seven, against the Netherlands, came on 12 October 1983 at Dalymount Park. This, regrettably, was a Jekyll-and-Hyde performance from us: great in the first half; abject in the second.

The game began at a brisk pace with the Dutch moving the ball around with great speed. Quickly, however, our snarling and snapping at their heels knocked them off their stride and they became ragged. Large spaces started to open up in behind them, particularly down their left side where Robinson and Stapleton were getting great joy from quick balls over the top.

Our pressure told. With only seven minutes on the clock, Grealish played the ball into Stapleton's feet. Frank used his strength to hold it up and then laid it off for Waddock, who was making a powerful run from midfield. Waddock received and burst through the Dutch man-marking to score with a low drive from twenty-five yards.

After this excellent start, we stayed on the front foot and continued to create chances. Soon after, Brady intercepted and crossed for Stapleton whose header was saved acrobatically by Piet Schrijvers in the Netherlands goal. The Dutch players were now at sixes and sevens and began dropping back into defence to stem the flow. In the thirty-fifth minute we were two up. Stapleton found space in the right channel and, like all good forwards, drove straight into the box and forced the tackle. He was upended by Gullit, who was playing as a sweeper, and the referee immediately pointed to the spot. Brady confidently dispatched the penalty to make it 2-0. Before half-time, it could have been three when, unluckily, an unsaveable shot from Stapleton smashed off the crossbar.

I could not have been more pleased with the first forty-five minutes. We had played with urgency and self-belief and had reaped the rewards. In the dressing-room, at half-time, Tony Grealish was struggling with a dead leg. I asked him and the doctor if he could play on and, despite not looking too comfortable on his feet, he insisted that he was fine and would continue. But during the course of the second half, it became obvious that Tony was not all right. Gullit was flying past him with ease and we were beginning to get overrun in midfield. Grealish should have admitted that he was not fit but it was absolutely typical of Tony – he was a warrior-player who would have run through walls for the cause. I had to take him off and replace him with Kevin Sheedy.

As good as we had been so far, it was obvious to me that the Dutch would hit us hard in the first fifteen minutes of the second half. We needed to ride out that storm. We didn't. Gullit came out from his sweeper role and moved up front. It made all the difference. Seven minutes in, Moran tried to clear with a weak header that fell at Gullit's feet. His first shot was saved but, very disappointingly for us, we were not alive to the rebound. Gullit got a second chance and this time he buried it with his other foot. Now the Dutch applied the pressure and the complexion of the game truly changed. We began to fall back and allow them to come onto us, and, as soon you do that, it becomes difficult to reverse the trend. Good opponents are not very obliging and, once you give them the initiative, they don't tend to give it back lightly.

The Dutch could still qualify from the group and so, understandably, once they had their goal, they went after the game with some tenacity.

Fifteen minutes later they got their equaliser when, from a corner, van Basten headed in superbly from fourteen yards. It was an exemplary header but a poor goal to concede. Waddock was marking van Basten (an obvious threat in the air) when it should have been one of our centre halves, Moran or Lawrenson. In the seventy-sixth minute the game was past us. Gullit ran on to a van Basten pass to calmly shoot across McDonagh and score his second goal of the evening, and the winner.

At the final whistle there was no escaping the fans' ire. They were displeased with the manner of our collapse. Dalymount was one of those old-style, claustrophobic noise-boxes where the fans were crammed right up against the pitch. I liked the fact that for the visiting teams it was a hostile venue when the crowd were in the mood. Lansdowne Road, however, although boasting a higher capacity, was, in comparison, large and airy, with the noise dissipating into the huge spaces between the stands.

At Dalymount, there were also no dugouts to give a manager any sense of distance from the crowd. Sitting on the touchline on a chair, I could have stuck my hand over my shoulder to shake hands with a fan. If the faithful were happy, you knew all about it; but if they were unhappy, you knew all about that too. At half-time, I was getting personal congratulations from supporters as I walked down the tunnel; at full time, the very same spectators were hurling volleys of abuse at me.

They were furious; so was I. From a position of great strength, at 2-0, we had squandered the game. This was a match that we should never have lost, yet we contrived to do just that. No international side expects to come back from being two down away from home.

Our final outing in Group Seven was a home game against Malta on 16 November 1983. With nothing to play for, it was gratifying to see how professionally we went about putting away the opposition. We won 8-0, with goals being spread throughout the team. The scorers were: Brady (2), Lawrenson (2), Stapleton, Sheedy, Kevin O'Callaghan and Gerry Daly. The result was also one for the anoraks: allied to our 7-0 defeat in Brazil in 1982, in terms of goals, I had now presided (and still do, at the time of writing) over the nation's greatest-ever loss and greatest-ever victory. Those fond of statistics can take what they like from that.

Spain would ultimately take the single qualification spot by virtue of a freakish result. The Spaniards went into their final game, in Seville, knowing that only a victory by eleven goals against their opponents, Malta, would see them nudging the Dutch off top spot. They duly walloped the Maltese 12-1! It was only 3-1 to Spain at half-time but thirty-six crazy minutes in the second half saw them net nine more times. It was a turkey shoot for the Spanish forwards: Santillana and Rincón alone scored four apiece. Spain and the Netherlands had finished level on points, level on goal difference and level on the aggregate score between them. Spain progressed only because they had scored more goals than the Netherlands. Given the outlandish nature of the result, rumours quickly circulated of how the Maltese players had apparently been taken out on the town and dined late into the Spanish night by their generous hosts. In the final standings, Spain topped the group with thirteen points, the Netherlands took second spot, also on thirteen points, while we finished in third spot on nine points, ahead of Iceland and Malta respectively.

Looking back on the Euro '84 qualification campaign, I can see now how the experience of the 1982 campaign weighed heavily on our minds. Because we had come so agonisingly close to World Cup qualification, there was now a widespread expectation at home that we would push on and secure a place at Euro '84. This, however, is simplistic logic and does not stack up when you look at the reality. Assessing the relative strengths of the teams we faced in both campaigns, our qualification group was no easier this time around. Moreover, given the fact that only one country qualified from each group for the European Championships, it was, realistically, an even more difficult task than attempting to reach a World Cup. In these tighter and more pressurised groups, the margin for error was significantly diminished. This means that a draw here or a draw there can finish off your campaign before it even gets up and running. Our 3-3 home draw with Spain early on in the campaign was one such pivotal result – it had us playing catch-up after only three games and it underlined that, at this level, to give yourself a fighting chance, you must win *all* your home games.

However, the big difference between the two campaigns was injuries. In 1980 and 1981 we generally had our major players fit for action, while in 1982 and 1983, when we were trying to make it to Euro '84, we had too many casualties along the way to sustain an assault on the top spot. Of course the other nations also had to contend with absentees, but we simply did not have the depth in our squad to slot in like-for-like replacements when our first-choice players were out.

We also fundamentally lacked experience at the highest level. Had we made it to España '82, the players would have been all the stronger for it and would have carried this confidence through to our Euro '84 campaign. We didn't, and so, in the 1984 campaign, we continued to make the kind of basic errors that get punished pitilessly against the heavy-hitters of international football. For example, the critical lack of concentration that we showed early in the second half of many matches (in particular, against Spain away, and the Netherlands at home) had cost us dearly and showed the ultra-fine margins in international football between being the best and merely being the nearly men.

In mitigation, you could argue that 'if only we had concentrated more and avoided those isolated lapses, we would have been flying'. That's all well and good but the reality of international football is that good teams force you to lose your concentration by controlling and keeping possession. You can get men behind the ball but, with almost robotic insistence, they will keep pushing until a weak spot is identified. Then they strike once you have been dragged out of shape. What may seem like unforced errors to the untrained eye are, often, very much forced errors. If a player's brain is addled from chasing shadows around for fifteen minutes, he is in a place where he is vulnerable to making mistakes. We knew that all too well. The 3-3 draw at home to Spain proved this point. Although it was an exciting seesaw contest, in which we certainly gave as good as we got, Spain's intelligent movement had tired us out mentally. The level of concentration required at this level of football is immense and when you have canny opposition darting here and there, almost in perpetual motion, it inevitably starts to test your psychological resistance.

I faced some criticism for allegedly showing naivety away from home. The charge was that I played dangerously open football when we should have been closing out games. My approach has always been to be as constructive as possible. While I never encouraged an incautious, reckless attitude in my players, my preference was to play and be positive in possession. Players should get goalside when we lost the ball, but I was never a park-the-bus merchant; it was just not in me. My belief was that the best form of defence was attack. Sitting back and absorbing pressure carries risks of its own: eventually good teams will run you ragged. At least if you are trying to play, you are upsetting the opponents' rhythm and making it more difficult for them to establish dominance when they are at home. You are also quietening the home crowd and so denying the opposition their twelfth man.

Despite any concerns I may have had, by the close of 1983, and after over three years in the job, I knew where we stood. Yes, we were the nearly men but we were dangerous and were still at the shoulders of some of the stronger teams in world football. I looked forward to the 1986 World Cup qualification with confidence. Before resuming competitive action, however, we would travel to Japan in May 1984 for a summer tour. In a competition called the Kirin Cup (named after the beer company that was sponsoring it) we participated alongside a number of club sides, such as Santos of Brazil, as well as the China national side.

From our arrival in Tokyo, on 24 May, the atmosphere in the camp was not as good as it should have been. Despite exemplary hospitality from the Japanese, the players were not happy. The FAI had failed to confirm what fees the players would be getting on the trip. Everyone was fully aware that the Association had received a hefty fee from the Kirin beer company for agreeing to come on the tour, yet the players, after flying to Japan, were none the wiser as to how they would be remunerated. Our first training session was barely over, on 26 May, when there was a dispute. Eventually, a series of stage payments were agreed, with a certain amount to be paid up front and the rest to be paid out depending on how far we progressed in the tournament. I hoped the matter was closed.

However, the days, and the games, went by with no sign or mention of any payments. The players' frustration was mounting; so was mine. We had all been here before. More promises were given – and then broken. It was 3 June and we had made it to the semi-final where we were due to play China in Sapporo. On the day of the game, the simmering tensions came to a head. Frank Stapleton, who was then captain, spoke on behalf of the squad. He asked if I had any news. I could tell him only that, despite repeated attempts, I did not. Although I fully sympathised with the players' position and agreed that the FAI's behaviour was not acceptable, this was not the time for distractions. 'For God's sake, you are due to play an international match. You are representing your country. Get out there and play the game.' They did and with real commitment put their concerns to one side and defeated China 1-0. After the game, and before the final, which we unluckily lost 2-1 to Santos, the fees were belatedly paid in full.

Despite its shortcomings, the tour was a valuable experience and gave the squad precious time to bond. It was also a rare chance for the players to enjoy a country boasting such a unique culture.

In all, it proved to be a positive, worthwhile lead-in to our forthcoming World Cup campaign, due to kick off that September.

6

From Russia ... with Regret

1986 World Cup Qualifiers

In December 1983 I travelled to Zürich to discover the teams we would be drawn against in the 1986 World Cup qualification rounds. Having contested difficult groups in our last two qualifying campaigns, I had hoped that, this time, we might land a berth in one of the less challenging groups.

No such luck. When the teams were taken from the pot, we ended up in Group Six alongside Denmark, the Soviet Union, Norway and Switzerland. There is generally always one so-called Group of Death; this time we were in it. In 1983 Denmark were well on the way to becoming the best team in Europe, while the Soviet Union were already established as one of the world's best sides. Norway and Switzerland, although not in the same class as the Danes and the Soviets, were tough, defensive sides who gave away little. With no obvious whipping boy there would be no comfortable games in Group Six. I knew, realistically, that Denmark and the Soviet Union were stronger than us and that to beat them we would have to be at the top of our game. Only the first two sides would qualify. Despite my reservations, I left Zürich feeling confident and fully believed that we could make it to the World Cup in Mexico. The other sides had plenty to fear from us as well.

For this, my third campaign, there were four key additions to the squad. In defence we were strengthened by Manchester City's Mick McCarthy. I had first capped Mick in a friendly match in May 1984, when we played out a scoreless draw with Poland at Dalymount Park. Mick was a warrior, a tough, lionhearted centre half who left nothing in the dressing room. He was also no respecter of reputations on the field of play, and that went for his own teammates as well as the opposition. Mick's vocal presence really shook us up. We had some excellent big-name players from major clubs; sometimes, however, I felt almost as if these players were too conscious of each other's standing in the game and, maybe, they showed a bit too much regard for one another on the pitch. Mick McCarthy changed all that. If someone cocked up, they got an earful from him; it did not matter whether you were the big star or the rookie newcomer. We needed a McCarthy in the team. Although Mick was not the quickest defender over the top, he compensated for this with his good positional sense and aggressive style of play.

Another key addition to our defence was Paul McGrath, whom I capped in a friendly match against Italy in February 1985. Although Paul would ultimately mature into a phenomenal footballer and become one of Ireland's greatest ever players, in 1985 he was still finding his feet at international level. Owing to no fault of his own, Paul's selection was, however, not without its complications. He had transferred from the League of Ireland's St Patrick's Athletic to Manchester United in 1982. St Pat's, seeing Paul's great potential, had insisted on receiving a further payment for the player if and when he made his international debut. Fast-forward to 1984 and now I am St Patrick's Athletic's manager (a position I held for the 1984/85 season only, alongside my Ireland duties) and Paul McGrath has still not been capped for the Republic of Ireland. With the Ireland manager in situ at Richmond Road, the St Pat's board spotted an opportunity that was too good to pass over. The club hierarchy approached me and suggested that I should give McGrath his first cap. This would trigger Manchester United's contractual obligation to pay up. I made it clear, immediately, that I would have nothing to do with the proposed arrangement. I would pick Paul when *I* thought he was ready for international duty and that decision would have nothing to do with the interests of St Patrick's Athletic.

Although I had dismissed the club's idea out of hand and moved on, it had placed me in an awkward position. The perceived conflict of interest was not difficult to grasp: pick McGrath for Ireland and I could be accused of collusion with St Patrick's Athletic. Unfortunately for Paul, it meant having to be very careful about how I went about giving him his first cap. Suddenly what should have been a straightforward football decision had become laced with political implications. Would I have picked Paul earlier had it not been for St Pat's unwelcome intervention? Maybe, but I cannot say for certain.

Another new option was up front where Tony Cascarino was added to our ranks. Although it was a protracted process to try and establish Tony's eligibility, it was eventually confirmed that he qualified for an Irish passport through one of his grandmothers. When I first picked him, in 1985, he was a relative unknown playing with Gillingham in the Third Division. When I scouted him, I liked what I saw. He was a tall target man but mobile and surprisingly fleet of foot for his height. Although the level of football that Tony was playing at then was well below the standard of the international game, I could see that he had an eye for goal and that he would trouble most defences.

By 1985, we badly needed an extra striker. My only real options up front at that point were Frank Stapleton, Michael Robinson and Mickey Walsh. A fully fit Frank Stapleton, our top centre forward, was always going to play. If Frank was injured, however, it left me with only Walsh and Robinson. Now both Mickey and Michael were a different sort of player from Frank and neither were regular target men. Tony was that, and because of our style of play, we needed that kind of backup option to Frank. Although we always tried to play good football and we had the talented players to do that, we lacked the technical mastery of the best international teams who could play out from the back, no matter what the pressures.

My solution was to make sure that, where possible, we had a centre forward who could receive an out ball when required. Target men like Frank and Tony gave us this extra dimension and, with their ability to hold up the ball and bring runners into the game, they allowed us to continue building attacks.

I took some flak from the press for bringing in an obscure lower-league player (one journalist criticised the selection under the headline 'Hand picks a Third Division Ice-Cream Man').

The final new addition was Liverpool's Jim Beglin. Jim was a fine attacking full back hewn in the modern mould and he gave me new options at left back. Because of his extra height, I would sometimes pick him over the reliably excellent Chris Hughton. This was one position where I was blessed with options and it was never an easy task to choose between Chris and Jim.

Our campaign began at home against the Soviet Union on 12 September 1984. Although they were a serious challenge, I was happy to face one of the strongest sides in the group early on, and at home. The momentum from a major win at this stage would be vital in propelling us forward in the group. I knew all about the dangers that this game would present, however. There were no easy games against the Soviets; whatever you got, you fought for. They were invariably fitter, stronger and faster than a lot of international sides and, although there was a certain robotic quality to the way they methodically went about their football, they had no shortage of skill. The USSR could also call on one of the finest goalkeepers in the world at that time, in the form of Rinat Dasayev.

Three months earlier they had ransacked Wembley with a commanding 2-0 win over England, a match from which I got valuable scouting information. The former Irish international defender Terry Mancini provided me with a good insight into the threats of the Soviet team. The English defence had been run ragged by the movement and pace of their two front men, Sergei Rodionov and Oleh Blokhin. Unconventionally, the two forwards liked to start from wide positions and drift infield into dangerous channels between the centre halves and the full backs. To counteract this tactic, David O'Leary and Mark Lawrenson were instructed to drop deep when required. This gave extra cover behind the defence if the elusive Rodionov or Blokhin managed to slip through the lines. I was also mindful of the USSR's midfield, with the Armenian Khoren Oganesian, in particular, being an excellent dribbler from deep positions. Gennadiy Litovchenko and Sergei Aleinikov were also accomplished midfielders.

Despite missing two important players – Frank Stapleton was recovering from a knee operation and Kevin Sheedy had injured his ankle playing for Everton – we began the game positively. We were playing with great commitment and were always looking to get in behind the Soviet defence. Tony Galvin was causing mayhem down the left with his speed and strength and, with a vocal Lansdowne Road crowd behind us, we had the Soviets rattled. At the back we were showing good composure, with Lawrenson doing a fine job of reading the play and intercepting any through balls. Liam Brady was also on top form, taking on and beating players at will.

In the second half, our pace dropped off a little, but then, in the sixty-fourth minute, came the goal that changed the course of the match. Ronnie Whelan released Michael Robinson on the right, who broke free down the Soviet flank. He beat two men before crossing for Mickey Walsh. Walsh, who had to check his run slightly to gather the ball, in almost one motion, flicked it up, swivelled and shot. Dasayev in the Soviet goal was

The highs: celebrating Ireland's 1-0 win over the Soviet Union at Lansdowne Road on 12 September 1984. (L–r): my assistant Terry Conroy, me, team doctor Bob O'Driscoll and Mickey Walsh. (Sportsfile)

a mere spectator as the ball sailed past him into his bottom right corner. Lansdowne erupted; these were the moments that made it all worthwhile. It was an exceptional counter-attacking goal and one that demonstrated the strengths of Robinson and Walsh. Walsh was a highly skilful, mercurial player. He could produce the unexpected moment of class needed to unlock opposition defences. Robinson, as this goal demonstrated, was at his best when running at defences and working the channels.

After this, with time slipping away from them, the Soviets turned the screw and came back into the game. They came close on two occasions, but our defence held firm. We won 1-0 – a famous victory for Ireland and an excellent start to our campaign. If anyone needed convincing, this was proof that Ireland, on its day, could topple the best in the world. It was the Soviet Union's first defeat in twelve internationals.

That evening, once the celebrations had died down, I had a surprise. I received a personal telegram from the Taoiseach, Garret FitzGerald, congratulating us on a fantastic victory. Although I went to sleep a happy man that evening, with a crucial win in the bag, I knew well that it was only one step on the road to Mexico.

Our second game would be away to Norway on 17 October 1984. Although the Norwegians were clearly not as strong as Denmark or the Soviet Union, they would not be a pushover. Norway was a compact, disciplined side who defended deep and in numbers. Seven days earlier they had held the Soviet Union to a 1-1 draw in Oslo. The result proved that the Norwegians were no mugs. We would have to be at our sharpest to break them down.

Tactically, I felt that we would get little change from trying to play through the middle of the Norwegians. Such a move would have suited their game plan well and their massed ranks were likely to soak up pressure. I had seen what they had done to the Soviet Union a week earlier and I was determined there would be no repeat of that. To counteract Norway's approach, our strategy was to attack from wide positions whenever possible. Lining up with my preferred 4-3-3 formation, with Frank Stapleton up front and being supported by Tony Galvin on the left wing and Michael Robinson coming in from the right, the plan was to get the ball out wide as soon as possible in order to stretch the play.

For the first twenty minutes the tactic worked. Galvin and Chris Hughton, from left back, were whipping in some excellent crosses from the left. After only eight minutes, a Michael Robinson header and a low drive from Tony Grealish had already tested Erik Thorstvedt in the Norwegian goal. The Norwegians were so intent on sitting back that they were allowing Brady acres of space in the middle of the park. This gave Liam the chance to orchestrate play and move the ball out to our wingers early. Around the twenty-minute mark Ronnie Whelan and Frank Stapleton, unaccountably, missed two very easy opportunities – chances they would ordinarily have dispatched without any difficulty. First, Frank headed low and centrally, for the Norwegian goalkeeper to save, when he could so easily have put the ball to either side. Then, in what was almost an action replay, Whelan did the very same from a Galvin corner. I began to wonder if this was not going to be our evening.

From a position of dominance, our play became tentative and, suddenly, we were no longer showing confidence on the ball. Our play was not quick enough and so, any time our players received the ball, there were plenty of Norwegians goalside. As so often happens in football, if you do not take your chances when they are presented, the pendulum of a game can swing away you from all too quickly. It was clear to me now that the players were anxious not to make any mistakes but, in the process, that is exactly what they did. With only two minutes to go before half-time, Norway took the lead. A rapid through ball was played into the path of Norwegian forward Pål Jacobsen, and Mark Lawrenson was caught square. Jacobsen was in behind him and, although McDonagh got his body in the way, the deflected shot had enough force to bounce in over the line. We went in at the break trailing 1-0.

In the second half, the same trend continued: we struggled to regain our poise and then began to force our play. The Norwegians had tactically retreated into a virtual eight-man defence. We were very much dominating play by this point but the Norwegians, camped inside their own half, were quite content to let us have what was mostly sterile possession. Playing against two banks of four meant that going wide was still very much our best policy. With this in mind, I introduced fresh legs out wide with twenty-five minutes to go. Mickey Walsh replaced Michael Robinson and Kevin O'Callaghan came on for Ronnie Whelan. But the changes did not bring the breakthrough. Our one last meaningful chance came from a dangerous cross from John Devine but Brady just failed to reach it. The Norwegians took the two points.

The game was effectively a repeat of how we had defeated the Soviet Union some weeks earlier in Dublin, except that this time the shoe was on the other foot. Norway defended deeply, stifled us, unsettled us, and then hit us on the counter-attack. After the great start we had enjoyed in Group Six, the result was a blow, but hardly a disaster.

After the Norway game, sections of the press criticised me for selecting Frank Stapleton, arguing that he was not fit and, moreover, that Frank had influenced my decision to pick him. This was a good example of uninformed journalists not letting the facts get in the way of a good story. In general terms, there is obviously nothing wrong with commentators questioning your choice of selection or your tactics; that is their job, and the public expects them to do it. However, when speculative observers are effectively taking potshots in the dark, without any command of the facts, you get a skewed picture. Snappy headlines tend to conceal the small print.

Frank had no role in his selection for the Norway game. The truth is that all my forward options came with complications. Frank was not fully match-fit for international football, but nor was my alternative, Mickey Walsh. Stapleton had played a handful of games for the Manchester United reserves but, because of the strong form of Mark Hughes and Norman Whiteside, he was struggling to break back into Ron Atkinson's first eleven. Walsh at Oporto was in the very same position except that he was playing Portuguese reserve football. Anyone with football know-how could have told you that Portuguese reserve football did not compare with the standard on offer at Old Trafford and so the decision was not a very difficult one to make. In any case, Stapleton was always my first-choice centre forward, and, on the night, given his reputation, I hoped that his presence would upset the Norwegian defence. Although Frank did unfortunately have one of his poorer games, his selection, in the circumstances, was justifiable.

On 14 November 1984 we travelled to Copenhagen to face Denmark. The Danes were a formidable opposition. A few months earlier, at Euro '84, they had gone all the way to the semi-finals where only a lost penalty shoot-out, against Spain, had denied them a place in the final. Denmark were well organised and they had an excellent manager in the German Sepp Piontek. Most importantly of all, however, they had exceptional individual players throughout the team. They were dangerous in almost every position. At the back, the imperious Morten Olsen conducted affairs from his sweeper role while in central midfield the combative Søren Lerby was accomplished at breaking up opposition attacks and ensuring quick turnarounds for his team. On the wings they had the pace and artistry of Frank Arnesen and Jesper Olsen, while up front, with Preben Elkjær and Michael Laudrup leading the line, they had one of the best forward combinations in the game. Elkjær, on his game, was as close to unstoppable as centre forwards come. He had a menacing combination of power, speed, deceptively quick feet and deadly finishing. Elkjær was also the ideal foil for the nimbler and even more skilful Laudrup, who was adept at ghosting into threatening positions while the bustling Elkjær occupied the centre halves' attention.

When, in September 1983, the Danes arrived at Wembley and nonchalantly defeated England 1-0 in qualifying for Euro '84, English manager Bobby Robson anointed them 'the best side in Europe'. Bobby was not far wrong. His view was confirmed when, in September 1984, they defeated Norway 1-0 in Copenhagen, courtesy of an Elkjær goal.

Although the assignment ahead was, of course, a daunting one, I knew that we had enough quality to hurt the Danes, provided we approached the game in the right way. Despite my confidence, I was not, however, intent on playing into the Danes' hands. They moved the ball forward at lightning speed to create dangerous chances. I knew that we had to keep numbers back to cope with the inevitable waves of attack. Looking at these strengths, I decided that the wisest strategy would be to contain and frustrate the Danes early on, and then try to catch them on the counter-attack as the game progressed. I knew that to get something from this game we would need an error-free performance.

When the match was in its early stages, I was pleased: we had a good share of possession and were coping with whatever the Danes threw at us. We were also giving them some problems. In the first fifteen minutes, a contentious call by the referee denied us a penalty when Tony Grealish was fouled in the box while bearing down on the Danish goal. It was one of those decisions that you do not get away from home. Had we been playing at Lansdowne Road, I felt sure, the penalty would have been given.

With twenty-five minutes on the clock, we were comfortable and looked like taking the Danes in at half-time scoreless. It was then, while under minimal pressure in the middle of the park, that Grealish uncharacteristically played a stray ball backwards, right to Elkjær's feet. Twenty-five yards from goal, and with plenty left to do, the big Dane rolled David O'Leary and bore down on Seamus McDonagh from the right wing. O'Leary attempted a last-ditch saving tackle, but to no avail. Elkjær shot across McDonagh to put Denmark one up. It was a dispiriting goal to concede. One momentary lapse of concentration had cost us dearly. Now the Danes had their tails up and we were on the rack.

At half-time, the main message was to stick to the game plan. At only one goal down, we did not need to panic. Disappointingly, barely sixty seconds into the second half, the curse of lack of concentration struck again. Frank Stapleton got caught in possession on the edge of Denmark's eighteen-yard box and the Danes swept up the pitch in a whirlwind move. Laudrup crossed into the six-yard box where Elkjær flicked up the ball, catching our defence flat-footed, and toe-poked it past McDonagh for a second goal.

Two down, away to Denmark: Mission Difficult was fast becoming Mission Impossible. Nine minutes later the game was over as a contest. After a quick-fire one-two on the edge of our box, Lerby broke free on the left and shot underneath McDonagh to make the final score 3-0. We had been soundly beaten but it should be emphasised just how good the Danes were: it was one of the best international performances I had witnessed in many years. Escaping with a draw would have counted as an excellent result in the circumstances.

Together with the defeat to Norway a month earlier, the Denmark result put us in a weak position at the end of 1984. We had gathered only two points from a possible six and sections of the media were calling for my head. I soon discovered that not everyone in the FAI was behind me either. My employers summoned me to Merrion Square to discuss the situation in front of the entire committee. Although I was happy to stand my ground before the FAI, these inquisition-style meetings were not for the faint of heart. You entered the committee room to find sombre faces staring at you. Just to add to the intimidating atmosphere, the officials, for these sorts of meetings, sat in a crescent shape, surrounding you on both sides as you sat in the middle of them. I felt as if I was on trial. After a lengthy discussion, the committee gave me their support. It was back to football.

This period underlined for me how rapidly fortunes shift – and how short memories are! In September, we were being hailed as heroes after our victory over the Soviet Union; now, just two months later, there were calls for my dismissal, as well as harsh criticism of certain players for an alleged lack of commitment.

After over four years in the job, I had no illusions about the media. When I had started as Ireland's manager, I had shown some naivety in my dealings with them. I felt that if I helped the press to do their job, they would help me to do mine. At the close of 1984, however, I knew better: it was obvious to me that a minority of journalists were bent on drumming up controversy no matter what the cost to Irish football. If we lost games, all the better; that would supply even juicier headlines.

Whatever about the invective aimed at me, it was the questioning of the players' loyalty to the cause that was hardest to accept. I knew how much it meant for these players to represent their country. Their desire was always beyond question.

As for the suggestion that some of the players were somehow money-grubbers, the reality was different. If getting rich quick was your game, you were in the wrong job playing for the Republic of Ireland. There was precious little financial gain associated with playing for this particular international side. The Irish players received a once-off IR£250 match fee, compared to the Stg£1,000 paid to English internationals. As well as that, the Irish players, owing to the lower profile of our game, lost out on the lucrative sponsorship deals enjoyed by their English counterparts. In fact, many Irish players could have earned more from personal appearances than they did while playing for their country. I know that in some cases, certain players, by joining up with us for midweek friendlies, actually missed out on Stg£500 appearance fees which had been arranged by their agents. The players even paid for their own costs up front before being reimbursed by the FAI – and sometimes only after a very long wait!

Before resuming competitive action, we played a friendly against Italy in February 1985 at Dalymount Park, the game in which Paul McGrath made his debut for Ireland, as a substitute. Although it was unusual for us to play home games away from Lansdowne Road, the lower rent at Dalymount, coupled with the FAI's acute lack of funds, meant that the old stadium was still considered to be a viable venue. Considering the quality of opposition in our own World Cup qualifying group, this fixture against the world champions was precisely what we needed to keep our competitive edge. Disappointingly, we went two behind in the first eighteen minutes, courtesy of a Paolo Rossi penalty and a strike from Alessandro Altobelli. Thankfully, in the second half, we upped our tempo and took the game to the Italians. Gary Waddock pulled one back in the fifty-third minute and, although we would ultimately lose the game 2-1, we had given a satisfactory account of ourselves against strong opposition. The other plus was that McGrath, who replaced the injured Mark Lawrenson in the tenth minute, looked comfortable at this level.

Whatever about any positives from the match, the main action was, unfortunately, off the pitch. Owing to the FAI's decision not to enforce an all-ticket policy, no one knew how many fans would show up. When the players and I arrived a few hours before kick-off, at 5.30 p.m., it was clear that all was not normal. The main approach to the ground, from Phibsborough church, was already thronged with fans. By kick-off, judging by the serious overcrowding at the turnstiles, it was becoming obvious that the situation was out of control. What had not helped the situation was the new sponsorship deal the FAI had agreed with the lager company Steiger. Steiger had run a huge promotional campaign across the capital which saw them advertising the match in almost every pub in Dublin. The marketing ploy worked. Nearly 50,000 fans had turned up for a stadium that could hold only 35,000.

Kick-off was put back by fifteen minutes while the gardaí and stewards grappled with the swelling crowd. Dangerous numbers of fans squeezed into the terraces and it was clear that if any more were funnelled in, a serious human tragedy might well have unfolded. To alleviate the crush, the gardaí acted quickly and removed fencing from the terrace perimeter, thus allowing fans to spill out onto the side of the pitch. And that's where they stayed, under garda supervision, for the ninety minutes of the game. It was a surreal experience but at least tragedy was averted. I had fans sitting down next to me on the ground, watching the action. I always remember how bemused the Italians were. They couldn't believe that fans would be sitting so close to the action. I recall Paolo Rossi imploring spectators to give him more room for a corner kick because he needed a longer run-up.

Our next game in the campaign was at home to Norway on 1 May 1985. The preceding six months since our loss to Denmark had been a long wait. In international management the sometimes large gaps between competitive matches can mean that if you end one sequence of games on a low note, you have to wait an age to redeem yourself. You are willing the next match to come along as fast as it can.

The Norway game was, regrettably, a very disappointing affair. Although we were not at full strength – injuries excluded from selection Chris Hughton, Kevin Sheedy and Queens Park Rangers forward John Byrne – I certainly expected a lot better than what we gave. It was probably the worst competitive performance that I had presided over as Ireland manager. Nothing seemed to come off. With the exception of Packie Bonner in goal, everyone had a day to forget. We knew that the Norwegians would arrive with a packed defence and seek to choke us, but, despite home advantage, we could not find the inventiveness to break them down. Stapleton had a goal disallowed for a marginal offside call against Robinson and we barely even protested. I felt that summed up how much our self-belief had dwindled away. A highly damaging 0-0 draw was the result. Liam Brady had the worst game I had ever seen him play and, in the second half, I replaced him with Ronnie Whelan.

We were now in serious trouble in the group, and with some fans turning on us at the final whistle, Lansdowne Road was not a happy place to be. After the match, with emotions still raw, I told the players that I was going to resign.

Since I was not delivering the results, I suggested they might be better off playing under a new manager. They urged me to stay on, arguing that it was just as much their responsibility to perform well. At a time when I was being pilloried by sections of fans and the media, the players' genuine support was inspiring. I resolved to stay on and complete the campaign. Since we still had an outside chance of qualifying, I decided to give it my very best effort.

A few hours after the Norway game, I discussed with Liam Brady the decision to substitute him. He took it in a thoroughly professional manner, making it clear that he understood. He spoke about his performance with admirable honesty. He said he knew we had to win this one but that the harder he tried, the worse he got.

Although many of the players were disparaged at various times during my tenure, I believe that Liam Brady and Frank Stapleton came in for especially unfair attention. With their dedication to the cause sometimes publicly questioned, both players felt under a lot of pressure. Liam's below-par performance in the home match against Norway was a case in point. There were repeated attacks in the media, casting doubt on his passion for playing for his country, and he went out to prove a point. The outcome was one of his worst games for the Republic of Ireland. It was a tough decision to make to substitute Liam. He was also, at this stage of the game, being targeted by pockets of the crowd. Nobody likes being substituted, and even less so when the occasion is international football and you are playing in front of a home crowd.

The one plus for us, at this point in the campaign, was that the Soviet Union had not yet found their form: a loss (to us) and two draws ensured that they remained a point behind us at this stage. Allied to this was the fact that I believed two winnable games awaited us: at home and away to Switzerland.

Before facing the Swiss, we played a friendly against Spain on 26 May. The teams played out a 0-0 draw at Cork's Flower Lodge. The real show, however, was in the background, with rumblings, once more, of politics at Merrion Square. I would discover in the days after the match that the fixture had precipitated a failed attempt within the FAI to oust me from my position. An FAI delegate had led the unsuccessful coup, apparently hoping to get a bumper gate by having the publicity of a new manager installed in time for the game. It was a demoralising revelation but I stayed focused. I had four games left as Ireland manager and that's what my mind was on.

We faced the Swiss at Lansdowne Road on the afternoon of 2 June. The majority of the squad had been together for ten days before the game – a rare luxury I was very pleased to have. The only complication for our preparations was the fact that Mark Lawrenson, Jim Beglin and Ronnie Whelan joined us from the Heysel Stadium disaster which had occurred five days before when their club, Liverpool, had faced Juventus in the European Cup Final. Obviously, the enormity of Heysel completely eclipsed the significance our own match but, given that Lawrenson, Beglin and Whelan expressed their desire to play against the Swiss, I had to assess whether or not they were in a fit state mentally to play. My fears were ungrounded. They were able to put the tragic events (in which thirty-nine fans died and 600 were injured) to one side, at least for long enough to concentrate on our game.

The Swiss were fond of employing limpet-tight man-marking, so we were going to need to play with real pace to find openings in their closely marshalled formation. If everything had gone wrong against Norway two weeks earlier, thankfully, on a balmy day at Lansdowne, everything went right for us. We ran out comfortable 3-0 winners, to keep our chances in the group alive. We even briefly occupied top spot in the group after this game. For me, this match proved beyond doubt how well we could perform with a proper build-up in place. The outcome was a coherent, self-assured display that showed all our attacking abilities. From the first whistle, we imposed ourselves on the match and took the game to the Swiss.

We were ahead after only seven minutes and deservedly so. In a rehearsed training ground routine that worked to a tee, Kevin Sheedy played a free-kick to the Swiss back post where Dave Langan crossed first time, on the volley, for an onrushing Frank Stapleton to drive in from close range. The sun was shining at Lansdowne Road, the supporters were in high spirits, and I was feeling good. Before half-time we went two up, courtesy of a break from deep by Tony Grealish, who managed to slip through the Swiss man-marking and score with a lovely flicked header in off the post.

In the second half I was particularly pleased at how we closed out the game and controlled the tempo in a thoroughly professional manner. Midway through the half we crowned an accomplished performance with a third goal when Kevin Sheedy ran onto a long pass and coolly slotted past the Swiss goalkeeper. After this victory we were on five points, with Denmark and the Soviet Union both on four. That was round one to Ireland; two months later we would travel to Berne for the second encounter with the Swiss.

By now it was clear what we had to do to in order to have a realistic chance of qualifying for Mexico. We had to beat Switzerland, hope that the Soviet Union would beat Denmark in Moscow and then not lose to the Soviets in Moscow ourselves, before defeating the Danes at Lansdowne Road in our final game. It was no easy assignment but it was where we found ourselves in the group.

For the return game against Switzerland, I was without Ronnie Whelan and Dave Langan. The match proved to be a suffocating affair, with tight marking squeezing out any available space. The Swiss, whose home form was very good, could also still qualify at this stage so, as you would expect, they gave precious little away. Switzerland lined up with five in midfield, and as the first half wore on, it was clear that we were getting overrun in that part of the pitch. I decided to withdraw Brady from the more advanced role that I had given him, bringing him back into midfield. Cascarino, who was making his international debut, was performing well in attack with Frank Stapleton. The first half ended without either side making a breakthrough.

The game remained tight in the second half but we managed to create three excellent opportunities, all of which we failed to convert, however. The easiest of these fell to Stapleton who, uncharacteristically, did not take his chance.

The contest ended 0-0, a result that damaged both sides as it simply paved the way for the Danes and the Soviets to take the top two spots in the group.

After the disheartening draw with Switzerland we had two games remaining, both of which we now *had* to win to qualify. It is fair to say that they were both crunch matches: away to the Soviet Union in October and at home to Denmark in November – our two most difficult opponents in the group. But first, the Soviets and the Danes were playing each other on 25 September, so I made arrangements to travel to Moscow to see the game. I also arranged to stay in Moscow's Sport Hotel, the same hotel we would later use for our trip there. Because the Danes were also billeted there, it would be an ideal chance to assess the hotel and get the opinion of my opposite number, Sepp Piontek, with whom I had struck up a good relationship.

Even though the Soviets had agreed, when the draw was made in Zürich, that all visiting managers would receive full co-operation and be assisted in every way, the reality was somewhat different. With the Soviet authorities, it was often a case of fine words but shabby deeds. Before my trip was authorised by Moscow, there were problems obtaining a visa and it was only settled after numerous telexes back and forth. Like all travellers to the Soviet Union at that time, I was required to use the official Soviet travel agency, Intourist, to organise my trip and I was promised that an official would meet me at Moscow's Sheremetyevo Airport on arrival. Travelling with Swissair, my route took me through Zürich, where I met the Swiss manager, Paul Wolfisberg. He was also heading to Moscow to watch the game.

When we landed in Moscow, the vaunted co-operation was not immediately apparent. Orientating yourself in a city as vast as Moscow, armed only with the English language and some native pluck, was not a straightforward affair in the Cold War Soviet Union. Our promised contact was nowhere to be seen. He arrived thirty minutes later. It quickly became apparent that the assistance on offer was going to be token. The official coldly handed me a match ticket and told me to get a taxi to the city's National Hotel where my accreditation would be waiting for me at the hotel's reception. I objected. This was not the hotel that our respective football associations had agreed upon in discussions. Obviously, staying in the Sport Hotel, as planned, was an important part of my trip. I wanted to inspect our proposed accommodation at first hand to be sure of its suitability. My claims fell on deaf ears: this figure of Soviet officialdom was unimpressed and unmoved. He had done his job. He repeated: '*Go* to the National Hotel and you will find that everything *will* be in order.'

I was not filled with confidence, but, with fingers crossed, I made my way to the nearest taxi. The car was standard Soviet-issue: a beaten-up Lada, badly in need of love and affection. I sat into the back and instantly felt something odd. Before I could move, a spring came right through the seat and ripped the backside out of my trousers. The very awkward situation I was in dawned on me: I was travelling alone, and light, with only the suit on my back to rely on. There was no one to meet me at the stadium. I had to think of something. How could I present myself at the match in this state? It would have been some sight: the Ireland manager sheepishly sidling up to the officials' section of the Central Lenin Stadium with a great big rip through the back of his trousers.

First, however, I had to secure my accreditation for the match. When I went to the reception at the National Hotel to collect it, why was I not surprised to learn that no one there knew anything about it? I was being given the run-around by the Soviet authorities. Leaving the hotel empty-handed and frustrated, I wondered 'what next?'

Getting into any international stadium without accreditation is a tricky affair but in the case of the Central Lenin Stadium doubly so. The stadium (now called the Luzhniki Stadium) is, in fact, a sprawling complex and, in those days, on match day, the surrounding area went into lockdown mode. Roads to the complex were blocked off for kilometres around and no one moved anywhere without the correct paperwork being produced.

My only choice was to seek help from the Irish Embassy. I got in touch with the First Secretary, Joe Hayes, and to his immense credit, he was a great help. I also pursued a backup plan. With the embassy's help, I phoned the Sport Hotel to speak to Sepp Piontek. We may have been rivals on the field of play (and still competing for the final two spots in Group Six) but, outside the fray, the German was a model sportsman. A genial Sepp came on the line and was, as I expected, more than happy to help me out, once I had outlined my predicament. Without hesitation, he agreed to my travelling to the stadium on the Danish team bus. And, even though I now had no choice but to stay at the National Hotel, Sepp was open to me paying a visit to the Sport Hotel to view the accommodation.

When I reached Denmark's team hotel, I got talking with the Danish Football Association secretary, Erik Hellstrup. Erik gave me a tour of the players' rooms and also told me about the various problems they had encountered since their arrival. At least I was not alone in being messed around by the Soviet authorities.

On the day of the match, as planned, I took my place on the Danes' bus to travel to the stadium. There was still, however, that small matter of the tear in my trousers to resolve. I hit on a solution – a bad one but I was hardly blessed with options: with so little time it was not realistic for me to go shopping in a city as vast as Moscow. I had a quiet word with Sepp. It was surely an unusual request from a fellow international manager but, once again, Sepp came good. He had trousers for me. He disappeared into the dressing room and re-emerged with red Danish tracksuit bottoms. Oh Lord, I thought. Red tracksuit bottoms underneath my suit jacket and shirt. But beggars can't be choosers. I thanked Sepp and got into my colourful get-up!

Before kick-off, I went out onto the pitch along with the Danish players to inspect the surface and sample the atmosphere. On a freezing cold night, the stadium – with its 100,000 capacity, forbidding Soviet architecture and Red Army soldiers lining the perimeter of the pitch – was an experience. We would soon have to deal with all these factors ourselves. Not being pressed for time, I lingered on the pitch a little longer than the Danes. It was a mistake. When I walked back to the tunnel, I found its entrance blocked by mute, stone-faced, armed soldiers. Despite explaining that I could only have got out onto the pitch via the tunnel in the first place, they would not budge. In the end, I climbed over a wall and finally got to my seat. Although by the end of evening I was freezing and soaked (oh, the glamour of it all!), the aim of the trip had been achieved.

In a closely fought contest the Soviet Union won 1-0, thanks to a second-half strike from the deadly Dynamo Kyiv centre forward Oleh Protasov. The result left both the Soviets and the Danes in a strong position in the group, with everyone else playing catch-up.

For me, and for many of the senior players, Mexico '86 would be the last chance of appearing at a World Cup. I knew that if we did not qualify, it was going to be time for me to call it a day; as for the senior players in the squad, many might well be too old by the time the 1990 World Cup came around. For these reasons I was determined that preparation for the Moscow trip would be of the highest possible standard; if we lost, I wanted it to be for footballing reasons alone, and not for any want of organisation.

I had played away to the Soviet Union twice with the Republic of Ireland, so I was well aware that a trip behind the Iron Curtain came with its own unique perils. Food poisoning (or 'Moscow tummy' as it was known) was a common affliction of players on away trips to the Soviet Union. The food in Communist-era Russia was very poor, compared to what footballers ate on away trips within Western Europe. If you did not prepare for this eventuality, you could find yourself with a spate of sick players.

My time with the Danish squad had been an eye-opener. Sepp Piontek told me that when the Danes had travelled to Moscow, they brought their own chef, selected from a top Copenhagen hotel, as well as a plane-load of their own carefully chosen food. They then used the kitchen facilities of the Sport Hotel for the duration of their stay.

This approach made sense. Sepp pointed out that, as far as the players were concerned, with familiar food morning, noon and night, the hotel became a virtual home away from home and, on top of that, the risk of sick stomachs was avoided. I had to convince the FAI of the merits of this approach, but before proposing it I did my homework. I sounded out the Burlington Hotel in Dublin and asked if their chefs would be willing to prepare and then cook our food in Moscow. I knew that Liverpool used the Burlington chefs for away trips, so this was a good option for us.

I put the idea to Peadar O'Driscoll and Charlie Walsh. The response was not good. They were against it on financial grounds. They didn't fancy our chances of getting a positive result in Moscow and felt that the outlay was unnecessary. This was a negative response that only served to undermine my best efforts for a vital game. It *was* a costly option. I understood that, but my attitude was that if we wanted to count ourselves amongst the best, then we should do as they do. The Danes were doing it; other nations were doing it, so why not us?

I pressed my case. The arrangement would be needed for only three days, I explained: one meal on the Monday of our arrival; two on the Tuesday; and pre-match food on the Wednesday. They agreed to postpone a decision until the following day.

I went home and mulled over the situation. My then wife, Pat, asked what the matter was. I outlined my hopes of having a chef travel with the squad and the resistance my employers were giving to the idea. It was then that an unorthodox solution hit me. I asked my wife if she would come to Moscow and cook for us, provided the FAI would deliver the food to the team hotel. 'Why not?' she replied. The next day I ran it by the FAI. Walsh agreed, without a moment's thought, chiefly because my wife would be doing it at no cost. It was a long shot and I did not believe for a moment that the FAI would actually go for it. I had proposed the notion as a ploy only because I believed that it might finally embarrass them into submission and give me my professional chef after all. I had certainly misjudged this one. Mrs Hand was coming to Moscow; she had just become the official cook for the Republic of Ireland international football team.

A few days later O'Driscoll, Walsh and I travelled to the Burlington Hotel to arrange for the preparation and delivery of the food consignment. By the time we made it back to Merrion Square, it was late and we still had a few points to iron out on how the food would make it to Moscow. There would be no chance to deal with the outstanding issues, however. In the middle of settling mundane organisational matters, a stormy argument erupted between O'Driscoll and Walsh. They could not agree on who would make up the official party. Both wanted different delegates on the trip. O'Driscoll marched out, slamming the door behind him. Moments later, Walsh also stormed out. I was left all alone in the FAI's offices, wondering if these guys were coming back. I waited, and then I waited some more. There was nothing but silence in the old building. I let myself out, shut the door behind me and went home.

On the Saturday before the Soviet Union game I travelled to London to watch Chelsea play Everton at Stamford Bridge. I planned to get reports afterwards on the fitness of all squad players who were in action that day. As always, I hoped that no one would go down with an injury.

There was bad news from Old Trafford. Ron Atkinson rang me to say that Paul McGrath was doubtful after badly bruising his toe and instep in that day's game. Paul had become a valuable player for us. Later that night my fears were confirmed when Manchester United withdrew Paul. I rang him and underlined how important this match was to us. I told him that only he could persuade Ron to change his mind. 'Big Ron', however, was not for turning. McGrath was out.

I also had a scare when Arsenal told me that David O'Leary had been taken off injured towards the end of the game against West Ham. Luckily, it was only a superficial knock and David reported for training the next day. Because we were flying out from London, I arranged with the Brentford manager and former Arsenal player, Frank McLintock, for us to use his club's training facilities on the Sunday.

When the squad assembled at Heathrow Airport we ran into the Northern Ireland squad who were on their way to an equally crucial qualification game, on 16 October, against Romania. The players, many of whom knew one another, mingled before going their separate ways. I wished their manager, Billy Bingham, the best of luck. Looking at both squads side by side and the array of fine players in each one, I could not help but ponder what we might achieve by pooling our resources and fielding a single international line-up. Of course, Northern Ireland, after their quarter-final showing at the 1982 World Cup, had every right to believe that they did not need the assistance of the Republic; they were managing just fine on their own. Still, it was a tantalising thought.

The food consignment had been placed on a separate flight from us and I had been worrying whether or not it would make it to our hotel.

In Moscow before our 1986 Word Cup qualifier against the Soviet Union. (*L–r*): John Byrne, Tony Cascarino, guide (unknown), Dr Bob O'Driscoll, Kevin Moran, me, guide (unknown), Packie Bonner, Tony Grealish, Terry Conroy, Kevin O'Callaghan, Seamus McDonagh, Kevin Sheedy, Gary Waddock, Chris Hughton, Ronnie Whelan, Frank Stapleton, Jim Beglin, Mick McCarthy, Mark Lawrenson, Mick Byrne (physio), David O'Leary and Liam Brady.

Thankfully, it arrived on time. The players were also very happy with our new cook – at the end of the trip they would christen her 'The Chef'. On our first morning, however, I overheard Charlie Walsh – the same person who had originally opposed my food plans – pulling my wife aside and asking her to make sure that he got a proper breakfast – by which he meant, he wanted some of the meals that the Burlington had prepared and not the local Russian fare. I told Pat that he was not to get a morsel. He could make do with what the hotel served up.

The day before the match I announced my team to the squad. The big call for this game was my decision to leave out Kevin Sheedy. Sheedy was an up-and-coming player for us but, for the game ahead, despite his undoubted ability, I felt we needed runners who could cope better with the Soviets' athleticism. Kevin was not this kind of player. Besides, his performance had been average in our draw away to Switzerland. Kevin, I'm sure, was disappointed but the matter was left at that. He did not express an opinion on it either way.

That is why I was surprised to hear Kevin's comments in subsequent years, suggesting that he apparently barged into my Moscow hotel room and had a 'blazing row' with me over being dropped. Now anyone who knew Kevin could tell you that he was a quiet, introverted type. As a rule, Kevin did not barge in anywhere and I have no recollection of any 'blazing row'.

On 16 October, we arrived at our do-or-die encounter with the Soviet Union. We knew the scale of the challenge. With 100,000 home fans looking on and soldiers placed everywhere around the ground, including in the crowd, the atmosphere was guaranteed to be intimidating. The Soviets had not lost a competitive international fixture at home for fifty years. If that was not enough, they had not conceded a goal in Moscow in twenty years. It was an exceptional record. To progress, we were going to have to be record-breakers but, considering that we had already defeated the Soviet Union at home eleven months earlier, we could hardly believe it was an impossible feat. One thought, however, gnawed at me: in the past we had shown a worrying inability to win key away games and now, in the bear pit that was the Central Lenin Stadium, we were trying to reverse that trend.

At this point, having already seen the Soviets play in Dublin and having watched them another five times, I knew that their greatest threat lay in midfield. For this reason I opted for a 3-5-2 formation with our full backs pushed forward to provide extra width. However, in order to maintain defensive solidity, the formation could revert to a 5-3-2 as and when required. When the game began, we were playing well. The players were giving their absolute all and the tactic of urging our full backs to get forward was bearing fruit. Our opponents were also on their game, but I was happy that we were turning this into a proper contest. Jim Beglin, in particular, at left back, was proving to be a thorn in the Soviets' side. Given the USSR's unblemished home record, I knew that we had to give them something to worry about in attack. If we had sat back and hoped for a winner to come from a set piece or some random moment of luck, we would have been overwhelmed. The first half was definitely our best performance away from home in that campaign. We went in at half-time scoreless but looking composed and, perhaps, poised to strike in the second half.

The next forty-five minutes began well. The Soviet players were feeling the pressure in front of the huge home crowd and they began to look edgy. I felt optimistic that now might be the time for us to take the initiative. However, in the sixtieth minute, we fell on our own sword. Protasov broke free far too easily down our right side and played a high, looping cross to the back post where the onrushing Cherenkov caught the ball on the half-volley. McDonagh got a hand to it but could only deflect it into the bottom corner. For the remainder of the game the Soviets retreated into a shell and protected their lead. Those final fifteen minutes will stay with me for ever. All the endeavour, all the striving, all our hopes, across the entire span of the previous five years, had now boiled down to this. 'Can we do it?' I kept thinking, over and over. I was willing the players to find a goal from somewhere. We had two late chances, but the goal would not come.

In the ninetieth minute, with our players overcommitted and chasing the game, the USSR caught us with the classic sucker punch: catching us on the break, Protasov scored the goal that sealed victory.

Our efforts, although heroic, were not good enough. It was a spirited and hugely impressive performance which had pushed our opponents to their limit, but the USSR still had enough to overcome our resistance. We had put everything into this match, both on the pitch, and in our meticulous pre-match preparations, but we fell short – and it was bitterly disappointing. Mexico was gone; I counted the great players in our squad who would now, in all likelihood, never taste the experience of a World Cup. That saddened me greatly.

I felt nothing but immense pride towards my players. After offering my congratulations to the victors, I made my way to our dressing room and told a disconsolate squad: 'You gave it everything you had. You can hold your heads high and be proud of yourselves.' I also made it clear to the players that I would be resigning after the campaign's final fixture in November.

At the press conference afterwards, I cut a dejected figure. I knew that I had reached the endgame and by now I was a spent force. The pressures of the previous year in particular had left me drained. Now that it was all over, the emotion and tiredness flowed out unchecked. I was forthright and honest with my answers to the waiting press pack and admitted that it was the saddest night of my managerial career.

Whatever about the disappointment, we still had our game against Denmark to play on 13 November. Denmark had already effectively

The long walk: Moscow, October 1985. We have just lost 2-0 to the Soviet Union. The result meant that we would not qualify for the 1986 World Cup in Mexico. (Sportsfile)

qualified and we no longer could, so the outcome would be merely of academic interest. I went about preparing for my last match, and although I tried to be as professional as possible, it was hard to summon my usual passion.

In the build-up to the game a particularly silly and ultimately regrettable incident took place. John O'Shea, then a journalist with the *Evening Press*, and later the chief executive of the charity GOAL, was getting on the players' case in his weekly column. O'Shea had criticised Mick McCarthy repeatedly for not having enough pace for international football. It was such a bugbear with O'Shea that he even called me the day before we were due to train in Dublin to say that he, himself, would beat McCarthy hands-down in a sprint. I was sick of O'Shea's posturing so, on the spur of the moment, I challenged him to put his money where his mouth was. He jumped at the bet. O'Shea said to expect him at training the next morning. Instead of ignoring him, I said, 'Come on down if you want to, John'. I didn't think for one second that he was actually going to turn up.

The next morning, at training, sure enough, there was O'Shea, fully kitted out in his tracksuit and runners, enthusiastically putting himself through his warm-up exercises on the side of the pitch. If O'Shea wanted to take on a professional footballer and embarrass himself, who was I to stand in his way? I went over to Mick McCarthy. Would he race O'Shea and shut him up? He would. Mick was only too glad to have an opportunity to humiliate him.

The contestants lined up. Mick Byrne blew the whistle. They took off. McCarthy was yards in front. 'No, no, stop, stop. That was a false start that time. That was a false start', O'Shea protested. The starting whistle went for the second time. Same result again: McCarthy tore into the lead, with O'Shea getting a clear view of his opponent's heels. Suddenly, a flagging O'Shea pulled up again: 'Aghh, aghh, my hamstring, my bloody hamstring, I think I've done my hamstring,' O'Shea complained. He coughed up the money, left and we got on with training.

It didn't end there, though. McCarthy tweaked his groin the day after, and was not fit to face Denmark. In the aftermath of his defeat, O'Shea seized on the chance to make his story. He wrote about how reckless I was to allow a professional player race a journalist in the days before a World Cup qualifier and suggested that McCarthy's injury stemmed from that race. I couldn't win. When he lost the race fair and square, he twisted the story for his own ends. In later years, Mick said that I was a plonker to allow the race to take place, and he was right. I should have known that it was stupid and realised that, one way or another, O'Shea would have created controversial copy out of the incident. Because it was my last game, I just was not thinking straight.

The night before the Denmark game, the players presented me with a gift of a Waterford Glass bowl in the lobby of the Airport Hotel. It was a genuinely touching gesture and one that confirmed for me that the players had been in my corner throughout the twists and turns of the previous five years.

For my final game as Ireland manager, I opted again to play with the unfamiliar 5-3-2 formation. Although we had lost in Moscow playing this way, our performance had been very promising, so I chose to try it again. This time, however, the tactic backfired. The movement of the Danes was too good and our three centre halves were not comfortable enough in this relatively new line-up to cope. In the 1980s, the majority of English clubs played with either a 4-4-2 or a 4-3-3 formation. This meant that centre halves were schooled in the habits of playing with one partner immediately beside them and two full backs on either side. It was a simple set-up and one in which everyone knew their role: if one centre half moved towards the ball, the other stayed back; if attackers got down one flank, the opposite full back came across to offer cover if the centre half was dragged out of position. With 5-3-2, however, the old certainties went out the window.

Even though we got out of the traps early and stunned Denmark with an excellent goal from Stapleton, we ultimately got pulled to pieces in a deflating defeat. Our three centre halves, Lawrenson, Moran and O'Leary, were at sea. We went in at the break 2-1 down. Elkjær, again, was murdering us, with Kevin Moran, especially, having a torrid time trying to rein in the big Dane. The second half was little better and we lost 4-1 to a rampant Danish side who were almost on a victory lap now that their place in Mexico was guaranteed.

With nothing to play for, in my last game in charge, it was a moment of self-indulgence on my part to experiment against such quality opposition. It did, however, prove to me, once and for all, that in international football you cannot make major changes with the short time available to you.

The result meant that, in the group's final standings, we finished on six points, and in fourth position, behind Denmark, the Soviet Union and Switzerland respectively.

That night we had a squad get-together at our hotel with Sean McGuinness, Pete St John and the Wolfe Tones providing the music. Pete, aware that I was leaving the Ireland job, recited a farewell poem that he had written for me. It was very moving and, although I certainly felt sad to be going, I also felt relief that I would no longer have the stress of being Ireland manager.

7

For the Love of the Game

Looking Back on My Years as Ireland Manager

Looking back now, I feel honoured that I am one of a select number who have managed the Republic of Ireland international team. It was a huge task, but one I embraced wholeheartedly. I have no regrets and many fond memories.

However, to truly understand the challenges of being Republic of Ireland manager in those years, all the constraints that I worked under should be made clear to readers. Chief among these were, ironically, my bosses. You trusted the FAI to do basic organisational work at your peril. Repeatedly, throughout my term, so much of my time and energy went into checking and rechecking that the FAI was fulfilling its obligations. Everything became an uphill struggle because I could not rely on them. The reader may not realise it, but in the 1980s the FAI had few full-time officials on the payroll. It was a threadbare operation that had very little capacity for coping with the demands of international football.

Although generally the FAI staff did their best, too often the organisation showed itself to be consistently amateurish. It left me always wondering what new problem lay lurking around the next corner. With inveterate penny-pinching a way of life at the Merrion Square headquarters, there were numerous ways in which the FAI could not see the bigger picture of international football. Many of the organisation's decisions were infected with a debilitating short-sightedness and so lacked any coherent long-term perspective.

The farce of the South America trip was a harsh eye-opener for me, but the problems did not stay in Rio; they were a feature of my entire time as Ireland manager. I should emphasise that my point is to give a truthful account of all the circumstances of my years in charge of the Republic. Some further examples will show the reality of what it was like to work under this regime.

Peadar O'Driscoll, as the general secretary, was the official with whom I dealt on a regular basis and the one who was responsible for ensuring that various off-field matters were tended to. Unfortunately, in my opinion, he did not grasp the importance of his role. O'Driscoll was invariably all smiles but when the practicalities needed looking after, he struggled – certainly in my dealings with him. So often, he did not understand my viewpoint and so failed to see why measures that were obvious to me were necessary for our success. O'Driscoll could also be very challenging to deal with – when I could get hold of him, that is. He was so hard to pin down. Any time I made a visit to the office in Merrion Square, I felt that he was doing his level best to avoid me.

His office had an opaque glass front. This meant that once I came through to the reception area, I could clearly see his figure behind the glass moving across the office. To O'Driscoll, the sight of Eoin Hand crossing his threshold must have signalled imminent questions. And that meant that he would have to provide answers. Before I would get in the door, he would have the receptionist primed. I would go through the motions and deliver my line on cue, every time: 'I'm here to see Peadar.' To which his receptionist would always mechanically reply: 'I'm afraid that Mr O'Driscoll is not in at the moment.' This was frustrating, to say the least: we both knew that Mr O'Driscoll *was* in.

Furthermore, I could not trust Merrion Square to complete mundane tasks like contacting clubs to confirm the availability of players for forthcoming matches. If any of my squad had picked up an injury, this was something I needed to know about as soon as possible, so that I could immediately call up a replacement. Early on in my role, I got left hanging a few times when O'Driscoll either failed to inform me of injuries to players or simply told me far too late for me to do anything about it.

The other problem was that the FAI offices shut up shop at 5.30 p.m. on a Friday evening and did not open for business again until Monday morning. This meant that, if it was in the week before a Wednesday-night match, there was no one available over the weekend at Merrion Square to confirm with the clubs each player's availability. Discovering on the Monday morning that a certain player was injured may have been sufficient notice for a home game, but if it was an away game, the information was practically useless – we would typically leave from London for these games on a Sunday! As it was, we had only one full squad-gathering, on the Tuesday, because Liam Brady, after playing in Italy's Serie A on a Sunday, would travel on the Monday.

In order to have control over this vital part of match preparation, I established a routine in the week before international matches. I would travel to watch a match in England on the Saturday, when most squad members were playing. This allowed me to assess some of my players' performances but it also gave me a way of keeping tabs on injury news for the whole squad. After each game at, say, Highbury or White Hart Lane, I would make my way to the club secretary and ask for permission to use his office. I would then ring around to various grounds in England to get immediate updates on any injuries to our players. Getting through to switchboards at grounds just after the final whistle was not always easy. I had about forty-five minutes (from 4.45 p.m. to 5.30 p.m.) to contact all the locations. I covered a certain number of grounds while my assistant, Terry Conroy, would be going through the same process at another ground in the north of England. It was a hectic time. Together, we would assemble a full understanding of our squad's readiness, and in the quickest possible time. In one instance, the Spurs secretary, Peter Day, asked me with disbelief, 'Do you always have to do this?' My answer was straightforward: 'If I don't do it, no one else will.'

I knew from talking with my England counterpart, Bobby Robson, that none of this work fell to him. During one match, which I had watched with Bobby, I got up to say goodbye and explained that I was on my way to begin my usual post-match phone-calling routine. He was surprised and told me that the FA offices were open on a Saturday, so staff there made all the phone calls on his behalf.

Scouting trips abroad was another situation where the FAI and I were not reading from the same script. For example, in 1980, when I had just been appointed to the job, I told the FAI that it would be important for me to travel to Italy to watch the European Championships. I was particularly interested because Belgium and Holland were competing – two teams we would face in our 1982 World Cup qualification group. I wanted to find out as much as possible about these opponents. The FAI agreed to my going and so I asked them to send the required telex to the Italian authorities to obtain my official accreditation. Without this, I could not gain entry to the various stadiums to watch the games. 'No problem,' I was told, with an assurance that the matter was in hand. All I had to do was travel; they would see to the rest. (Incidentally, there was no telex machine at the FAI headquarters, but there was one in a travel agency nearby. That was where all Irish football's official messages were sent from.)

Looking forward to the scouting assignment ahead, I arrived in Milan on 17 June 1980 and made my way to the San Siro Stadium to watch the Netherlands v. Czechoslovakia. There were many hours to go before kick-off but, taking no chances, I went to the stadium early to make sure that everything was in order with my accreditation. I approached the official entrance to complete the formalities. A small hitch: no request had been received. For the next few hours I hung around in torrential rain arguing with increasingly exasperated Italian officials, telling them that a telex had been sent. They were equally insistent that no such message had been received. The proper official approach was not working, so, as usual, the back door would have to do for Irish football. By sheer luck, the deadlock was broken only when a Maltese journalist recognised me and managed to get me access with him. Once inside, my next saviour was Martin Tyler. Tyler, in his pre-Sky days, was doing commentary work for ITV. With no official accreditation, I was not entitled to sit in the officials' section. Thankfully, Martin brought me into the commentators' area instead where I finally was able to watch the game.

From Milan, I travelled south to Rome to watch Belgium play tournament hosts Italy on 18 June. I arrived at the Olympic Stadium with my fingers crossed, hoping that this time, at least, I would get my accreditation from the officials without any added drama. Déjà vu: no telex received; no accreditation available; Ireland manager ducks and dives into stadium, hanging on the coat-tails of a few pals – in this case the RTÉ commentator Jimmy Magee and the then BBC commentator George Hamilton.

During my stay in Italy, the accommodation that the FAI booked for me in both Milan and Rome was appalling. In Milan, it was not even a hotel. I was put up in the equivalent of a hostel that was well off the beaten track.

When I got back to Dublin, I let the FAI know what had happened in Italy. They did not seem all that upset and then proceeded to blame the Italians for everything. The telexes had been sent, they insisted, so the problem was obviously at the other end. I accept, of course, that it is possible that neither party was to blame and that the telexes simply got lost in the ether; however, the FAI should have confirmed receipt of their messages before I travelled.

When the 1982 World Cup in Spain came around, the same old problems resurfaced. I told Peadar O'Driscoll that I should attend the tournament. All I got back was a mixture of bafflement and resistance. 'Why do you need to go to the World Cup, Eoin?' O'Driscoll asked. I really did not think that, as an international manager, I would find myself having to justify this request, but things rarely worked according to normal rules at Merrion Square. I impressed upon O'Driscoll that this was the most important event in international football, and one that every other international manager would be attending. I had to be there to learn about our next competitive opponents, watch the world's best teams and to keep abreast of changing tactical patterns. The FAI truly was the world upside down: in any other association, the manager would have been ordered to attend these tournaments as part of his duties. To be fair to O'Driscoll, he was surprised by my suggestion precisely because no other Ireland manager had made such a request. Neither Liam Tuohy nor John Giles before me had had the time to travel to such tournaments. This was brand-new territory for the FAI and so a certain opposition was to be expected. I was lucky that Limerick United had no problem with me going since it was the close season.

O'Driscoll tried to dissuade me, claiming that, apart from the managers from the competing nations, there was no accommodation available for visiting managers, so there was no point in going. I decided to go anyway. I arranged to stay with some press people in accommodation that they had already booked in Madrid. I was grateful to Charlie Stuart of the Irish Press Group and Peter Byrne of *The Irish Times* for offering me a place in their apartment.

As far as my own football association was concerned, heading to Spain was my idea and so I would have to just make do without the FAI's official assistance. I had somewhere to stay, but I still had no accreditation because the FAI had not applied for it; I was also ticketless! Because the simple option was not available, further tiresome strategies would have to be devised for this international manager to get inside a stadium. Security at the World Cup was, naturally, very tight. Everyone had colour-coded security passes. If you didn't have one, you were not going anywhere near a match.

One option available was to contact Northern Ireland manager Billy Bingham. His Northern Ireland side was also based in Madrid and would soon face Austria in the second round of the tournament. I rang Billy's hotel and explained my situation. Thankfully, Billy, whom I knew well, did not hesitate to invite me to their team hotel. It was on this visit that I made my first acquaintance with the current Ireland manager, Martin O'Neill. Martin, then a player with Northern Ireland, was always articulate and intelligent in his thoughts about football. His subsequent success in management does not come as a surprise.

Bingham allowed me to travel on the team coach to Atlético Madrid's Vicente Calderón Stadium on 1 July. In this way, I was able to skirt the security requirements and gain access to the match. Although I saw ninety minutes of international football, the manner of my achieving this made me very uneasy. Having to tag along for a free ride on the Northern Ireland team coach was embarrassing. I wondered how much more bizarre this trip could get.

The next plan would involve me reprising my impersonation as a match commentator, first ventured at Euro 1980, and this time I would have a badge to prove it. Again, RTÉ provided me with a solution. I got in touch with Jimmy Magee, who was, as usual, commentating at the tournament, and Tim O'Connor, who was heading up RTÉ's coverage of the World Cup. Tim and I paid numerous visits to the World Cup headquarters in Madrid and eventually I managed to get an official commentator's accreditation. Clearly, if the football management game did not work out for me, a second budding career in the commentator's box was in the offing. Now, with this accreditation, I could watch matches from the commentator's box, a vantage point that was better than anywhere else in the ground.

For the second-round match between Spain and England, even more extreme measures were called for. Although I now had access to games as a 'commentator', Billy Young, the Bohemians manager, who was also in Spain for the tournament, asked if I could source a ticket for him. Tickets were next to impossible to get hold of and so entry to the game was being strictly controlled. I decided that I would ring England manager Ron Greenwood to wish him and his team well in their forthcoming game. Of course, I hoped that Ron might give me a way out, and offer tickets, without me having to ask straight out for the favour. Once the pleasantries were over, I could tell that this conversation was coming to a close. With Jimmy Magee beside me, egging me on and desperately trying to hold back

With Seamus McDonagh (*centre*) and the current Ireland manager, Martin O'Neill (*right*), at an awards dinner in 2016. Seamus was my regular Ireland goalie and is now goalkeeper coach of the national team.

the laughter, I bit the bullet. Just as Ron was ready to hang up, I asked: 'Ron, you wouldn't happen to have any spare tickets, would you?' He did have a ticket but getting my hands on it was going to be tricky. I was to be outside the entrance to Real Madrid's Santiago Bernabéu Stadium at an agreed time where I would wait for the England team coach to arrive. Finally, the coach came but, because security was so strict, there was only time for Ron to hand me the ticket through an open door while the coach was still moving through the gate. It was a drive-by ticket drop-off, with bemused security officials and Spanish police looking on. I can tell you that I was not too pleased to discover that, after all that, Billy Young had decided to watch the match on television.

Despite some of the inconveniences of the trip, I enjoyed my stay in Madrid immensely. Meeting and talking football with other international managers in the city's restaurants and bars was a great experience. The company of Jimmy Magee was highly enjoyable. Jimmy and I first crossed paths in 1967, when he was working as a commentator on a Drumcondra match. He remains a friend to this day and I can personally vouch for the encyclopaedic nature of his mind, both on sports and on many other subjects.

In Spain, we got used to meeting up at the same bar, the Negresco, and one evening, when we had settled in, Jimmy decided that he was going to treat the locals to a bit of authentic Irish 'culture'. The room was hushed as I motioned for the audience's reverent attention. He would sing a traditional Irish folk song. Jimmy could not sing a note if his life depended on it, but he proceeded to launch into a couple of minutes of sheer wailing gobbledygook with a rapt audience listening on. Just for a touch of credibility, at the end of each verse, deliberately dragging the words, he would always whine 'the factory waaaaaall'. Then, finally, Jimmy paused. Had he finished? Not likely. I jumped in. 'Now, for the second verse.' Jimmy struck up again, on cue. This time, though, the owner had had enough. 'Out, out. You are drunk, you are drunk.' Jimmy protested, but to no avail. We both ended up being asked to leave. Little did the irate manager know but, Jimmy, a committed teetotaller, had hardly touched a drop of alcohol in his whole life.

These trips showed once more that anything was good enough for the Irish. I was not royalty and I certainly was not expecting to be pampered, but in order to have any chance of doing my job properly, I needed these administrative tasks to be carried out competently. Was it too much to ask? Unfortunately, in the case of the FAI, yes. Later, I found out that the majority of managers in world football had been officially represented at España '82.

Although the persistent organisational difficulties never helped matters, it was the double standards applied by FAI officials that tossed salt into an open wound. Because I usually operated without any cash advances to cover my expenses, I would cautiously book economy-class flights five to six weeks before flying, just to get a better price and so limit my costs. Then, when the day to fly came, I would discover that the FAI officials had booked late, paid a premium price *and* had booked themselves into first-class seats!

The players and I were used to seeing this kind of behaviour, but even we were surprised by the FAI's antics in Poland in 1981. We were due to play the

Poles in a friendly match in Bydgoszcz on 24 May. Ordinarily these matches would be played in Warsaw but, I believe for political reasons, it was moved to the north of the country. We flew to Warsaw but then had to travel on to our destination. There would be no connecting flight, however. The FAI had booked a bus to make the five-hour journey. The rickety contraption that was to carry us turned out to be a clapped-out old labourer's van with no springs, no proper suspension and no air conditioning. It was an awful trip in the intense humidity of a Polish summer. We were bounced around like rag dolls in a blazing hot furnace. Players were getting sick. My own stomach was in bits.

Once at Bydgoszcz, things deteriorated further. The hotel was spartan, to say the least, and the rooms were not even properly clean and tidy. On top of that, there was no hot water, no towels and no toilet paper.

Poland was experiencing political upheaval at the time, with the communist government seeking to repress the Solidarity trade-union movement. When we arrived, the country was actually under martial law; its effects on Bydgoszcz were all too obvious. There were queues in the streets because of the serious food shortages. No one told us before we travelled that food might be in short supply. The rationing in place meant that the fare on offer was of a very poor quality and the result was that four players quickly went down with serious stomach aches.

The rub, however, was that, while we had to endure these conditions in Bydgoszcz, the FAI officials had booked themselves into luxurious hotels in Warsaw. Not even the full complement of officials bothered to travel to Bydgoszcz for the match – perhaps the Warsaw nightlife was a better bet than roughing it in a dour outpost of communist-era Poland. The officials who did show up, rapidly scarpered back to Warsaw after the final whistle rather than share our fate. The game, in which I gave Packie Bonner his debut, ended as a forgettable 3-0 defeat.

Suitably embittered by the whole affair, we got back on our ramshackle bus and hunkered down for the five-hour return trip to Warsaw.

Our friendly match against England at Wembley, in March 1985, was another example of the FAI's lax approach to organisation. For any footballer, playing at Wembley is a career ambition. I had narrowly missed out on the honour as a player when my international career ended shortly before Ireland played England in September 1976. I was excited now to at least have the opportunity to manage my country in this historic stadium.

Although a close game, it ended in a disappointing 2-1 defeat for us. I played Packie Bonner in goal in this game, a decision I would later have cause to reconsider. Seamus McDonagh was still my first-choice keeper, and would have ordinarily played, but I felt that I needed to see how Bonner would cope with the rigours of a major international game. Bonner was playing in the Scottish First Division with Celtic and, owing to the Glasgow club's dominance, was part of a team that invariably won every week. This was not a serious test of Bonner's ability. He did well against England and, obviously, went on to become a great goalkeeper for Ireland. My regret, however, stemmed from having robbed McDonagh of his chance to line out at Wembley. The evening after the match Seamus came to me and expressed his bitter disappointment at not getting the opportunity to face England at Wembley. Seamus was, after all, our number one goalkeeper and the one who had gone through everything with us over the previous five years. I should have given him the honour and introduced Packie later in the game. Seamus deserved it.

It was not just football matters that left a bitter aftertaste, though. The accommodation arranged for us in London had, once more, been dire. When we arrived at the hotel, problems were immediately obvious. There were not enough rooms available for us, the staff politely informed me. Why? The FAI had forgotten to book a room for my assistant, Terry Conroy. Terry had no choice but to sling his bag over his back and find himself accommodation in another hotel.

It also quickly became clear that what we were being put up in was a budget-grade establishment – and that description was being generous. It was also apparently a favourite of package-tour organisers and with large groups of tourists everywhere you looked, I knew that there would be no hope of privacy for the players during our stay. The other glaring issue was the fact that the hotel was actually a construction site. Major renovations were being carried out to the building and there was an incessant din of hammering and drilling. Most of our players liked to take an afternoon nap on the day of an evening match. Not in this hotel. The rooms were also way below the standard that the players were used to at hotels booked by their clubs. I remember Frank Stapleton telling me that whenever he travelled to London with Manchester United, they always stayed at the upmarket Lancaster Hotel.

The then FAI treasurer, Joe Delaney, and I spent a wasted day contacting London hotels to hastily find alternative accommodation. This was the dispiriting routine that the FAI put you through: you wanted to think about football, but instead you found yourself ringing hotel receptionists the day before playing England at Wembley.

Unsurprisingly, it was far too late to find somewhere that could fit such a large group as ours. Some hotels said that they could take a few guests but none could manage the entire party. It was hopeless; we stayed where we were with builders, tourists, jackhammers – the lot. When I asked the FAI for an explanation, they threw up their arms and said: 'Talk to the people at the English FA. It was they who booked the hotel'. I decided that I *would* talk to the English FA.

Amazingly, I discovered that we were, in fact, supposed to have stayed in a far better hotel until someone at the FAI decided to intervene. The FA secretary, Ted Croker, told me that an Irish official had approached them and asked for a larger match fee in exchange for cheaper accommodation. It made no odds to the English. If that's what the Irish wanted, then that is what the Irish could have. Some things never changed: it was a chance to make a bit of money, with the players and me being, once again, the losers.

On another occasion, when we were due to travel from the Green Isle Hotel in the Clondalkin area of Dublin to our training base several kilometres away, there was no bus laid on to take us. The official charged with looking after this small detail had forgotten to do it. With twenty-odd international footballers hanging around impatiently in a hotel car park, I had to hurriedly book a fleet of taxis to get us to our destination.

One final incident will show how the FAI officials would so often let the squad down. It took place in October 1980, before our match against France in Paris – an important game in our 1982 World Cup qualification campaign. Each player had been given two complimentary tickets for the fixture. In addition to these two, the players usually had the option of buying extra tickets for family and friends. Because this was such a vital match and the distance between Ireland and Paris was relatively short, many players were eager to buy further tickets, none more so than Michael Robinson, who, because he was making his debut, was keen to have tickets for his family and friends who had already made the journey to Paris. When we approached the FAI, we were blanked. No tickets and no explanation. The players were extremely unhappy to have to tell their family and friends that no tickets could be bought. This had never been a problem before.

The incredible solution was that we found ourselves trying to track down tickets on the Paris black market. We eventually located a tout and got our tickets, though at a hugely inflated price.

These experiences created understandable ill-feeling in the squad and did nothing to build a healthy working relationship amongst myself, the players and the FAI. And although it would be going too far to suggest a direct link between FAI mismanagement and our sometimes poor results, the routine problems hardly helped our efforts.

Furthermore, since the squad were sometimes treated almost like second-class citizens, while the officials enjoyed the best of travel and accommodation, it was made all too clear that it was a case of 'Us' and 'Them'. This was a distinction that a power-conscious executive tacitly perpetuated. It had not been long since Irish football managers had to take orders from the Big Five. As noted, only eleven years before I took over, Mick Meagan, in 1969, was the first Irish manager to select a team. Some of the executive members who were active in my day remembered the good old days of the Big Five all too well and, I believe, resented the evolutionary process that had seen their power slowly but surely diminish. Ensuring that they sat in first class while players and managers put up with a berth in steerage was one small way for these officials to hang on to a sense of prestige.

Even though the standards at Merrion Square in my time were uniformly amateurish, there were still some good people in the organisation who did what they could to help. Treasurer Joe Delaney (father of John Delaney, the FAI chief executive at the time of writing) and FAI President Des Casey were two genuinely forward-thinking officials. They were typically in agreement with my approach, but their hands were tied – invariably, the FAI executive would usually overrule any worthwhile attempt on their part to move with the times.

By the time I left the job of Ireland manager in December 1985, it had taken its toll on me and my family. I found out that my son had even been hassled at school because of the way in which I had been demonised in the press. The tyres of my son's bike were slashed on several occasions. When things get to that point, football no longer has any relevance.

Being an international manager comes with tremendous pressures; I accepted that fully, but what I could not accept was the visceral personal abuse that I took from certain quarters of the media. I should make it clear, however, that, then as now, I have no issue at all with my management record being scrutinised. Those challenges come with the job. Football allows for numerous viewpoints and, if someone disagrees with your football philosophy, you need to grow a thick skin and live with that fact.

However, in the case of Eamon Dunphy, it was difficult for me to accept that his well-documented and what felt to me like personal attacks on me were based on anything resembling reasonable footballing logic. Dunphy and I had known each other very well from our youth. We both grew up in Drumcondra and even went to the same pre-school. We learned to play football together. Throughout our youth, we would have regular kick-abouts together and often play with and against each other in casual matches in Drumcondra's Griffith Park. Dunphy was always a very skilful player but highly temperamental and strong-willed. He had a serious dislike of being dispossessed of the ball and had an intense desire to win. I remember one game where he lost possession and he stormed off home in a huff. The only problem was that he took the ball with him, so that was the end of game.

For as long as I knew him as an adult, Dunphy was exceptionally argumentative and adopted a consistently left-wing line on most topics. I should know his character: we played together for Ireland for many years, as well as regularly facing off against each other at club level whenever Portsmouth played his club, Millwall.

Before one match against Italy, when we were both in the Ireland squad, Dunphy took an unusual approach to preparing himself mentally. While everyone else was busy focusing on the game ahead, Dunphy was spoiling for an intellectual scrap. He ended up getting into a heated row with RTÉ commentator Philip Greene. The topic was politics, of course, with a splash of religion thrown in for good measure.

Dunphy's political stances did not always sit well with his life as a professional footballer. When the Irish squad was preparing to travel to South America for its end-of-season tour in 1974, Dunphy became very agitated. The problem was that one of our chosen opponents was Chile, a country, which, as already mentioned, was then suffering under the despotic rule of General Augusto Pinochet. The fixture was obviously controversial, and some elements of the Irish press were arguing that the game should not proceed. They believed that the match, if played, would in some small way recognise and legitimise Pinochet's dictatorship. When we gathered in London before our departure, Dunphy began staging a one-man protest against the game. He had even printed anti-Pinochet leaflets to pass around and was actively encouraging our players to boycott the game. When the time came to leave, the rest of us got on the bus. Dunphy, however, was still handing out leaflets to all and sundry. Player-manager John Giles had had enough. He was, after all, trying to manage a football team. As the coach was about to pull away, he said to Dunphy: 'Are *you* coming or not?' He came.

When Dunphy got his big break at fifteen and joined Manchester United as an apprentice, I was delighted for him. It was a huge achievement for a lad from Dublin's northside. Everyone in the Drumcondra area was talking about it. As well as that, my mother was friendly with Dunphy's parents. There was a normal neighbourly relationship between our two families. Once he began in journalism in the early 1980s, however, Dunphy quickly set about taking a flamethrower to any goodwill that existed between us.

When Dunphy began coaching, again, I found him to be a difficult character to fathom. I saw the reality when I played for Shamrock Rovers in the 1977/78 League of Ireland season. Dunphy's approach to coaching the club's youth players was not one that I shared. Promising young players sometimes make mistakes. That is normal. They are in a development phase. It is the job of the coach to coax the good qualities from the players while also trying to smoothe out the rough edges. This is a dexterous balancing act. As a coach, you either have these skills or you don't. In place of sound advice and encouragement, in my view, all Dunphy brought to the table was a predominantly coarse, abrasive style – not exactly a recipe for nurturing talent.

In my opinion, Dunphy's criticism of my tenure as Ireland manager was motivated not by neutral football arguments, but by a desire to advance his writing career. The bad blood became worse after an encounter I had with him in 1983 in Quinn's pub in Drumcondra. At this stage Dunphy was already on my case in his weekly column, so we were not exactly bosom buddies. We had been involved in a charity match at Dublin's Parnell Park. A selection of former Irish international soccer players played a Gaelic football match against the Dublin Gaelic football team. Afterwards, we all gathered in Quinn's. Dunphy started on me in front of everyone. I had recently resigned as Limerick United manager and he suggested that I was manoeuvring to get the Shamrock Rovers job now that it was common knowledge that John Giles would be stepping down. I told him that, if he must know, I was busy planning to open a sports shop in Dublin with Tony Ward. Dunphy was having none of it. He then argued that the shop idea was all just a crafty ruse to mask my true intentions and, what is more, he was going to expose my subterfuge. He was making great hay out of his piece of 'investigative journalism' and, it seemed to me, acting like someone who had just unearthed a national conspiracy.

I was not going to let this one go. I thought it was high time to deliver some home truths. I told him what I thought of his daft theory and his ridiculous articles about me. Dunphy replied, with vengeful spite: 'I'm going to get you.' By which he meant, of course, that he was going to get me in print. After this, his writings on me became even more toxic.

To make headlines Dunphy seemed to chase controversy wherever he might find it. In me, the Ireland manager, he found a target. Liam Brady was also described by him, during my tenure, as a 'monument to conceit', no less. Why not? Liam was Ireland's highest-profile player.

Usually you could bet on Dunphy's output being in bad taste, but sometimes it was plainly libellous. In one example, printed in the now extinct *Sunday Tribune*, this self-appointed Grand Inquisitor of our game proclaimed that I was no less than 'the Richard Nixon of Irish soccer'. For that remark I took legal proceedings against the *Sunday Tribune*. Ideally, I did not want to have any dealings with Dunphy. Up to that point, I had been putting up with him while I got on with the work of managing Ireland. The implication of his likening me to the disgraced US president was very serious, however: no longer content to settle with commenting on my ability as a football manager, he was now effectively suggesting that I was a liar and morally corrupt. We were only talking about football, weren't we? It was another example to add to Dunphy's over-the-top style of journalism. And the *Sunday Tribune* seemed to agree. They promptly settled out of court.

Ultimately, although Dunphy had it in for me after the Drumcondra incident, I was just the straw man set up to be the convenient object of his journalism. Positioning himself as the perpetual naysayer, as far as I am concerned the guy's bread and butter has always been about targeting Ireland's managers with snappy sound bites. I think it is his default strategy:

Ireland managers are relatively big news and so, by saying controversial things about them, he extracts reflected attention. Once I was out of the frame, Jack Charlton became the new target, then Mick McCarthy, Giovanni Trapattoni and so on, ad nauseum. The list grows.

The late Tim O'Connor, who, while in charge of RTÉ Sport, gave Dunphy his first break on television, made a revealing admission to me. He told me that he brought Dunphy in to join Bill O'Herlihy for the station's football coverage just to add a dash of controversy to their coverage. O'Connor used an example. 'Imagine a crowd of lads in a Dublin bar,' he said. 'They are watching Ireland playing on the pub's screen and then it's half-time. They say to each other "It's the break. Let's get in a few more pints". Then, suddenly, they spot Dunphy on the TV and one says "Hold on one minute, lads. Dunphy's on. Let's see who he's going to slaughter today."'

Once John Giles joined the panel, with his excellent analytical, football mind, O'Connor had his desired mix. Dunphy, with his often contradictory, off-the-cuff views, would be the loose cannon to Giles' more considered approach. And it has never mattered how many times Dunphy might contradict himself. The more the better – it's all showbiz.

The volte-face that Dunphy made in my case proves just how easily he pulls off alarming shifts of opinion. When I was appointed to the Ireland job, his praise for me was glowing. In his column he confidently informed the Irish public that 'If you are going into football's trenches, there is no one better to have by your side than Eoin Hand.' It was quite a rapid transformation then for me to be subsequently cast as Public Enemy No.1. This, of course, is the well-worn strategy of the sensationalist scribbler: build 'em up, knock 'em down.

Dunphy was also very careful to try and stand out from the flock of Irish sports journalists. During my reign, he came up with the notion that almost the entire group of Irish sports writers, by failing to share his extreme views about me, were buying into what he called 'decentskinsmanship'. In Dunphy's world, this term was shorthand for a wholesale sell-out by his journalistic colleagues. Because I was such a nice guy (a 'decent skin'), apparently, journalists just could not bring themselves to tell the truth, as Dunphy saw it, and criticise me. Dunphy, allegedly, had unmasked a mass conspiracy of mediocrity afflicting the ranks of Irish sports journalism, yet, miraculously, he alone remained untouched by it.

The truth is that the majority of journalists, like Peter Byrne, to name only one, were properly trained and behaved with great dignity and professionalism but, somehow, for Dunphy, this was a bad thing!

Before I became Ireland manager, I had always liked Dunphy. I could also sometimes enjoy his writings – when they were not given to excess. This was why I was so disappointed at the venom of his subsequent opinions.

Nowadays, we have no contact at all. In fact, if we ever happen to end up at the same event, he tends to stay well away from me.

Some might assume that Dunphy was effectively the cause of me not being offered a fourth term by the FAI, when the organisation and I parted ways. Although he certainly influenced public opinion, he had no power over the FAI. To do so would be to suggest that his unbalanced writings had actually held some sway over the FAI Council. The FAI's decision not to extend my contract was made for footballing reasons. I oversaw three campaigns and I did not make the big breakthrough. I had had my turn; when I stood on the turf at Lansdowne Road, looking up into emptying stands after the 4-1 defeat to Denmark, I knew it was over. And, at that time, I had no desire to carry on.

In 2013 Dunphy brought out his autobiography, *Eamon Dunphy – The Rocky Road*. It made for interesting reading, with his memory conjuring up some obvious inaccuracies. For instance, in 1986, after my involvement with Ireland had ended, I came across Dunphy in Joy's nightclub on Lower Baggot Street. I was out with a good friend, the professional golfer Arnold O'Connor. Dunphy was standing in the middle of the floor. The negative emotions all came back. I walked over and emptied my glass of beer over his head. I do not make a habit of pouring drinks over people and it was genuinely out of character for me to do something like this, but, after all that had gone on, it was an instinctive moment of release. Dunphy was shocked and went in search of the club manager, Frank Conway, to get me thrown out. Conway questioned me. 'I don't know what happened,' I replied. 'Someone must have nudged my elbow by accident and I spilt the glass.' It ended at that, with Dunphy leaving the place very quickly. Onlookers must have wondered what was going on, but, for me, it was a small act of retribution for the hell that he had put me and my family through.

This is all that happened, nothing more. That is why I was surprised to read Dunphy's account of the meeting in his book. Here Dunphy recalls the incident with him as the innocent, friendly chap who was grievously accosted by my uncivil behaviour. In his hail-fellow-well-met account, he has himself gesturing kindly to me to come and join him and Colm Tóibín for a chat. I graciously accept his offer, sit down, and then throw his hospitality back in his face in the form of an unwelcome glass of wine. None of this happened. Dunphy has reconstructed the incident to cast himself as the all sweetness-and-light victim of my 'unprovoked' attack. Considering all the water that has flowed under the bridge between us, this is a ridiculous pose for Dunphy to strike.

This, however, is not the only objectionable passage in the book. In 1977 when, as mentioned, I returned to Dublin after playing in South Africa, I contacted John Giles about joining Shamrock Rovers. In Dunphy's book, however, he takes full credit for getting me into Rovers at this time, suggesting that *I* rang *him* for help and that he then pulled all the necessary strings to dig out an old pal. No such thing happened.

Throughout the pages of his book, Dunphy also cannot suppress his obvious antipathy towards the late, great Con Houlihan. Con was one of the best sports journalists this country has ever produced and an exceptional writer. He held the English language in the palm of his hand and made it do his bidding. You would always look out for what Con had written, no matter what game he was covering. It could have been an awful match, with little or nothing to speak of by way of entertainment but Con would invariably find the unexpected angle and give you an enthralling description of the game. His writings were also frequently hilarious.

Con came to my defence on numerous occasions in the mid-1980s when Dunphy's criticisms were at their fiercest. I was very grateful to him for his support. Con was a one-off: a highly educated man, whom you might just as easily overhear speaking in Latin (in his strong Kerry accent) as you would in English. I always had great time for Con. He was a genius. When he passed away in 2012, I made a point of attending his funeral. It was a truly sad occasion.

I was unhappy that my term as manager of the Republic of Ireland senior team should end with the disappointing low of failed qualification for the World Cup in Mexico in 1986. Although I was proud to have been the

Ireland manager, I must confess to feeling some relief, however, when it was all over.

Unlike John Giles before me and all Ireland managers after me (with the exception of Brian Kerr), I lived in the country throughout my term as manager. I was not expecting a medal for this, but it meant that, as the results failed to improve, I could not get any respite from the pressure cooker of negative attention. In my last year in the job, I was regularly taking verbal abuse, much of it very unpleasant, from random members of the public. I remember, in one case, while managing St Patrick's Athletic, how a Shamrock Rovers fan just walked up and spat on me. I inevitably became more cautious about my movements. Before I went out anywhere in Dublin, I had to think about it first. Certain places, unfortunately, became out of bounds for me. Even something as simple as going for a quiet drink with my wife became a potential nightmare.

Although my home phone number was ex-directory, a handful of unhinged 'fans' managed to get hold of it. This led to a number of threatening calls to my house, usually late at night or in the early hours of the morning. Although I had tried to keep these calls secret from my family, I found out later, however, that they were aware of the abusive calls all along but, to their credit, they stayed silent and allowed me to deal with the situation in my own way.

Whatever about the security of my home phone number, since I owned a sports shop for a part of my time as national team manager, I became easy pickings for the crackpots who wanted to have a go at me. I received death threats by mail and over the shop phone. One caller told me: 'You will not see the end of the week.' Another caller, focusing on the non-Irish-born players in the squad, said: 'If you play any more of those English bastards, the only capping they'll get is a knee-capping.' These calls were obviously disturbing, but I decided not to bother reporting them to the police. I felt that if I took them seriously, I would have been ready for the asylum.

The situation, unfortunately, affected my mother. If I visited her at her home in Drumcondra on a day when there was a big Gaelic football match in Croke Park, some of the yobbos passing her door would chant all manner of abuse, knowing that I was her son.

Eventually, such a burden comes to dominate your life: it is what you think about first thing in the morning and last thing at night. A particularly unsavoury incident happened in Dublin after our scoreless draw with

Norway in May 1985. The then Southampton manager, Lawrie McMenemy, attended the game and, as he left the ground with me, the aggression and threats from a group of so-called fans became very serious. Lawrie was targeted because he was English. What really infuriated me about that day, however, was the fact that some of the Irish team were spat on as they made their way to the team bus.

Near the end of 1985, with the pressure on me growing, I met journalist and friend Dave Guiney for lunch. I was feeling overwhelmed by the negative reaction towards me. Dave gave me advice that I needed to hear. He said that, in the long run, 'time and silence' would be my friends. 'The silent majority,' he assured me, 'know that you have done your very best. However, the vociferous minority is all you hear.' It was difficult to believe Dave's words but he was right. In subsequent decades, wherever I have travelled in Ireland, I have met with only genuine generosity and goodwill from ordinary football fans.

When I assess my time as Ireland manager, I can see the positives and the negatives. Although my last two campaigns did not meet expectations, the truth is that, when I left the Ireland role (looking at the country's football history up to then), I was the manager who, in the 1982 campaign, had come closest to qualifying the team for an international tournament.

We also played progressive football that took advantage of the qualities of the players available. Although Jack Charlton, after me, insisted that his players conform to a strict tactical plan, my philosophy has always been that the players' abilities should dictate the chosen tactics. I was lucky enough to be able to select talented players and so I viewed it as my job to ensure that they could express themselves to the absolute best of their ability in a green shirt.

Furthermore, behind the scenes, I had worked constantly to try to bring the support structures of Irish football into line with proper professional standards. My attitude and aims were at all times to improve everything concerning the national team and I was the first national manager to tackle the endemic shortcomings surrounding travel and accommodation. I did not expect thanks for this from the media; it was unseen work but, nonetheless, of genuine value to Irish football. As for the players, some of whom have suggested that I was not strong enough to stand up to the FAI, they would not know. I consciously kept my efforts from them. My attitude was that they did not need to hear about the latest organisational cock-up minted at FAI HQ. These were professional footballers tasked with winning games for their country. I wanted them thinking about football, not the humdrum minutiae of accommodation and flight schedules.

Although the major strides in the modernisation of the FAI and of Irish football's structures have obviously arisen as a result of the fallout from the Saipan affair in 2002 (more about this later), the truth is that Irish football was slowly progressing from a very low base throughout the previous decades.

Of course, for obvious reasons, in public opinion Jack Charlton's success has overshadowed the positive aspects of my tenure. Being unlucky to be the manager who came before Ireland's greatest period of success began, I was, to some degree, whitewashed out of history. In the unsubtle narrative that some commentators repeatedly emphasised, 'Eoin Hand' became shorthand for 'failure', while 'Jack Charlton' meant 'success'. Fair or unfair, it is a fact of life that the international manager who delivers qualification for tournaments goes down in the history books, while everyone else is effectively forgotten. Football, however, is always more complicated than these black-and-white theories suggest; and so I will stand over my achievements, whatever about the glory that Jack Charlton would eventually bring.

I have no difficulty in applauding what Charlton did for Ireland. Although I have never fully agreed with the long-ball game that Jack favoured, his record of qualifying Ireland for two World Cups and a European Championship is beyond compare. There has, however, been a lack of balance in the treatment of our respective periods in the Ireland dugout. In a few cases, the press analysis has been downright offensive, both to me and to the players with whom I shared those five years.

For example, when Jack Charlton turned eighty in 2015, there was, rightly, plenty of glowing things written about him in the Irish press. There were also some blatant misrepresentations published. Pushing the easy line that Charlton, with the Midas touch, inherited a rabble and turned it into a football powerhouse overnight, some writers sought to consign the record of my players and myself to football's scrapheap. Two journalists, writing in the *Irish Daily Mirror*, proclaimed that 'Charlton took a group of misfits and expats and turned them into a team'. This is plainly insulting to the many top-class players who put on the green of Ireland during my five years in charge.

This before-and-after-Charlton version of Irish football history might make a good story but its effect is to unfairly denigrate what preceded him, including the reigns of Liam Tuohy and John Giles before me. Football supporters who followed the Irish team throughout the 1970s and 1980s know that Charlton inherited foundations on which to build his success. For all his undoubted talents, even he could not have turned Ireland into a heavyweight of world football overnight, if what he inherited was really that bad.

Although Charlton's success was, clearly, in large part down to his managerial ability, luck played its part. Charlton's era was kick-started by qualification for the 1988 European Championship but, as everyone knows, his team got there only with a large slice of help from Scotland, who, against all the odds, defeated Bulgaria in Sofia in November 1987. In everyone's form book, the talented Bulgarians (needing only a point to qualify) were odds-on favourites to be comfortable winners against a Scottish side with nothing to play for. When, in the eighty-seventh minute, the Hearts player Gary Mackay buried a left-footed shot beyond the Bulgarian keeper, Mihaylov, it would seal Scotland's first away win in five years and Bulgaria's first defeat at home in three and a half. Before this now legendary goal was scored, Charlton was on the brink. Even Jack did not think his team's chances were very good; he went fishing instead of watching the game in Sofia.

What the general public do not know is that (before the intervention of Gary Mackay) things had got so bad for Charlton during the Euro '88 qualification phase that I was actually contacted in Saudi Arabia, in mid-1987, by members of the Irish press asking me to comment on Jack's imminent departure. At that time, I was coaching a side in Saudi. I was even asked if I would put my name forward again as his replacement. I quickly said no to that suggestion.

The message that I was getting was that the FAI executive was worried about the supporters' negative reaction to Charlton's brand of route-one football and, since qualification for Euro '88 was not looking likely, a change was being considered. The point of this is not to try to take the sheen off the subsequent glory years that Charlton would usher in. He earned what he achieved and brought Ireland to where the team had never been before. The point is simply to highlight how fine the dividing line is between success and failure in international football. Ireland went to Euro '88 when they so easily might not have; Ray Houghton headed a brilliant winner against the

English in Stuttgart, and the Charlton era took off. Euro '88 was also the first time that an Irish squad had a four-to-five-week period together for training and bonding.

People have asked me so many times if I felt envious of Charlton's success and if it was difficult for me to watch Ireland doing so well under him. Although I can understand why people might ask such questions, I was delighted to see Ireland succeeding in international football. I knew many of the players very well. They were excellent footballers and deserved to play at World Cups and European Championships, whether under me or under another manager. Why would I not be happy for them? I admit that I did not agree with Charlton's style of play, but that was a matter of different football philosophies. It did not mean that I was not behind the team in the way that any other fan would have been.

In my own case, qualifying for the 1982 World Cup would have obviously been an enormous event for the players and the country, but it would also have had other important knock-on effects. Decisively, it would have allowed me to get my players together for four or five weeks of training and preparation, a spell of time that I could only dream about. Generally, the squad was together for one day only before a match. If we had spent a month or more on the training ground at a pre-tournament camp, so much more could have been achieved. I believe that this would have been a turning point in our fortunes. Sadly, it never happened.

A criticism that I have often had to contend with over the years is the idea that I lacked sufficient authority over the senior players in my squad. Specifically, the accusation has often been made that Brady and Stapleton exerted excessive influence behind the scenes. The truth is that I ran the Ireland set-up just like any other manager would, with complete control over team selection, tactics and all the other aspects of the role. While I was open to getting the opinion of an experienced player, the final decision was always mine. I would never have accepted the notion that one of my players should dictate to me how things should be done. When I took over from John Giles in 1980, although I fully believed in my ability to do the job, I was also aware that what I had been appointed with was a Second Division pedigree. It was important for me to earn the respect of my players, not demand it, so I adopted an open and communicative style with them. At no stage did this amount to any player exercising control over my decisions.

When I became Ireland manager at the age of thirty-four, I was one of the youngest managers in international football. Was I too young for this responsibility? Maybe I was. Perhaps, if the FAI set-up had been more professional at that time, someone with my background in the English Second Division and the League of Ireland would not have been appointed. I accept that, but it does not mean that I did not deserve to get the job. I competed with the other candidates who put forward their names and, after an interview process, was adjudged to be the best. In no sense did I take on the task with any inferiority complex. I looked at the role as a wonderful challenge and, to this day, I remain grateful to the FAI for giving me the opportunity to manage my country's team.

When Jack Charlton took over from me, he quickly realised, like I had before him, that all was not exactly normal in Irish football. The job of Ireland manager was not quite as well-paid as he had expected. Jack, as a World Cup winner, came to the role with a strong presence and was determined to negotiate hard with the FAI and get for himself what he considered was a proper financial package. He asked what money I was on, expecting that he would, at least, get the same amount. When he was told what I was actually earning, £17,500, Charlton, in characteristically forthright fashion, told his new taskmasters: 'I'm not bloody well working for that.' He would get a significant increase on my leaving salary.

Before I moved on to the next phase in my career, I had one last job to do. It was February 1986 and Charlton had just been appointed in my place. The then FAI president, Des Casey, asked me if I would be willing to meet Charlton and offer whatever advice I could. I agreed and travelled to the Westbury Hotel in Dublin to meet Jack.

In a two-hour conversation I outlined the challenges he would face. Charlton, understandably, was short on local knowledge. I recommended that he should keep Mick Byrne on as his physiotherapist. Mick had always done a great job for me. He was very popular with the players and, because Jack would not be living in the country, there would be an added benefit in having Mick based in Ireland. I warned him about the pitfalls of dealing with the FAI and just what to expect from Merrion Square. I also said that he, with his high profile, had a real chance of influencing the FAI for the better. I had stood up to the FAI when I felt it was necessary, but the fact that I had a lower profile than Jack meant that he started on a stronger footing. I also gave him tips on some players who had recently come onto my radar but had not yet been selected. I told him about Ray Houghton and John Aldridge at Oxford United, both of whom Dave Langan had brought to my attention.

When I left Jack that day, it was with a strong sense that an important phase in my life was ending. The Eoin Hand era had run its course; it was over to Jack. I had to now gather myself and consider the next stage of my career.

8

Lost in Translation

Teaching the Beautiful Game in Saudi Arabia: 1986/1987

My next move in football was an unusual one. By the time I left the Ireland role in late 1985, my sports business in Firhouse had, unfortunately, folded. Despite having an excellent manager in Karen Reeves (daughter of comedian and friend Shaun Connors), my business was up against it. The financially straitened times of the 1980s meant that few punters had spare cash lying around for branded sports goods. With no income, and a wife and young family to support, I had to get back into football as quickly as possible. It is always easier to get a job when you are in a job; that truism holds good for any line of work, including football management. Now that I was temporarily out of management – I had also departed from the St Patrick's Athletic role in 1985 – it became more difficult to present myself to clubs as an attractive option. I applied for numerous jobs in England without success. There were some offers but, for one reason or another, none of them was right. The closest I came to landing a position was when Wolverhampton Wanderers invited me for an interview, but this also proved to be a dead end. I strongly felt that the English club chairmen did not look favourably on the thought of an Irishman running their teams; they had a very obvious bias towards English managers at that time. It would have been an easier task to pick up a management position in the League of Ireland, but there was just no money in that league.

The solution to my financial woes would come from an unlikely source. I got a tip-off from a journalist at the *Manchester Evening News* that there was a management position being advertised by a club in Saudi Arabia. The former Scotland and Manchester United manager Tommy Docherty, I understood, had just turned it down. The club was Al-Taawoun FC, based in Buraidah in north-central Saudi Arabia. The club owner wanted an established European coach to develop its players, all of whom were Saudi nationals. The contract would be for three months and, of course, I would have to move to Saudi Arabia for its duration.

The prospect of uprooting to the Middle East, while my family stayed behind in Dublin, was far from ideal. My children were still young. However, Saudi being Saudi, the money, compared to what I had previously earned, was exceptional and it would all be tax-free. If I could not live at home in Ireland with my family, I could at least support them by working abroad. I decided to put myself forward for the job. It was not strictly a football decision, but a short-term solution. Had money not been an issue, I would have bided my time in Dublin and waited for further positions to come up in the English and, perhaps, the Scottish League. Time was one thing I did not have a lot of, so it was imperative to make a move.

I flew to London to be interviewed by representatives of the club. I was offered the job and accepted it. My brief was to improve the skill levels of the squad, train them in all aspects of the game and get them winning games. But also (and this was very important to the club), I was expected to bring enhanced prestige to the club, qualities held in very high esteem in Saudi Arabian society. For Al-Taawoun, being able to attract a foreign coach with international experience was a big deal and something they thought would significantly raise the club's profile in the Saudi game.

Before making the move, however, I had the welcome diversion of travelling to New York in March for a St Patrick's Day indoor soccer tournament. I was invited as a manager and asked to form a team to compete. I brought a selection of mainly League of Ireland players, including Johnny Walsh of Limerick City (formerly called Limerick United).

Although we failed to win the tournament, the atmosphere in the city was superb. Once the football was over, we joined in the celebrations and went to the well-known Irish bar Rosie O'Grady's in Manhattan's Times Square. A group of us, including Johnny, were having a drink and mingling with the crowd when something suddenly occurred to me. My cousin, Jamie Hunt, a high-ranking officer in the New York City Drugs Enforcement Agency, was also in the bar. Now Johnny had travelled with myself and the

Limerick United squad to Fort Lauderdale, Florida, on our end-of-season tour in 1982. For a laugh, I took my cousin aside and gave him a fictitious story about Johnny smoking a joint in Florida in 1982. He knew where I was going with this one. I then returned to the players and waited. A few minutes later, a booming, official New York accent interrupted our revelry: 'John Walsh? Limerick?' Johnny visibly taken aback, meekly nodded yes. 'We've been waiting for you to come back into this country since 1982 and now we finally have got you.' Johnny was getting paler by the second and, at this point, having overheard my cousin, some nearby women tried to intervene. 'Ah, leave him alone', they pleaded. 'He's on his holidays.' My cousin was having none of it. 'Ladies, ladies. Stay out of this. This is official police business.'

By this stage, Johnny was white with worry.

'Mr Walsh, I'm with the New York City Drugs Enforcement Agency. You have two choices: either you come down town with me right now *or* I can buy you a drink? What's it gonna be?' Everyone turned to Johnny to hear his response. He stuttered and stumbled and finally said 'Ah, am. I need to go to the toilet.' At that point, my cousin's imperious demeanour was shattered and he broke down laughing, along with the rest of us. Johnny is still waiting to get his revenge.

In May of that year I took up my new role in Saudi Arabia. Although the country's facilities were exceptional (all-weather pitches and modern stadiums were par for the course), the standard of football certainly was not. The players under my instruction were somewhere between amateur and, at best, semi-professional level and, while some of them possessed a degree of raw natural ability, overall they lacked a rudimentary training in football. On the whole, the general standard of player was well below what I was accustomed to working with. After a few training sessions I realised that the very fundamentals of the game itself would have to be explained to the squad. I was earning six or seven times more in Saudi, in a remote football outpost, than I ever made while working with elite professional players in my previous role. The irony was not lost on me.

I quickly realised that not only did the players and I not share the same language – all communication was through an interpreter – we also had no shared football vocabulary. Getting my message across sometimes required a little linguistic gymnastics. Through the interpreter I did my best to deliver basic instructions in training: 'Track your man,' I would say. 'Track your man? Track your man? What is "track your man?"' a confused bunch of players would ask in return. It suddenly dawned on me that they did not have a concept of marking and that even such an elementary notion as that would have to be drummed into them. I rephrased: 'Well, basically, if the man that you are nearest to runs towards our goal, you need to follow him and try to stop him from doing anything with the ball.'

Marking was an idea that would cause even further confusion. When I told them to get tight to their man, they were clueless as to the meaning of my words. They seemed to think that it meant that they should literally climb on top of the opposing players. Again, when I told them to 'fill the hole', they were lost. 'Hole? What hole? There is no hole in the pitch,' they responded. It was back to page one of the coaching manual: 'The hole', I explained, 'is the space between our midfield and the front players – a dangerous area where the opposition will find it harder to mark you.'

Set pieces presented further challenges. On one occasion, when practising how to defend corners, I told our six-foot-tall attacking midfielder to take up his position at the front post and to head clear any crosses, if he could. 'I am sorry but I do not head the ball,' he replied. '*What?*' I asked, in disbelief. 'I *do not* head the ball', he repeated. It was difficult to believe what I was hearing. 'But you *have* to head the ball. Heading is a part of football. Footballers *head* the ball.'

The players were unpredictable; sometimes I just did not know what was coming next. I remember a particular match where we went 1-0 up after ten minutes when our centre forward scored a beautiful volleyed goal. The goalscorer was understandably delighted. He ran over to the touchline to celebrate with me and the bench in typical fashion – or so I thought. In fact, he had actually made a beeline for me because he was demanding to be taken off. I was completely thrown. 'Are you injured? Are you hurt? What's the problem?' 'No. No injury but I must come off *now*'. 'Why?' I asked. 'Because I cannot do anything better than that in this match,' he explained. I had certainly never heard that one before. In the end, I just ordered him back into the fray. It was, however, a waste of time. Subsequently, I had to take him off anyway: he was so chuffed with himself that he was just strolling around grinning like a Cheshire cat and not trying at all.

Thankfully, we won the match but I still had a word with the player afterwards. It was clear that he felt like a hero for scoring that one goal and saw no point in bothering after that. 'OK, that's fair enough,' I started. 'But what if you had stayed on and scored two goals, or maybe even three. Just think how much of a hero you would have been then.' His face lit up; he had not thought this one through.

The squad was not used to the demands of professional training and not fond of tough training sessions. Whenever I planned heavy fitness work, the excuses started coming out. The reasons given usually had a convenient religious angle, the one sacrosanct sphere that they knew I dare not question. 'Training tomorrow? No, no, we cannot do tomorrow. Tomorrow is a *very* important holy day.' Or else, if the running was getting a bit too strenuous for their liking, it was: 'We have to leave immediately. It is prayer time. It is prayer time.' What could I do? I knew that I was not going to change the prevailing culture. I could only flow with the situation and do my best to insist on high standards where possible.

The job also required me to develop entirely new management skills, including how to deal with the fact that two of my players were overly fond of each other. In order to make sure that they got a proper night's sleep before a game, I decided to separate them and make sure that they did not room together. It did not work. One way or another, they would always finish up in the same room.

In the case of another player, I just could not figure out why he had suddenly dipped in form. He was a promising young forward and, as one season ended, I was really pleased to see how he was developing. By the time I would return for the next season, I was confident that I would have a proper player on my hands. Instead, however, when the new season started he was lacking in spark and a shadow of the player he once was. In training, his performances were acceptable enough, but he was making little or no impact in matches. I was looking at a changed player and person. Eventually, I decided to ask the club doctor if there was maybe just something wrong with the boy's health. No. It was just that he and a male friend were going into the desert every Friday evening to spend the night together. I had to ask the doctor if he was joking. He was not.

After three months, the players were beginning to respond to professional-level training and it was clear that the team was making progress. My sponsor, through whom I had obtained my entry visa, was very happy and

The players and staff of Al-Taawoun FC pose for a pre-match team shot in 1986. Although my decision to manage in Saudi Arabia was born out of financial necessity, the experience, which came with no little amount of culture shock for me, was ultimately a rewarding one.

asked me to remain for another year. I hesitated. My plan had been to get in, complete my contract and get out. It was difficult for me to ignore the prospect of extra work and money, however. I agreed to the contract extension but only on condition that he would give me my own car, on top of my salary, as well as pay for my family to visit me on a few occasions during the year. He agreed and the club gave me an almost-new Mercedes. My association with the country was going to be a lot longer and more significant than I had at first anticipated.

Although my relationship with the players grew stronger as I spent more time working with them, the religious sensitivities of Saudi Arabia meant that I always had to be vigilant. One incident taught me just how precarious my position was and how rapidly things could spiral out of control. During training, I kept impressing upon the players that they needed to be more physical in matches. In the previous game, I felt that we had been bullied by the opposition and so I told the players that I expected them to stand up for themselves more in future. In order to demonstrate how they might make themselves look more imposing, during a training routine I put my arms and elbows out to show the players what I meant, but, just as I did so, one of the players accidentally turned his face right into my elbow. It was an innocuous incident but his nose began to bleed. I apologised and thought no more about it, and believed that we could move on. I was wrong on that count. The very next day I was brought before the club committee and accused, in very serious tones, of having drawn blood from one of our players. I explained that the whole thing was a harmless training-ground accident but they were not having it. I got out of the situation only after apologising to the committee, accepting its warning and promising that it would not happen again.

The players also often tried to persuade me to convert to Islam. Because I had got to know them well and had won their respect, they said that they wanted to give me the opportunity to save my soul. They meant it, and with deadly seriousness. I had to stealthily dodge the issue every time it was brought up. Saudi Arabia is an intensely religious country. This meant that every time I refused, it had to be done in such a way that there was no perceived insult to Islam implicit in my refusal. I found myself saying 'no' politely in so many circumstances. I would always respect the religion and culture of any country I worked in and it mattered not a jot what faith my players held, but while I was always respectful of the country's religious practices, my view was that I was in Saudi Arabia to coach a football team. I was determined not to get dragged into any theological and potentially controversial discussions.

The public beheadings that sometimes took place in the city's square was another topic that required cultural deftness on my part. Any time one was taking place I was often asked to come and watch it. 'We'll show you how we dispense justice in this country,' someone would say. They wanted me to know how the world should be and, obviously for them, the end justified the means: their country had very little crime. This extreme punishment was ordered for offences such as murder and rape; and it was invariably a public event. I could not bring myself to attend. I would make my apologies and stay well away from what I saw as a grisly spectacle. Some of the other westerners in the compound had witnessed beheadings previously; their descriptions were quite enough for me.

Another aspect of the law which caused me genuine worry concerned the rules governing car accidents. If someone walked out in front of my car and I accidentally killed them, the victim's family had an automatic legal right to sue me for the person's death. It did not matter a whit that I may have not been at fault; if there was a collision, I would have been sued for everything I had. It certainly gave me food for thought as I drove around in my shiny Mercedes.

With the many taboos and strict religious laws in place, I had to catch on quickly and become savvy about how I conducted myself. What did not help matters was the fact that Buraidah was a centre of fundamentalism – even by the already extreme standards of Saudi Arabia. Take a relatively minor wrong turn, innocent or not, and it could lead to a jail sentence, and there was nothing the Irish embassy could do to help you. It was certainly a society to help bring your powers of diplomacy bang up to speed.

I found out very early on in my stay how serious the consequences could be if you put a foot wrong. It was very warm on one of my first days there, so I decided to wear a pair of tennis shorts and a T-shirt before heading out. I had not been told that the wearing of shorts was not permitted in public. While minding my own business browsing in the camel *souk*, I was suddenly apprehended by a group of policemen. I was shocked. I had no idea what was going on. Unable to communicate with them properly, I just kept repeating the name of my sponsor. But, instead of listening, they bundled me into the back of a truck and took me straight to a police station. They then left me alone in a room for hours. It was scary. I had no idea of how this would end. When a policeman who could speak some English arrived, I finally got the message across and was released. They rang my sponsor, who explained the reason for my indiscretion. They sent me on my way with a stern warning to respect the country's dress code.

Once was enough to fall foul of the religious police. From now on, I was going to be scrupulously careful. When my then wife, Pat, came to visit me, I warned her about the strict dress code and of the dangers of disobeying it. Pat, as required, wore the abaya, a religious robe-like dress, with a hood, that covered most of a woman's body except for the hands, feet and face. Even so, trouble still came our way. Once when we ventured out together, although Pat was wearing the abaya as required, she momentarily forgot herself and pulled the hood down from her head to look at some silks in a shop. The ultra-vigilant religious police (or *Muttawa*) were never too far away and one suddenly appeared behind Pat. 'Madam,' he began, in chilling, perfect Oxford English, 'you would be very wise to keep your face covered when in our country. Show respect for the laws of this country.' I thought that was the end of it. Unfortunately, human nature being what it is, when we went to another shopping centre, my wife forgot herself again and once more uncovered her head while looking around in a shop. I was in a different part of the shopping centre and, when I heard some shouts, I feared the worst. I ran as fast as I could through the shopping centre to get to Pat before the police did. Just as a van pulled up, I shouted to her to cover up. To my great relief, she did, and the police were too late.

Although the religious police patrolling the streets strictly enforced sharia law, in private, behaviour could be far more relaxed. One example was alcohol consumption. It was illegal but, in fact, private drinking sessions took place regularly at the homes of wealthy persons. Officially you could not buy drink locally but the rich always seemed to have a plentiful supply of Johnnie Walker whisky. I would sometimes be invited to these social gatherings but I always made sure to have a credible excuse on hand to stay out of trouble. Because of the obvious risks of putting a foot wrong when under the influence, I made it a rule not to touch alcohol during my time in Saudi Arabia. The point is that if they had reported me for drinking, I could not have counter-accused them. I would have been the lone guilty party.

The rigid rules on male-female relations also created some frankly weird situations. I lived in a compound throughout my stay. This restricted area was for expatriates only. We had a swimming pool, but because it was used by western women whose bikinis would clearly infringe the Saudi Arabian women's strict dress code, it had to be surrounded by a high corrugated iron fence. The local men were forbidden to see what by their own standards were very scantily clad women. This did not stop them from trying. I would sometimes see young men cutting peepholes through the iron perimeter to steal a look.

Saudi Arabia is also a strictly hierarchical society: you had to know who was important and exactly how they expected to be treated. For me, an outsider trying to cope with local customs, the consequences could sometimes be comical. One evening, the players and I were invited to a formal dinner, with the local prince who sponsored the club being the esteemed guest of honour. I was very hungry by the time the food arrived and was more than ready to begin eating. The protocol in place, however, made this a trickier assignment than I had imagined. I was told that no one could start eating before the prince and, furthermore, once he began eating, you had to stop as soon as he did. We were sitting on the floor, as was the tradition, and because of my dodgy knee (a souvenir from my playing days), try as I might I could not find a comfortable spot. What made the manoeuvre all the more difficult was the fact that it was forbidden to show the soles of your feet to the prince.

I was twisting and turning for so long that, by the time I had found a suitable position, the prince had already finished his meal. He had no interest in being there. This was just a ceremonial appearance, so he had just picked at a few morsels and got up and left. That was it. My food was in front of me, but the protocol dictated that it had to go in the bin, without me eating a single mouthful. The prince had had his fill, so it was sayonara to my dinner. As soon as the event was over, I drove straight outside Buraidah to find somewhere to eat. Eventually, I found a Wimpy and ended the night dining on a fast-food meal of burgers and fries.

The ostentatious wealth was something that no visitor to Saudi Arabia could help but notice. Oil money had turned many Saudis into overnight multimillionaires. There was no sense of the old rich here. Only the most garishly expensive items were stockpiled as status symbols by these newly enriched tycoons. My sponsor, with whom I became friendly, gave me the grand tour of his enormous, lavishly decorated home. It had all the trimmings and, more often than not, with diamonds or gold encrusted as standard. He was particularly proud of showing me his private vineyard and his fleet of luxury cars and quad bikes.

Even casual aspects of life in Saudi Arabia reminded you of just how much money was floating around. If you flicked through the classifieds section of a newspaper, you would frequently find private jets for sale – as in jumbo jets! Oil was so cheap that it actually cost me more to go to a carwash than it did to fill my car with petrol.

Many of the mundane pleasures of life, which I had taken for granted in Ireland, were absent from Saudi Arabia. Because of religious mandates, pork meat was strictly banned. Luckily for me, I befriended a Filipino chef working in the compound's canteen who would secretly fix me up now

I visited Lisbon in 1987 and, as John Mortimore (a previous manager at Portsmouth) was now manager at Benfica, he kindly introduced me to Eusebio (*left*) – one of the greatest players of all time – at Estadio da Luz.

and then with a breakfast of bacon and eggs. It was a small thing, certainly, but when you miss home, like all familiar things, its significance becomes magnified.

When I was finally ready to leave the country, I began to make arrangements to have my Mercedes shipped home. I went to the club's chairman before departure and told him of my plans. He surprised me by stating that 'the Mercedes stays in Saudi Arabia'. The club were not happy because I would not stay on in the role and this was their way of showing it. I protested, arguing that it was mine because I had received it as part of my contract; I had earned it, in other words. 'No', he told me. 'The car is yours while you are in Saudi Arabia. You are leaving now, so no car.' I was inwardly furious but there was little that I could do. They could have made it very difficult for me to obtain the exit visa that I required to get out of the country. They had me over a barrel and knew well what they were doing. I could only drive the car straight back to the compound. I knew that there were others living there who also owned Mercedes cars, so I told them to take whatever parts they could find a use for.

Before I departed, the players presented me with a gift of a beautiful gold watch. It was a lovely gesture and a sign of the genuine friendship that had developed amongst us. I sometimes look at that watch and wonder how they all are.

When I left Saudi Arabia, it was with a sense of 'job done'. The team had improved and had begun to win more matches and I had earned the money that was needed to get me back on course financially. Although my time there was often filled with loneliness and boredom, it was far from a fruitless adventure. I was thrown into an alien culture and given no choice but to adapt – and I did. Given the option, I would obviously not have gone to Saudi Arabia, but the fact is that, ultimately, it became an education for me.

In the autumn of 1987, after a year and a half on the margins of the game, it was time for me to get back into top-level football, preferably in England, but at least closer to home. The experience that was Saudi Arabia was over.

9

'Call into Scruffy Murphy's'

From Huddersfield to South Africa: 1987–1996

In November 1987 Malcolm Macdonald, the former Newcastle United and England centre forward and then the manager of Huddersfield Town, offered me a route back into professional football. Malcolm had been appointed to the Huddersfield post the previous summer. I took a call from him as I was preparing to leave Saudi Arabia. Malcolm wanted me to come back to England to be his assistant.

Although Huddersfield, at that time, was a struggling Second Division side, I was very happy, and relieved, to be getting back into the professional game. I had first become acquainted with Malcolm in South Africa in the mid-1970s. We were both guesting for Lusitano at the time. Later, while managing Limerick United and when Malcolm was retired from the English game, I had brought him over to guest for us in a friendly match. We got on well, initially.

The 1987/88 season was not a happy one on the pitch, however, and the pressure was telling on Macdonald. A bizarre incident that occurred towards the end of the season would see our relationship falling apart. We were in desperate need of a goalscorer and, after receiving good reports of an English striker, Mark Payne, who was playing for SC Cambuur in the Dutch league, Macdonald sent me to the Netherlands to assess him. On a Friday evening, I made my way to a town called Leeuwarden in the central part of the Netherlands to watch the lad play. However, when I got to the venue, all I found was a locked gate and an empty stadium. There were no signs of any football match taking place there that evening. I looked around and eventually found someone. I asked about the game only to be told that I had missed it and that it had, in fact, taken place the night before.

Macdonald, I could only assume, had got the date wrong. When I returned to Huddersfield the next day, things became clearer. I took a call from one of the club directors asking me if I had seen the player and whether or not I liked him. Once I told him about the mix-up and that I had not been able to watch the game, the situation became more serious. 'Well, that is very interesting, Eoin,' an audibly irritated voice responded. 'The Huddersfield board was told that you gave a very favourable report of the player. You are suspended until we get to the bottom of this.' It turned out that, without my knowledge, Macdonald had told the directors that I had scouted the player and that I had liked what I saw. Events moved quickly after that. Macdonald was called to the boardroom and promptly relieved of his duties. Everyone knew that Macdonald had his personal problems at that time. By the close of that season he was not thinking straight.

Disappointingly, Macdonald, in subsequent years, has blamed me for my alleged role in his dismissal when, in truth, he was the architect of his own downfall.

With Macdonald having departed, once I had been exonerated of any wrong-doing, the board appointed me as caretaker manager for the remainder of the season. Unfortunately, Huddersfield was relegated at the end of the season but I had done enough for the board to give me the job on a permanent basis.

On 8 June 1988 I took over as Huddersfield manager. My brief was to stabilise the club, balance the books and slowly develop success on the pitch. Huddersfield was a club with a proud history. It had, in its heyday in the 1920s, been the first club to win three consecutive First Division League titles and, in the 1950s, Bill Shankly had managed the club for three years before moving on to Liverpool in 1959. When I became manager, the club had been playing in the lower leagues for a long time. The 1971/72 season was the last time Huddersfield Town had played in the top flight. After having spent so many years outside of the First Division, the fans were thirsting for success.

I appointed the former England and Aston Villa striker Peter Withe as my assistant. It proved to be an excellent appointment. Peter was hard-working and genuinely passionate about the job. Peter and I had become friends in 1973, in South Africa, while I was guesting for Port Elizabeth City and he was appearing for Arcadia Shepherds. Another appointment I made was George Mulhall, the former Scottish international and Sunderland winger, as my youth-team manager. His experience in the role was invaluable.

In the summer of 1988, for my first pre-season tour, I took my squad to Ireland to play a number of friendly matches. I wanted to get to know the players' characters as well as help the group to bond before the coming season. The trip provided me with valuable knowledge on the strengths and weaknesses of the squad.

Huddersfield was the first time that I was managing professional players on a full-time basis, an opportunity that I relished – with Limerick, the players were part-time; with Ireland, I obviously saw my players only when international matches were played; and, in the case of Saudi Arabia, the players were not professionals. I had the time to make my mark and to slowly establish my way of playing the game. Huddersfield Town, however, was not rich. Money was tight and so, like the majority of lower-division clubs, balancing the books was an ever-present concern. This meant that I was forever on the lookout for good deals and would use any contact available to unearth a promising player. Generally, the luxury of spending generously in the transfer market was not there, so, for example, if a player presented himself at the gates of the training ground looking for a trial, I generally let him train with us for a few days. I felt that there was nothing to lose in giving players a chance to impress.

In one case the gamble paid off. Scottish-born Iffy Onuora, who had appeared at training one day, turned out to be a real find. His qualities were immediately obvious. Iffy, who had never played professionally before, was a powerful and lightning-quick forward. With those traits, I knew he could do a job for us. He would go on to make 165 appearances for the club and score thirty goals, before being sold at a profit to Mansfield Town in 1994.

Being a full-time club manager brought me into closer contact with players and their personalities. One player, Phil Starbuck, whom I signed from Brian Clough's Nottingham Forest in 1991, did not exactly fit the footballer template. Phil, a forward who had come through the youth ranks at Forest, had made an early impact under Clough before fading. I hoped

Back in the management game, at Leeds Road. In 1988 I returned to management in the professional game when I became manager of Huddersfield Town. I would remain in the position until 1992.

to revive his career and get him back scoring goals. He was a reserved and well-behaved lad, who used to read the Bible before matches, presumably in order to draw some strength and inspiration for the contest to come. This was an interesting twist on the usual motivational techniques.

Another player, who was not quite as pious as Phil, and who was exhibiting the behaviour to prove it, gave me an unusual problem to handle. The player, I was told, had been seen having oral sex in a local nightclub one Saturday night and it seemed that half the town was talking about it. I called him into my office and warned him that if his behaviour did not change, things would not end well. 'If I am going to hear about you, I want it to be because of your exploits on the pitch and not because of your high

With the Huddersfield Town squad, 1989. I am in the middle row *(far right)*; Iffy Onuoura is in the back row *(fifth from left)*.

jinks in the local nightclub. Which do you want to be remembered for?' The message got through. There were, at least, no further reports of similar behaviour. This certainly ranked as one of the less comfortable conversations I ever had with a player.

In the case of Onuora, I had to deal with the challenges of his adjustment to the professional game. Although he had the talent to hurt teams, he had the habit of drifting out of games. At half-time, if I thought that he was not doing enough for the team, I would deliberately provoke him in the hope of stoking the fire in his belly and get him motivated again. Iffy was a good lad but you did not want to get him worked up and hang around for the aftermath. As soon as I saw the red mist descending on him, I made sure to get right out of his way. Then, standing at a safe distance, pointing to the pitch, I'd say: 'Don't look at *me* like that; go out and look at *them* like that.'

Inevitably, my time at Huddersfield brought me into close contact with agents. I quickly learned that although most agents behave with integrity, there are also a minority who are damaging to the game. Agents make money when players move clubs, so, fundamentally, it is not in their interest to have contented one-club men on their books who remain at their boyhood club for their whole career. The agent feeds on transfer activity, and the conditions for that are discontented players who are quarrelling with their clubs.

In some cases, if the desired movement is not materialising, the agent himself will artificially set the process in motion and begin a series of events that could eventually lead to a lucrative transfer deal. He will do this by working with key contacts in the press. Out of thin air, a story will appear in the sports pages of a daily newspaper about how such-and-such a club is interested in the agent's player. This will be the first the player and his club will have heard of it because, of course, no enquiries have actually been made. Then, predictably, if the mooted club is a big one and the suggested money involved considerable, the player's head will be turned. He then goes to the manager, with his agent in tow, and says that he wants to know more about the other club's interest.

If the situation has gone this far, then the agent usually has won. He has created conflict between his player and the club. These initial discussions, with their differences of view, may then harden into an impasse and eventually lead to a breakdown in the relationship. A player who, until recently, may have been an integral part of the club, now wants to leave. Few clubs can tolerate an unhappy player on its books, so the word is put out to other clubs that he is available for the right money. This is when the agent starts looking for the best deal for the player and, of course, for himself.

Obviously, the above tactics do not always succeed but, through flattery and with the promise of more money, it can be effective in unsettling a player.

Compared to today's game, agents were not as prevalent in the late 1980s and early 1990s, but all the same they were steadily working their way into even the lower echelons of English football. I was not always tolerant of dealing with them. In one example, a young player whom I took on trial had impressed me. I told him afterwards that I wanted to offer him a contract and spelled out the terms. I was expecting enthusiastic assent but, instead, as cool as you like, he said, 'Sounds good, but I'll have to run that one by my agent first and see what he has to say. I'll get him to call you.' I pulled him up short. 'Hold on a second, son. I am giving you a way into the professional game and you need to tell me now if you want to play for Huddersfield Town or not. I am not dealing with agents.' It finished at that, without the player joining us. From my perspective, it was just not right that a young, unproven player should be carrying on like that. He needed to grab his chance, succeed, and *then* perhaps earn the right to make such demands of Huddersfield or any other professional club.

I found the Yorkshire people to be salt of the earth and I always enjoyed mingling with them. After each home game, once I had completed my press duties, the last task of the day was always to make my way to the supporters' bar underneath one of the stands to have a drink with the fans. In the modern game, managers do not often freely socialise with the fans, but, in those days, I saw it as part and parcel of my job. The football club was at the centre of the community and had to play its role. This interaction meant that I heard everything. After a win, things were fine but, if it was a defeat, showing your face was not always the most pleasant of experiences. Although I would not accept getting unfair abuse from fans, if someone wanted to express their dissatisfaction, then I listened. Everyone could have their say.

Dealing with the club chairman, Keith Longbottom, presented its difficulties. He had an annoying habit of calling me at my office nearly every day. He would phone and always begin the conversation 'Eoin, I didn't know if you wanted me for anything.' Eventually I got sick of the routine and told him that if there was anything that I needed him for, *I* would contact him. I had heard of supportive chairmen but I could not work properly with him looking for daily bulletins. Try as I might, however, I could not shake him off. The calls kept coming.

As I had done at Limerick United, in order to maintain discipline, I established a system of fines. There were the normal fines for dissent and poor timekeeping but, in addition, I also fined players for diving. Diving is a part of the game that I have never been able to abide and I did not want any of my players engaging in it, even if it might bring us an advantage on the pitch.

Spitting was another offence that I did not look kindly upon. When I caught one player doing it to the opposition, I fined him and suspended him. It is behaviour that undermines the most basic respect and dignity between players.

One of the least enjoyable parts of the job, which also fell to me, was to break the news to academy players that they were not being kept on by the club. I was well aware that it was devastating news for them to hear, but you had to try to be constructive. You would emphasise that they had ability and that there could be opportunities for them elsewhere. Leaving Huddersfield Town did not have to be the end of their career.

In 1990 I travelled to Ireland with Huddersfield for a pre-season warm-up match against Drogheda United. Returning to Ireland unexpectedly brought me into contact with a character from my past, Charlie Tierney. Charlie was a simple soul, a football fanatic and a devoted St Patrick's Athletic fan who used to sell programmes outside the club's Richmond Park ground. The sight of him pacing outside the ground before kick-off, armed with a bunch of programmes, was etched in the minds of anyone connected with the club. I knew Charlie from my time managing St Pat's in the 1984/85 season.

When we were training in Dublin in the days before the game, I found out that Charlie was not well. His health had never been the greatest and he suffered from diabetes and bad circulation. He was a patient at the Mater Hospital and had just undergone an operation. On the morning of the match, I had time to spare before travelling to Drogheda, so I decided to visit Charlie. He was glad to see me and I was happy to be able to cheer him up a bit. After discussing the old times, I said my goodbyes and wished him well. I explained that I was in Ireland to play a friendly match against Drogheda that evening and so would have to leave. I made my way out of Charlie's ward and started walking down the stairs when I heard a voice calling me. I turned to see Charlie hobbling down the stairs, struggling to catch up with me, in his pyjamas and shoes. 'Ah sure, Eoin, I'll come to the match with you. I'll be fine.' His innocent enthusiasm was genuinely touching, but I obviously could not take him out of hospital in his condition. I tried to persuade him to go back to bed but he was not giving up. 'It'll be grand, Eoin. The doctors won't even know and sure we'll be back early enough, won't we?' I offered a compromise. 'Look, Charlie. Here's what we'll do. I'll come back tonight after the game and tell you exactly how it went. How about that?' 'Fair enough, Eoin.'

I left, confident that Charlie was placated and that the next time I would see him would be later that day. I met up with the squad at our arranged point and we began driving north to Drogheda on the team bus. We were about halfway to our destination when someone pointed out a taxi beside us on the road that was behaving strangely. It was flagging us down. I looked out the window to see Charlie waving furiously at me from the back seat of the taxi! The taxi then manoeuvred in front of the bus and forced us to pull over. A frantic Charlie jumped out, still in his pyjamas, with his coat hastily thrown over it, and ran up to the bus door where he starting banging to be let in. I told a dumbfounded bus driver to let him in and that it was OK, I knew the man. I was stunned. 'Charlie, what are you doing here? Do the doctors know that you are out?' 'Yeah, yeah, of course, Eoin. They said it's fine.' I knew well that he was not being truthful but what could I do? We couldn't leave him on the side of the road halfway between Dublin and Drogheda. We took Charlie to the game and dropped him back to the Mater that evening.

The next day, I visited him in hospital again; it was not long afterwards that I was attending Charlie Tierney's funeral.

The Huddersfield job was never anything less than all-consuming and I found it difficult to switch off. I might be sitting at home in front of the television with my family, but I was there only in body: my mind was elsewhere wrestling with some issue affecting Huddersfield Town AFC. Inevitably, on occasion, my immersion in the job conflicted with my family life. In one instance this was brought home to me starkly. In the 1990 pre-season, Huddersfield was scheduled to play away to the Fourth Division side Lincoln City in a friendly. My son Warren, who was thirteen at the time, begged me to let him come on the bus to the match with the squad. Ordinarily I would not have allowed this but, considering it was only a warm-up game, I relented and let him sit up front with me.

The game did not go well. Lincoln beat us and we played poorly. I was in a terrible mood afterwards and ordered the players to get straight onto the bus. It was a Saturday evening, but there would be no post-match drinks for the players. I told everyone that they were to report for training the next morning, on the Sunday, where we would try and put things right. We got on the bus and took off. It was a sombre atmosphere. I sat at the front stewing, while the players maintained blanket silence behind me. After about twenty minutes one of the lads plucked up the courage to approach me. 'Ah, boss,' he began nervously, 'I think you've left your son in Lincoln.'

The bus was turned around and we drove back to Lincoln immediately to pick up a distraught Warren. Luckily, the staff at the stadium had been good enough to take him in and look after him until we arrived. Warren sat down beside me on the return journey and told me that he had actually been running after the bus when it had first left. Thankfully, he and I can have a laugh about it now.

On 5 March 1992, after nearly four seasons as Huddersfield Town's manager, I was let go. It was a bittersweet day. After being told that I no longer had a future at Huddersfield, I went home to find out the wonderful news that my son Gary had got his first commission as a commercial pilot with British Airways.

I can only assume that I was a casualty of regime change in the Huddersfield boardroom. A new chairman was taking over the club and, presumably, wanted to bring in his own man. Although the club released a press statement with the usual 'leaving by mutual consent' tagline, the fact is that I was pushed. I found out almost by accident. I was going to the outgoing chairman, Keith Longbottom, to see if my assistant, Ian Ross, could be given a new contract. I had appointed Ross, a former Liverpool and Aston Villa player, in 1990, after Peter Withe had left to become reserve team coach at Aston Villa. I had not realised that it was, in fact, my own contract, and not Ross's, that the chairman wanted to discuss. A bad run of form since the turn of the year, which saw us winning only two out of twelve games, ultimately cost me my job. The club, I was told, 'were keen to move in a new direction' and that the new manager would be Ian Ross.

I was not all that happy that Ian Ross, the man for whom I was trying to get a new contract, was now unexpectedly replacing me, but I could only bite my lip and accept the club's position. Talks had obviously already been held between Ross and the club without my knowledge, but that's often how things work in football. I had always enjoyed a good working relationship with the club board and we parted on good terms.

In my four seasons, although we had failed to win promotion, we had made progress and I was certainly disappointed not to be given the chance to take the club further. In 1991/92, my final season – for most of which I was at the helm, before Ian Ross replaced me – the club finished third in Division Three, just missing out on promotion in the play-offs.

In regard to transfer-market activity, the club made a net profit during my term. Players like Iwan Roberts and Phil Starbuck were sold on at a considerable profit to the club. My best signing, however, was Craig Maskell, who was also sold, to Reading, to the club's benefit. I had signed him from

Southampton in 1988 and he went on to score forty-three times in eighty-seven appearances. It was an excellent return on our investment.

Throughout the summer of 1992 I began applying for jobs all over England but was getting nowhere. I decided to reach out to contacts in the game. I met Sir Alex Ferguson for lunch at Manchester United's training ground, The Cliff. I had first met Alex at a coaching seminar in the early 1980s when he was manager of Aberdeen. Alex is a likeable down-to-earth character. He expressed his surprise that Huddersfield had let me go and asked me what I was going to do next. I mentioned that I was considering returning to South Africa and so he suggested that I should do some scouting work for Manchester United if I was going out there. He gave me a letter of authority to bring with me. If someone Alex knew was going to be in South Africa, then it made sense for him to ask them to keep an eye out for players. I really appreciated Alex's help.

At the beginning of the 1993/94 League of Ireland season I briefly managed Shelbourne. The club's director, Ollie Byrne, asked me to come in to steady the ship on a temporary basis. It lasted for thirteen matches and, with Shelbourne's results improving, I told Ollie that I was moving on. He asked me to consider taking the post full-time but I declined.

In early 1994 I moved to South Africa to begin what I hoped would be a new life. I wanted to investigate the possibilities of working in the South African game. Before leaving Ireland, I had found out that the country's national side were looking for a new manager. I made enquiries and the South African Football Association asked me to fly out to interview for the position.

I travelled to Johannesburg's Soccer City stadium at the appointed time to meet the Association's general secretary, but he did not show up. I left and returned a few days later when I finally met him. The reception was not warm. In what was little more than a five-minute conversation, he told me that they were no longer interested in my application. I was not too pleased with having travelled to another continent for an interview only to be fobbed off with the pat line, 'we have decided to go another way.' I have no idea if my candidacy had ever been taken seriously.

Soon after, in the spring of 1994, thankfully I managed to pick up some casual work as a football commentator on South African television. While commentating on a pre-season friendly in Johannesburg between Kaiser Chiefs and Liverpool, I was lucky enough to be introduced to

Nelson Mandela. I can, without any doubt, say that he was one of the most charismatic human beings I have ever met. As soon as he walked into the lounge area of the Chiefs' Soccer City stadium, his graceful presence took over the room. It was as if Mandela was surrounded by a halo that radiated calm authority.

It was through my media work, and a mutual friend in Tony Ward, that my long friendship with the former rugby union player John Robbie began. John had played for Ireland and the British and Irish Lions at scrum half. After touring South Africa with the Lions in 1980, John came back in 1981 and signed for Transvaal. On retiring from rugby, he moved into media work and subsequently became a highly respected radio broadcaster on one of South Africa's major radio stations. John was a good friend to me at a time in my life when I was adjusting to major changes. Our golfing outings were reliably competitive affairs. John would insist that he could not beat me while I had my trusty driver in hand. He christened it 'the Green Mamba' and, because of the results I got with it, swore that I had put a spell on it. John's will to win eventually got the better of my magic.

As much as I enjoyed my media work, I could not rely on it for a regular income. Months passed without me finding permanent work and in May 1994 I was in a risky financial position again. I had staked my financial future on getting a position in the South African game but found myself rapidly running out of options. Geraldine, whom I was now living with, had also given birth to our daughter, Shannon. My marriage with Pat had unfortunately broken up before I left for South Africa.

I also already had a son with Geraldine, Jason, who was born in 1977. My return to South Africa was now a chance to spend more time with him. Although the birth of Shannon was a great joy, it underlined my need to find work and quickly.

Joe Frickleton, a Scottish former professional footballer and then a manager of the Johannesburg club Orlando Pirates, had put the word out that I was looking for work and, thankfully, in early June I heard that the Durban-based club AmaZulu was interested in talking to me. I made the journey south to meet the chairman. We agreed a good deal and I became manager of the club in May.

It was to prove to be one of the more challenging management positions in my career, with quite a few culture shocks for me to adjust to. Some of the players were believers in a kind of magic that they called muti and, for this purpose, they used to consult with their community witch doctor. The witch doctor's job was to try to conjure up sufficiently vigorous magic to guarantee the right result for the team. Usually, before the match, a concoction of herbs, and maybe a chicken's heart, would be burning in the corner of the changing room for some time as we prepared and then, with each player waiting expectantly, the verdict on the power of the magic would be delivered.

This was a critical moment for the players because they were convinced that, without favourable omens, it would be very difficult to defeat the opposition. It added a whole new dimension to my team talk and my efforts to rally the troops. I might instruct the players that if we followed a certain tactical plan and did X, Y and Z, we should be able to capitalise on the opposition's weaknesses and perhaps win the game. But even my most inspired moments of motivation were under pressure if the muti had already indicated that the wind was, in fact, blowing the other way.

I was in a running battle with the witch doctor. The players were in awe of this man and his influence counted for more than mine. Some days the situation was even more drastic. I would be told in no uncertain terms that victory was unlikely against such-and-such a team because the magic of their witch doctor was far more powerful than that of our own. It was no longer only about eleven footballers against eleven footballers; it was also about sorcerer versus sorcerer. This was one dressing room where superstition and football logic went toe to toe at about a quarter to three every Saturday afternoon.

I, a white manager who had pitched up overnight, could not change these players' superstitions. Magic was an ingrained part of their communities and played a role in solving countless everyday problems. This was how they dealt with the uncertainties of life, whether the issue was a game of football or a matter of life and death. As absurd as the situation was to me, it was where I found myself and, if I wanted to win football matches, I had to find a way of suspending my disbelief and adjusting to their mindset. With strange smells emanating from the corner of the dressing room and auguries being revealed by the witch doctor as I addressed the team, I did my best to instil a parallel football message in my players' minds. My attitude was that, yes, they may be running out for action with the gloomy words of the witch doctor having convinced them of the futility of it all, but, if they could just remember and follow the tactical instructions I gave them, then we might still win.

After a few months of managing AmaZulu, things took a turn for the worse. It was clear that the fans and the wider community did not want a white man in charge of the team. Apartheid may have been officially over, but underlying racial tensions proved far harder to uproot and so I became the unwitting subject of what was, effectively, reverse apartheid. I began receiving anonymous phone calls to my hotel room telling me: 'We do not want you here. Leave or you will die.' When I reported these threats to the police, they advised me to change hotel rooms regularly and to ask reception to keep my room number confidential.

The situation got worse. There were disturbances at the training ground and, in some cases, rocks were thrown at me during matches. In one game, for protection, I took my place in the dugout with a motorcycle helmet on!

When your own fans are hurling rocks at you, it's obvious that you are in a bad situation. I went to the club chairman and told him that something had to change. He suggested that I take a few weeks off and travel back to Johannesburg. In the meantime, he would attempt to cool the tensions and work things out with the supporters' club. He assured me that the situation had nothing to do with me and that it would be fixed. I went back to Johannesburg and, while there, gave serious consideration to quitting the AmaZulu position.

Intent on doing the job that I was contracted for, however, I hung on in, and, despite the bad omens, returned a few weeks later to take control of the team again. Matters, however, very quickly came to a head and I realised that nothing had changed.

I was at training one evening when a group of about thirty Zulus walked out onto the pitch to confront me. Their message was not subtle: 'You must go or we will kill you.' I was sick of being harassed and was exasperated to realise that the very same problems were resurfacing. I tried to explain that I was Irish and that whatever issues they were experiencing had nothing to do with me. 'I'm a professional and you are stopping me from doing my work,' I shouted. Then the crowd suddenly parted and the tribal chief walked right up to me. '*You* are *not* listening. If you *do not leave*, we *will* kill you.' I looked around, only to find that my players, to a man, had vanished. It was only me, the tribal chief, and an angry mob behind him, standing in the middle of an otherwise empty pitch. I knew this was no idle threat. I was so scared that I actually walked backwards across the training pitch to where my things were. I left the ground, shaking, and made my way back to my hotel.

The next morning I went to the chairman and told him what had happened. It was clear to both of us that I could not continue as manager in these circumstances, and so he agreed to pay me for three more months of my contract.

On the day after, I began to plan what I would do next. I was sitting alone by the pool on the hotel's rooftop when a man came out of the nearby lift. He did not greet me but I knew he was there for me. Without looking at me, he pulled out a gun and began to pace slowly around the pool, every few steps, pulling the trigger on an empty barrel and aiming into the distance. I got up immediately and, walking towards the lift, said out loud, 'I'm leaving Durban now. I'm leaving.' I got no response from the gunman, not even a glance. He was as cool as be damned and every bit as sinister. Following me, he got into the lift next to me and brandished the gun in front of his body but remained a picture of silence. The lift was going down to my floor at what seemed like an interminably slow rate. It reached my floor and before getting out, once more, I said again that I was leaving Durban. To my great relief, the lift door closed behind me and he continued downwards. When I got to my room, I threw everything into my suitcase and went straight to reception to check out. I told them that there had been a man with a gun in the lift with me and they called the police. He, however, was long gone by the time the first police officers arrived.

When the police told me afterwards that professional hitmen would kill for as little as 500 rand in Durban (about €40 in today's money), I realised how lucky I was to get out of the encounter unharmed. Once I had left the hotel, I went to my brother Eamonn, who lived in Durban, for advice. He knew South Africa better than I did. His advice was unequivocal: get out of Durban and go straight back to Johannesburg. I drove there that day.

In Johannesburg, in the autumn of 1994, I was looking around again for work. It came from an unexpected source. While having a drink in a pub, a friendly man at the bar engaged me in conversation. He was a fellow Irishman and the landlord of the establishment. He then said that he had an idea to set up an Irish bar in Johannesburg but that he needed a partner to invest funds with him. Would I join him in the venture? I was frank and told him that I had very little money to put forward. 'How much do you have?', he quickly asked. I told him that I could raise about

50,000 rand (about €4,000 today). He said 'OK, you can come in with me for that.'

The idea was that I would front and run the business day to day. With my background in Irish soccer, it was hoped that the location could become a popular sports venue. It seemed like a smart business move and, with financial concerns to the fore, I went for it.

In order to do things properly, I decided to research Irish bars and even travelled back to Dublin to take photographs of the interiors and exteriors of some of the more successful examples there. I went back to Johannesburg and decorated the bar with old-style wooden furnishings and, keeping to the sports theme, framed and hung my international jerseys on the walls. A large screen was also installed to show live sports. I called the pub Scruffy Murphy's. It opened at the end of the summer of 1995.

Although the first six months of trading were challenging, in the second year it was doing well. My pal John Robbie had given me some great publicity at various times on his radio show and it helped. With live Irish music most nights and English and Scottish football matches on the big screen, it became what all Irish bars abroad should be: a home away from home for the Irish diaspora. I was delighted that the pub was a hub for the Irish community. If anyone new emigrated from Ireland to Johannesburg, the message they were given was: 'Call into Scruffy Murphy's. The people there will sort you out.' And we did. If at all possible, I would introduce the new arrival to other Irish people who might help them out with settling into the country.

Being the manager of the pub, I kept a close eye on the accounts. After a while, I began to notice that stock was going missing. Eventually I figured out who was taking it. It was my business partner. Evidently, he was taking it for whatever other concerns he had going on in the city.

I confronted him about it but he was evasive. Then, a few days later, an unsavoury incident took place. A young woman walked in and asked for the toilets. I pointed to the back and she went. Then, as soon as I turned around, I was faced with a huge Afrikaans man bellowing and remonstrating violently. 'What did you say to my woman?' I quietly told him that she had gone to the ladies'.

He picked up a bottle from the bar and smashed it across the side of my face. I went down and remember nothing of the incident after that point. I am told that he hit me again on the way down. I was unconscious for a while and came to with a group of concerned faces looking down at me. They told me that an ambulance was on the way.

After being treated in hospital, I was in extreme pain with a head wound but, thankfully, not seriously injured. The doctors told me that I was lucky not to have lost an eye. Later some bar regulars asked me what I wanted to do about my assailant. Did I want him buried or just to have his legs broken? What good would that do? I wanted neither. What I wanted was to move on.

As I nursed my wound and recovered my health, I began to reflect on the fact that South Africa and I could not seem to get on good terms. I loved South Africa but it did not like me. In Durban I had been threatened at gunpoint and in Johannesburg I had been seriously assaulted. Now once more I had to give serious thought to my future.

I knew I could not go back to running the bar. That much was obvious. It did not require much thinking to guess who had paid this thug to scare me off. If that was the intention, it worked. In late 1996, once I was out of hospital, I went into the bar early one morning and took down all my jerseys from the walls. I left and cut all my ties with the place. Out of desperation to earn a living, I had made a very poor decision in getting involved in this bar business.

I no longer believed that I could make a living in South Africa and so I made plans to come home.

10

Last Rites, New Beginnings

1997

When I returned to Dublin in late 1996, I was not in a good place. I was financially and emotionally broken; it felt like everything in my life had gone wrong. I wondered how I had arrived at this point. My career in football management had hit a brick wall, my business in Johannesburg had collapsed and my personal life was in disarray. My life had fallen apart in South Africa. My relationship with Geraldine had become strained and I was now separated from my daughter Shannon. It was tough.

Whatever about my personal problems, I needed to think about money, so I staked my immediate financial future on securing a testimonial from the FAI. I had a letter from the organisation promising me a testimonial from 1986 and I hoped that it would now materialise. A number of years earlier, in 1993, I had investigated the possibility of arranging a match but it had gone nowhere. In order to garner support for the testimonial, I had travelled to Jack Charlton's home in England and asked if he might lend me his support. Jack grumbled and said that too many people, including current players, were asking him for help with their testimonials. He was not interested. I dropped it and left. I felt let down by Jack because I had, after all, helped him when he took over as Ireland manager.

In January 1997, after a few months of discussions, in which the then national team manager, Mick McCarthy, played a part, my testimonial was finally given the go-ahead by the FAI chief executive, Bernard O'Byrne. The Republic of Ireland national side would play a League of Ireland selection on 27 September of that year. Organising my testimonial was a great distraction for me. I was conscious that I had only one shot at this and so I wanted to get it right.

Throughout 1997 I had meetings with my testimonial committee to organise the match. I am indebted to them for the work they did on my behalf. The members were my brother Frank, John Givens, Liam Tuohy, Peter Byrne, former Shamrock Rovers player Eddie Cowzer, publican Charlie Chawke, local businessmen Krish Naidoo and Tom Scully, and banker Gerry O'Mahony. Pat Quigley, the then president of the FAI, was also very helpful, as was the Association's former president Michael Hyland. To secure a venue, I went to the Shelbourne club secretary, Ollie Byrne, and enquired about the availability of the club's Tolka Park stadium. Testimonial matches, far from guaranteeing you a lucrative retirement nest egg, come with their own financial risks. Ordinarily, you have to pay for the rent of the stadium, as well as all the associated match-day costs of stewarding, policing and the ambulance services. That leaves you financially exposed and hoping for a bumper attendance to put you in the black again. Some former players, failing to attract the punters, have actually lost money on their testimonial, so it was with some trepidation that I asked Ollie about the cost of using Shelbourne's ground.

It was a short conversation. Ollie, to his immense credit, insisted that I have Tolka Park free of charge. At this time, aside from some on-and-off football writing that Peter Byrne had managed to secure for me with the *News of the World*, I had no regular income. Ollie's kind gesture was a huge help.

During this period, the first half of 1997, I was travelling back and forth from South Africa to visit to my three-year-old daughter, Shannon. This weighed heavily on my mind. I was with her when she came into the world, and had been by her side for the first two years of her life – a time in which we had formed a deep bond. I wanted to see her but the uncertainty of South Africa meant that I did not know what future relationship I could hope to have with my daughter.

By mid-1997 I was struggling. Although I had slowly begun to drink too much, it was really only in June and July that I started to sink into depression and drink to a dangerous degree. The emotional problems I thought I had left behind in South Africa were following me around Dublin and, from where I stood, I could not see how things were going to work out.

Although, in one sense, understanding how I had become locked into this desperately unhealthy spiral of drinking was complicated, from another angle it was all very simple. Not a lot was going right in my life, I was tired of feeling bad and I wanted to feel good again. I was faced with a choice every morning: think my problems through or go drinking. The latter often won; it was the easier thing to do.

That it was the bottom of a glass of beer that gave me the lift I needed was almost beside the point; it was working, I didn't feel miserable, at least for those few hours spent in the pub. The reality, however, was hardly so rosy. There was no master plan here; this was not going anywhere. I was drinking myself into a hole.

There was also another reason for drinking. It was not only psychological pain that I was trying to forget, it was also physical pain. While I was in South Africa I had developed an intense pain on the upper left-hand side of my stomach. I'd had it examined in Johannesburg but the diagnosis was inconclusive. The pain, unfortunately, followed me back to Ireland. Alcohol, I found, numbed the feeling and so it quickly became my homespun anaesthetic. The soreness, however, was getting worse and so, in a deeply damaging cycle, I had to drink all the more to keep the growing discomfort at bay. I knew that my body was telling me there was something seriously wrong with my health, but I was not interested in hearing the message – I was not *able* to hear that message. The days were not too bad, but, then, during the night, I would often awake abruptly from my sleep with a ferocious pain in my stomach.

Whatever about the amount of alcohol being downed, I was still, at the end of it all, just a friendly, social drinker. This was the 'medicine' I needed.

Although I had a genuine problem during those months, I was not then and I never have been an alcoholic. I was drinking for a reason. Throughout my playing career, like most players of my era, I enjoyed the pub atmosphere. The most serious part, however, was that, by the beginning of August 1997, I had effectively stopped eating properly. Like most bad habits, consistent drinking slowly takes you over.

Whatever about dulling the pain in my stomach, the alcohol could not banish the depression – in fact, predictably, it only made it worse. When the black episodes came over me, my world contracted to almost nothing; everything appeared as a pointless dead end. I remember walking home in the darkness one evening, on deserted streets, past the Royal Canal. I stopped and wondered whether or not I should throw myself into the water. Having nothing to lose is a dangerous position in which to find yourself. What did *I* have to lose? What did I have to live for? I was struggling to find an answer to those questions and to grasp a reason not to jump. The longer I peered into the black water, the more tempting it became to finish it all there and then. The water seemed so serene, my life such a mess. There's an easy way out, I thought. Just jump, and you can pull the plug on all the suffering. No more pain – what a seductive thought!

As the seriousness of what I was contemplating began to sink in, my body started shaking. Was I going to do this? Could I really take this ultimate step? I stood there, rooted to the spot for what must have been at least five minutes until, abruptly, the fog lifted, and I became appalled at myself. *What the fuck are you thinking? You can't kill yourself, for God's sake. How would that solve anything?*

What stopped me from attempting suicide? There was no one definite impulse that persuaded me to walk away from the bank of the canal, but, thinking about it afterwards, I was clear that I did not want to leave a trail of suffering behind me for everyone else to have to deal with. It would have been a deeply selfish act. Yes, my problems would have been extinguished along with me, but everyone else's would have just been starting.

Looking back now, I understand how destructive my behaviour was. It is also clear to me that I was, in my own awkward way, trying to *make* myself sick, almost to force the issue and to bring about a kind of climax, however unpleasant it might be. Something had to give: I needed a breaking point; I was not happy with my life and I was going to force it over the edge of a cliff in the hope that something salvageable might emerge from the wreckage.

That breaking point came on 14 August 1997. The previous weekend of drinking had brought me to the brink. I collapsed in my mother's house in Drumcondra early in the morning. My mother wanted to do the sensible thing and call for an ambulance. I, however, despite being doubled over in agony and barely able to stand, still had my stupid pride intact. I insisted on taking a taxi, alone, a decision that served only to delay my arrival at the city's Mater Hospital.

Finally, I made it to the Accident and Emergency unit of the hospital and begged for something, anything, to end the intense pain. The staff asked me if I had been drinking. I said I had. 'How much?' they asked.

It was a Tuesday and, by taking them through the extent of my previous weekend's drinking, I laid bare the full seriousness of my situation. They quickly diagnosed possible acute pancreatitis.

Over the next few days I lapsed in and out of a semi-coma state with the infection starting to attack my other organs. By now the enzymes had spread so far that my lungs were at risk of collapsing. I stabilised somewhat when I was taken to the intensive care unit, but over the coming days things were still dicey. I asked the doctor straight out: 'Is my life in danger?' I wanted to hear the unvarnished truth, however uncomfortable it might be. He said 'Yes. This is very serious. You need to ask your family to come sooner rather than later.' After that, my mother, and my brothers, Frank and Brian, came to my side while my former wife, Pat, and our sons Gary and Warren travelled from England to see me.

Because it felt as if I was in death's waiting room, I decided to begin planning my funeral with my family. It sounds morbid but there was not a lot else to do. I organised my send-off from this world in an oddly matter-of-fact manner, even down to the songs that would be played at my funeral Mass. You would think that a brush with death might send you into ructions of anguish and self-pity but, in my case, it didn't. I stopped resisting and became almost calm. What could I do? I was practically out for the count and my life was now in the hands of other people. I accepted that. My mother had her own way of coping. She went to Mass every day and prayed for me.

On 22 August, my condition worsened and the decision was made to operate as a matter of urgency. At this stage the priest was called and it was then that I received the last rites. Despite it being a genuine life-and-death situation, I was reconciled to whatever would be. I am not a very religious person, although I do believe in God. The only way out of this situation now was the surgeon's knife.

The hospital rang my mother and told her to come as soon as possible. No one could say if I was going to live or die. The surgeon told me afterwards that four out of five patients failed to survive the operation. The operation took twelve hours. I was one of the lucky one-in-fives who eventually come out the other end.

I was over the operation but my health was still in a critical condition and I remained in intensive care for a few more weeks. I was conscious but not fully with it. Some days were better than others. I have hazy memories of familiar faces appearing at my bedside. I remember Mick McCarthy coming but not much of what we spoke about. The folk singer Patsy Watchorn, of Dublin City Ramblers fame, also visited me and this encounter I can clearly recall. Patsy, unbeknownst to me, once he had heard of my condition, had brought his Catholic cloth medal, the Green Scapular, to my bedside. He insisted that it was the healing powers of the scapular that had, in fact, saved my life. Whether or not I could fully agree with that assessment, I was truly grateful to have Patsy by my bedside.

As I was laid up in the Mater Hospital on 27 September, without my knowledge, my testimonial match was being played a few kilometres away at Tolka Park. It was an unforgiving wet and windy night for a game of football, and the public largely stayed away. Only 2,000 spectators showed up but I was grateful to the fans who had come and supported me. The following week, a greyhound race meeting also took place at Shelbourne Park as part of the fundraising effort. My friend John Givens and my testimonial committee had also organised this second event.

Once it became clear that my health had stabilised and that I was no longer in immediate danger, I was moved to the Caritas Convalescent Centre on Dublin's Merrion Road in October to regain my strength. Before discharging me from the Mater, however, the surgeon gave me a sobering account of how close I had been to dying. He said the one thing that had saved me was the natural fitness that had carried over from my professional footballing days.

He was only partly right. What also saved me was the support of my family and, in particular, the strength I drew from the person who sat by my side through it all, the reassuring, non-judgemental presence that listened to me, day after day in the hospital and in the recovery unit, as I poured out my most private thoughts. This woman, Pauline Doherty, always patient, always caring, who began as my friend in 1992, would become my wife. I know with certainty that I would not be alive today if it were not for Pauline. I also cannot forget the wonderful medical team, led by Dr Thomas Gorey, that worked ceaselessly to keep me alive.

During my recovery period at the convalescent centre, I had the opportunity to assess what had gone wrong in my life and how to ensure that I would not repeat those mistakes. The hundreds of get-well cards that I received made me realise that people cared. I was not alone, as I had been convinced I was in my darkest moments. I certainly chose a dramatic route to get this affirmation from the people in my life, but to have it now was of great significance.

The slow convalescence gave me plenty of time to think. I had been given a second chance and I resolved to use it. From now on there would be challenges, not problems. Once I got back on two feet, I would take practical steps to fix my personal life.

I had a life; now I had to lead it.

11

'Ah, Eoin, you're alive after all.'

Second Chances and Working for the FAI: 1998–2017

When I was released from care in October 1997, I slowly began to consider my next steps. My strength was returning and the business of reorganising my life was under way. Alcohol was off the menu. I was also now in a close relationship with Pauline.

On 15 November Limerick City played a benefit match on my behalf, with the then Limerick side playing a selection of club veterans. Before the match I received a guard of honour as I walked onto the pitch. I greatly appreciated the regard in which the club and the Limerick public still held me. After all the years that had passed, the connection and the camaraderie were very much alive. It was touching that the testimonial committee should be made up of my brother Brian and several of my former players, including the inimitable Mick O'Donnell.

In connection with the match, a dinner was also arranged. The great ballad singer Paddy Reilly performed at no cost. My good friend Frank Hogan, a former rugby player with Limerick's Garryowen and now a successful businessman, generously sponsored the evening. Also, towards the end of the year the Wolfe Tones were kind enough to play a tribute concert for me in Dublin. I was truly grateful for their help.

That Christmas I travelled to South Africa and finally managed to make the legal arrangements that would allow me visiting rights to Shannon, as

With my daughter Shannon (*left*), for her twenty-first birthday, and Pauline, at Cheetah Park, Johannesburg.

Pauline and me in 2016.

well as formalising the maintenance payments that I would send. It was a great relief for me to know that I would be able to see my daughter, and the end of a major concern.

I flew back to Dublin in January 1998 and began to think about work. I applied for the job of New Zealand national manager but did not receive an interview.

Luckily, early in the year, I got a break that, in the long term, would prove hugely significant for me. RTÉ's Head of Sport, Tim O'Connor, offered me work as a co-commentator on the broadcaster's television football coverage, while, soon after, Ian Corr asked me to work as a co-commentator on matches covered by RTÉ radio. What began as casual employment would eventually become more regular, especially in the case of the radio work, and represent a source of income.

Before beginning my new work, I took a big step in my personal life. At this point I was living in my mother's house in Drumcondra. I needed to have my own home but, because Dublin was way out of my financial range, I had to look farther afield. Moyvane, in Kerry, was the place that came to my mind immediately. I was drawn to the thought of returning to Glenalappa in Moyvane, the part of Ireland that had been so special to me in my youth. After my illness, the notion of living permanently in the beauty of Kerry was a healing one.

I made enquiries from Jimmy Kirby, a farmer, about buying a plot of land from him. His sister Josie was the woman who had first brought me and my brother Eamonn to Kerry. This was where I wanted to settle. Pauline and I made the journey to Kerry.

I met Jimmy and we began looking at a site in Glenalappa, just outside Moyvane. Jimmy asked, 'Are you actually serious about this?' I assured him that I was. What for him may have seemed like a nondescript piece of land was for me a little corner of heaven. I picked a spot, with a stream flowing at its boundary, and told Jimmy this was the piece of land that I wanted. I had lived in cities all my life, whether it was in Ireland, the UK or South Africa, so I knew what a big change it would be. For now, I was only buying a piece of land. I did not know when I would be able to actually build a new home on it.

When I was back in Dublin, and feeling very much alive, I was surprised to suddenly find myself, once more, discussing my mortality with the press.

I took a call from journalist and great friend Peter Byrne, then *The Irish Times* soccer correspondent. 'Ah, Eoin, you're alive after all', he began.

I was lost. 'What? Sorry, Peter, what do you mean?' 'Did you not hear? You're dead, Eoin. At least as far as the *Yorkshire Post* and the *Portsmouth Evening Post* are concerned.'

Somehow, with news of my close shave of the previous year slowly reaching various parts of Britain, wires had been crossed, and I was *now* being reported as dead. I was delighted to be able to clear that one up.

Some days later my false death reared its head again when I ran into journalist Charlie Stuart at Tolka Park. 'You're some bollocks, Eoin. You didn't die. You had to go and survive, didn't you? I read the reports of your death and was up half the night last week writing your obituary.' It was probably the most good-natured bollocking that I have ever received. I could only apologise for having the cheek to live.

I had a long-term idea for more permanent work which I began to consider more seriously in late 1998. There was no one to offer guidance to promising young Irish footballers who were moving from local schoolboy clubs in Ireland to sign for professional clubs in Britain. In many cases, they were making one of the biggest moves of their lives at the age of fifteen or sixteen, when they did not have the experience to cope with the challenges ahead. I discussed the idea with Liam Tuohy and some other football friends, and was encouraged to develop it and to make a submission to the Football Association of Ireland.

The proposal was that the FAI would introduce a career guidance type role and that I would fill it. The purpose of the job was to advise young players before, during and after their scholarship contracts had ended. It also involved a proactive element which would see me giving talks to players at local clubs and schools on what to expect from the dream of trying to become a professional footballer. Pauline and I drew up a business plan, submitted it and, after I met with the Association's chief executive, Bernard O'Byrne, the green light was given. Bernard was open-minded and pragmatic. He saw the merits of the role and said it was worth giving it a try for a year.

In early 1999 the work began. The career guidance role was all about advising talented young players and their parents. It was understandable that everyone involved should be excited when a youngster is signing for a major Premier League club but equally the realities and difficulties of trying to make it in an ultra-competitive world had to be underlined. I would wish the young lads the best but also try to arm them with the tools they would need to negotiate their new world successfully. In the case of teenagers who, overnight, were swapping a small rural Irish town for clubs in very large cities like London, Birmingham or Manchester, I was always particularly careful with my advice. The adjustment for them, in terms of homesickness and coping in an alien world, were much greater than for a kid who was leaving a capital city like Dublin and, maybe, signing for a small-town club in England or Scotland. The latter child was invariably far more streetwise and better able to integrate. And integration matters. The more secure and content a boy is, the better his chances of success.

Players also needed to understand the gulf in class between their old playing environment and the far more exacting professional game they were about to be dropped into. Coming from their schoolboy club, where they were usually feted as the undisputed star, they would now have to deal with the culture shock of finding out that in a professional club there are no weak players. Everyone is a potential star. The player goes from being a big fish in a small pond to simply being one more promising player in a large British academy. The levels are incomparable.

Dealing with players' parents sometimes presented its own obstacles. Mothers were always the grounded ones. They did not tend to have a deep emotional investment in the idea that their son might one day run out in front of Manchester United's Stretford End or become a Kop hero at Liverpool. Invariably, they cared only about the boy's education and his well-being. If he was to become a professional footballer, then that was a bonus, but certainly not the be-all and end-all.

Fathers, could, in some cases, be another story. That was where most of the pressure and the unrealistic hopes stemmed from. Sometimes, all they could see was that their boy was going to be a star. They were living the dream *through* their child and, on occasion, getting much too involved. Where possible, I had to gently outline the likely pitfalls and calmly explain that the player was at the beginning of a rocky road. That road could lead him to a career in football if he showed the necessary dedication. Although, in some cases, involvement with professional football can lead to other career options such as coaching and, maybe, physiotherapy, the majority of young players do not make the grade with the recruiting club – as is highlighted by the dearth of Irish players plying their trade at the top levels of the British game.

Inevitably, parents would sometimes ask for my opinion on the various clubs that were interested in their child. Because I was fundamentally an adviser, I tried not to get drawn on these questions. Although I did know which clubs looked after their youngsters very well and which ones did not do such a good job at it, I had to be tactful. If asked to choose, I would simply say that such and such a club was a good option. I would remain silent about the others.

I was also occasionally asked by parents whether or not their child should have an agent. If it was the boy's first contract, then I always advised that it was premature for agents to be involved. In my opinion, it was not appropriate for young players at the very outset of their career to be dealing with agents. It would serve only to introduce them to the commercial side of the game before they had even kicked a football in a professional club, and before they were mature enough to cope with these issues. At the development stage, players should be thinking about their football and, most importantly, about how they are going to prove themselves on the field of play.

If, however, the player impressed in his first few years at his new club and, as a result, was being rewarded with a new and improved contract, then, if asked, I would say that it might be helpful for him to have an agent. At that point, even though they are still very young, they have, at least, earned the right to go to the club with an agent by their side and discuss their financial future.

I tried to take a proactive role as much as possible. For example, I felt that dealings between scouts and players needed regulating. Essentially, there was nothing to stop anyone from calling themselves a scout and purporting to represent Arsenal, Chelsea or whoever. It was unregulated and entry to the field as easy as acquiring a long coat with a badge. This was open season. The profession, in the worst cases (thankfully a minority), was a plaything for fantasists who wanted to puff out their chests and play the role of the scout just for a day, and who could second-guess them? It was not acceptable that the player and club might not be certain whether or not the man making all the promises was actually an official representative of a British club. I knew that the genuine scouts would welcome regulation because

At home on the job in 1999. I worked with the FAI from 1999 to 2012, first as the association's Career Guidance Officer and then as Football Support Services Manager.

the move would essentially winnow out the shadowy fringe characters who served only to make their job more difficult. I decided to contact as many professional clubs as possible in Britain to ask them to confirm the names of their representatives in Ireland. I wrote to all Premier League and English Football League clubs and to many clubs in Scotland. When the majority of them had replied, I then had a list of names in which I, the Irish clubs and the parents could place our trust.

It was important for me to make sure that a boy was going to be looked after when he travelled to Britain, even if he was only travelling for a week-long trial. Most clubs had professional structures in place to properly care for boys on these trips, but not all. In one of the worst cases I came across, one Dublin teenager was invited for a trial by a lower-league English club. For months his mother had saved up the money that would allow him to travel. When he did make the journey, there was precious little football and certainly no trial. Without any supervision from the club, the lad was

Meeting President Mary McAleese with Pauline in 1999. Also pictured are the former president's husband, Martin McAleese, as well as Jimmy Magee (centre). The occasion was an event to honour figures from Irish sport.

allowed to fritter away his week drinking and partying, staying in a house that a club official had organised. His mother was heartbroken when he returned with his opportunity gone up in smoke. I reported the incident to the English FA in the hope that this one club, at least, would be forced to get serious about its obligations to underage players.

One of the most enjoyable parts of my career guidance work was the fact that it took me to all corners of Ireland. Sometimes schoolboy clubs might invite me to give a talk or to advise on particular issues. I would often travel to the club to help them. In the vast majority of cases I had only positive experiences of dealing with local football. I met all the unsung volunteers who gave up their weekday evenings or their Saturday mornings to train kids, or the local chairmen and club secretaries who were doing their best to support the game in their community.

In late 2001 I learned that a conference was to be held in Budapest that October, on the topic of new FIFA regulations concerning the international transfer of young players. These new regulations would set minimum mandatory compensation that professional clubs had to pay when they signed underage players. The regulations established the FIFA Solidarity and Compensation Payment scheme. I knew that this would have a huge impact on the movement of young Irish players to British clubs and so I asked Brendan Menton, the then general secretary at the FAI, for permission to travel to Hungary. He agreed and, after attending, I returned home and explained the importance of the new regulations to the FAI. Someone would have to ensure that the Irish clubs got a fair deal when the heavy-hitting UK professional clubs came looking for their best youngsters. I offered to be this person and act as a mediator who would facilitate the negotiation process between the two parties. I was well aware that because of the enormous success of Brian Kerr's Irish underage sides, assisted by the late great Noel O'Reilly, the UK clubs were more determined than ever to unearth talented footballers in Ireland. And, of course, if they could, they would pay as little as possible for the player they wanted. The FAI recognised the importance of this and so accepted my proposal.

Although I began my new duties immediately, in 2001, it was only from 2002 onwards that my role formally expanded to include the FIFA compensation work. There was a lot to be done. Customary practices were deeply entrenched. The UK professional clubs were used to calling the shots when it came to dealing with Irish clubs and, of course, Ireland had been a happy hunting ground for decades, with numerous top-class players being discovered and subsequently gracing major teams across the Irish Sea.

Schoolboy clubs, on the other hand, necessarily lacked bargaining power and were, therefore, more or less resigned to accepting what was offered for their players. The British clubs knew this and so, Ireland, in the worst cases, became a sort of bargain basement, a place where, if you were lucky, you could pick up a future star practically for a set of jerseys and a few training balls. It was a low-risk, win-win situation for the professional clubs: if it worked out, great, they had a new player at a rock-bottom price; if it did not work out, so what? The gamble was easily worth it because their outlay was so low. If you were the custodians of a schoolboy club in Ireland, however, it was often a lose-lose scenario: you watched your best young player walk out the door, and usually without any worthwhile compensation for the years of development put into his training.

The whole point of the FIFA compensation regulations was to redress this imbalance by compelling professional clubs to strike fair deals with schoolboy clubs, and, as a result, help to fund grass-roots development. I was fully intent on playing my part in this process.

When I began the work, I discovered that, even though the new regulations were already in place and had to be followed, most clubs in England and Scotland were not observing them. They still paid whatever they wanted. It was as if nothing had changed. There was a fundamental attitude shift needed and I knew that I would face challenges in getting the clubs in Britain to accept the reality of the new landscape.

Not all clubs did. Some persisted with their preferred way of doing business. One of the more unsavoury and frequently used techniques was to drive a wedge between the player and his parents, and the club. The professional club would tell the player that it thought he was a tremendous prospect and that it badly wanted him, but the only snag was that these new regulations that his club was insisting on were blocking the deal. Of course, these words were like a siren call for the young aspiring player and suddenly his own club, by apparently selfishly insisting on the observance of some distant FIFA red tape, had been transformed into the enemy. This, predictably, gave rise to a stand-off and, sometimes, actually led to the worst possible outcome: the deal collapsing and the player's dream going up in smoke.

In one particularly fractious case, a Scottish club deliberately drummed up conflict between a schoolboy club and the parents in a small village in Ireland. Rather than pay what they were obliged to, they worked on the parents' hopes and persuaded them that the local club was ruining their son's chances. In the end, the community was divided in two and the club, just to put an end to the discord, buckled and accepted a derisory sum for their player. It was a crude tactic for a professional club to employ, but one that was effective because of the huge disparity in bargaining power that they could rely on. It had to stop.

For these reasons, all parties had to accept from the outset that deals could happen only in an environment of fairness and transparency, and within the confines of the regulations. I always did what I could to enhance the Irish club's position. For example, often the British clubs would want the player and the local club representatives to travel to England or Scotland.

This, I felt, was a deliberate tactic. By taking the player, his parents and the club representatives out of their familiar world and forcing them to negotiate in the intimidating surroundings of a professional British club, it hoped to overawe, tip the scales in its favour, and sign up the player without much compensation. I insisted that it should be the other way around. The professional club's representatives had to come to the player's local area to show that they were serious. After all, they were the ones who wanted him.

Once we were all sitting down, I would then make it clear to the UK club that I was a facilitator in the process and that there was no financial incentive for me to ensure the passage of a young player to Britain. When that was understood, it was always possible to work out a fair solution.

At all times, the central focus of the negotiations had to be the young player's future. This meant that, if at all possible, impasses had to be avoided. A highly effective strategy for getting around the deadlock was to suggest progress payments as an alternative to the full compensation being paid up front. So, for example, if the compensation payable was €100,000 but the UK club was stalling I would suggest, instead, that they pay €50,000 on signature of contract but, if the player reached various milestones, such as getting into the first-team squad, then another, say, €100,000 would be paid. It created a win-win situation for all parties. The English or Scottish club paid less in the beginning but, if the player progressed and the club got its money's worth, then the Irish club who transferred the player was ultimately getting even more than it was entitled to under the compensation rules.

In the first years, a number of high-profile transfers served to highlight the importance of the regulations. I was involved in obtaining compensation for Irish clubs concerning the transfer of Robbie Keane from Leeds United to Tottenham Hotspur in 2001 and the transfer of Damien Duff from Blackburn Rovers to Chelsea in 2003. In the case of Robbie, Crumlin United, his schoolboy club in Dublin, was, I argued, entitled to a solidarity payment, and in Duff's case it was St Kevin's Boys, also Dublin-based, which was entitled to the same compensation.

Although Duff's transfer was straightforward enough, Keane's was not. Spurs had no clue whatsoever about its obligations under the regulations and so had not considered that the player's schoolboy club might be owed compensation. When I made their spokesmen aware of the requirement, they brushed it aside and pushed ahead with the transfer. According to the regulations, in the case of such a transfer, a club like Crumlin United was entitled to a percentage of the fee for their contribution to the development of the player in his formative years.

I reported the matter to FIFA and they advised me to make the submission. On the other side, however, Spurs had made their own efforts to contest the FAI's claims and so, on the London club's behalf, the English FA, the FA Premier League and the English Football League lined up to contest the interpretation of the regulations. All parties regarded it as a test case. For the UK clubs, it was viewed as a floodgates moment: allow this payment and every club in Ireland will come looking for their share of the latest big-money transfer. On the other hand, we wanted a positive verdict to send an unequivocal message to all clubs that the regulations were here to stay. Thankfully, FIFA ruled in our favour and Crumlin United received substantial compensation. It was a landmark ruling and one that established the relevance of the regulations.

Although many cases were challenging, when it went right, the process could be very smooth. For instance, I recall the transfer of Robbie Brady from St Kevin's Boys to Manchester United in 2008 going off without a hitch.

The protocol for transferring funds, however, was not perfect. Once acceptable compensation had been agreed between clubs, the money was then transferred from, say, Aston Villa to the FA in London. Then the money would be transferred directly to the Irish club's bank account. In order to improve the transparency of these payments, I had suggested to the FAI that this money should be transferred to the Association where it could be ring-fenced, before then being passed on to the appropriate club account. The problem was that the English FA would transfer the money to whichever account they were given the details of. The lack of transparency in the process was obvious. To my surprise, the FAI did not agree that there was a need for the measure.

A further suggestion I made was the idea that the FAI should set up a players' fund to assist youngsters who had been released by professional clubs. The money would have helped these players to get back on their feet after suddenly finding themselves unemployed and surplus to requirements at their former club. Most of these young boys did not know much else besides football and although, nowadays, many continue their education, in their own minds it is still football or nothing. When the hand they are dealt is the 'nothing', they struggle to cope.

They need a financial cushion to help gather themselves and, perhaps, to start the task of going for trials to lower-division clubs. This process, itself, can be very upsetting. Having been used to the thought of one day lining out for a glamorous Premier League club, many will have to make do with trying to catch the eye of an unspectacular lower-league club. Worse still, they may have to endure the dreaded exit trials, the annual last-chance saloon, arranged for recently released young players to impress in front of a throng of scouts. Usually, I would assist the Irish players who took part in these trials. I proposed to the FAI that the money for the fund could come from holding back a percentage of the player's original compensation fee paid to the training club but, again, there was not sufficient interest in the organisation for such an initiative.

In 2005, to reflect my expanded role, my title changed to Manager of Football Support Services. In the same year, my remit extended to the Irish professional scene when I became heavily involved in the creation of a domestic compensation scheme. I organised a seminar to inform clubs of the new rules. This ensured that Irish schoolboy clubs would receive appropriate compensation if a League of Ireland club signed one of their players. In order to research how best to run such a scheme, I visited other countries similar in size to Ireland – Portugal, Denmark, Austria, Belgium, Switzerland and Norway – and then presented my findings to the FAI. If I was in one of these countries to cover an Ireland game with RTÉ Radio, then, on my time off, I would arrange a meeting with representatives of the relevant football association.

On occasion, as the profile of my work grew, I was also able to help out with negotiations in other football jurisdictions. In one case, the Northern Ireland football governing body, the Irish Football Association (IFA), contacted me in 2005. It was proposed that a young Kyle Lafferty (now an established international player with Northern Ireland) would transfer from the County Fermanagh-based NFC Kesh to Burnley, then playing in English football's Championship. There being no equivalent of me in Northern Ireland, the IFA asked if I could assist with the transfer. Thankfully, a solution was arrived at which satisfied all parties and the player moved.

Our mother Monica on her ninetieth birthday party with: (*l–r*) me and my brothers Brian, Frank and Eamonn.

Pauline and me on our wedding day in 2008 with Pauline's mother, Clare.

In 2008, nine years into my new career, and six years after moving to Kerry, Pauline and I were married. We had moved into our new house in Kerry in 2002. At the wedding reception the music was supplied by the incomparable Gerry O'Connor duelling on the banjo with Mickey MacConnell and on the piano by the multitalented George Hamilton. Our wedding made it a joyful year but, unfortunately, it would be followed by a time of sadness.

In April 2009 my mother, who was still living in Dublin, underwent heart surgery in the Mater Hospital. When she came out, I went to see her in a convalescent home in the Phoenix Park. Acting under orders, I brought her dog Ross with me, whom my mother was anxious to see. Ross was an old warrior of a Jack Russell who had seen many winters come and go. My mother and he were a fixture on the Drumcondra streets. If one was ever spotted without the other, an inquisition always arose about the other's whereabouts. When, on one rare occasion, Pauline's brother Pat took Ross for a walk instead of my mother, he was stopped on the street numerous times to explain where Monica was. My mother had always said that when Ross died, she wouldn't be long after him.

Ross, owing to his old age, had many health problems, including arthritic hips. He was also deaf and blind. When my mother saw him dutifully shuffling towards her in obvious discomfort, she immediately said that she thought he should be relieved of his suffering and put to sleep. It was a Friday and so I told her that I would take the dog to the local vet in Moyvane the next morning and get their opinion. She agreed.

On the Saturday, when I took Ross to the vet, he also felt that Ross would be better off being put to sleep. He administered an injection and I stayed with the old dog until he finally passed away. I did not ring my mother because I wanted to wait until the Monday when I could return to Dublin and tell her in person that Ross was gone.

The next morning I got a call at about eight o'clock. It was the convalescent home. My mother had passed away some minutes earlier.

In the previous three weeks I had been busy organising the renovation of my mother's house. A new kitchen was installed and her bathroom was modernised. Sadly, she never got to see her newly refurbished home.

For her funeral, the decision was made to bring her home and wake her there. Although this was unusual for the city, I felt it was what my mother would have wanted. The wake was a poignant experience. People came and went, offering their condolences. I was particularly touched to see my mother's former boarder, Gerry McHugh, arriving on the doorstep – the same man who had been like a father figure to me in my youth. After coming in and greeting me, Gerry walked out into the back garden and returned with a handful of red roses – he knew my mother loved to keep them in the garden. Without saying a word, he gently placed the flowers between her fingers, underneath her rosary beads. It was a gesture that moved me.

Working for the FAI meant that, on occasion, I would get a chance to help out with the national team in a limited way. In February 2003, Brian Kerr, who was then the Ireland manager, asked me to travel to Georgia to cast my eye over the Georgians, who were playing Moldova in a friendly. The Georgians were due to play the Republic on 29 March in the 2004 European Championship qualifiers and Brian wanted me to assess their strengths and weaknesses. It would prove to be an eventful trip, with most of the action, from my perspective, taking place before I even got to Tbilisi's Mikheil Meskhi Stadium.

When I flew into the city's airport, it was late at night. A scruffy-looking fellow walked up to me and simply said 'Marriott?' The Marriott was my hotel so I followed him. When we got outside the airport building and into a shabby-looking Lada, with a silent man sitting in the front, my suspicions began to be aroused. The car pulled away and I asked if we were going the right way, but I got no answer. When the car began to leave the city limits and head towards open country, suspicion turned to fear. It turned out that I had fallen for a classic local scam. There were only two major hotels used by tourists in Tbilisi: a Sheraton and a Marriott. The man who, by this stage, was now driving me into dark woods in the middle of nowhere, took a lucky guess when he asked me if was I staying at the Marriott. He had a 50 per cent chance of being right and he had hit the jackpot.

I wondered if I was going to be robbed, or worse, right here in such absurd circumstances. I demanded again to know where we were going. They asked me how much money I had. I emptied my wallet and gave them the contents, which amounted to fifty dollars. The car turned around and I was dropped off at my hotel. I was never so glad in my life to be just ripped off.

Once he became chief executive of the FAI in 2005, John Delaney improved the Association's organisational structure and made it more professional in many ways. However, he was not always the easiest of persons to fathom. I discovered this when I invited the then Premier League Director of Youth, Dave Richardson, over from England to share his knowledge with the FAI.

I had already run Dave's proposed visit by Delaney in February 2006 before our guest arrived in Ireland. The hope was that, with Dave's invaluable experience and advice, a national academy for the development of home-grown players could be created in Ireland, along the lines of the academy structures in England. The knock-on effect of such an academy would have meant that young Irish players could go through at least part of their development phase in Ireland and, perhaps, remain there until they were eighteen years old. The academy would also allow players to finish their second-level education in Ireland, while still receiving top-level coaching. They would then be more rounded and more mature individuals and, if the break came, better able to cope with the rigours of a professional contract in England or Scotland. Not all promising players are ready to sign with a professional club at the age of sixteen but, with the help of an academy, they might be ready for that step two years later. I knew from travelling to Norway to speak with the Norwegian FA just how well such an academy could work. In Norway, the association's education officer, Andreas Morisbak, assured me that there was no perceived conflict between a player becoming a professional footballer and completing his education. They complemented each other.

I collected Dave at Dublin Airport and we travelled to meet Delaney in Merrion Square on 24 May. Dave began to outline his experiences, but Delaney was not really engaging with us and seemed to have other things on his mind. Dave and I cut it short, gave our brief thanks and left.

As soon as the door closed behind us, Dave asked me for an explanation. He could not understand why he had been asked to come all the way from England only to be treated so discourteously. I was as perplexed as Dave as to why the meeting turned out to be such a pointless exercise. When I had first aired the notion of getting Dave's assistance, Delaney had seemed genuinely enthusiastic. I have no idea what had changed in the meantime.

I took Dave straight back to the airport and apologised to him. That was all I could do.

In March 2012, I decided that I wanted to cut back on my workload and focus more on the FIFA compensation part of my role. Now that this element of my job had grown, it was becoming difficult for me to continue my career guidance work – a role that was requiring increasing amounts of travel. I was sixty-six, and past retirement age, so I felt that it made more sense to make the most of my energies by concentrating on one important thing.

I sat down with the Association's human resources officer, Stephen Driver, and explained that I wanted to reduce my workload. What I did not know was that he also had some news for me. My contract, I was politely informed, was not being renewed. I was being let go. I was stunned; at no point had there been any inkling that my position might be in jeopardy. The country was in the middle of a recession at that time, so I could understand why the FAI might have needed to make cuts, but their decision still needed explaining.

I asked who would do the work in my place and was told that it would be divvied up between the compliance officer and the children's officer. That meant that, though the career guidance work would continue in a limited way, the compensation work would be heavily watered down. My long-term plan was to ease out of the role and, in the meantime, to train in a successor. That notion was gone now, though. I felt that the Irish clubs were on their own again and, when it came to negotiating compensation packages, they could be at the mercy of the British professional clubs. I could not leave the matter at that, so I asked to see John Delaney.

I met Delaney on 16 April 2012 and told him of my concerns. I explained to him the importance of the compensation work and why I thought it should be continued. I was involved in numerous projects that would simply fall away if no one was specifically assigned to them. I also emphasised that the work was actually bringing money into the Irish game by ensuring that domestic clubs were properly paid.

I then suggested that if saving money was the issue, in the interests of the work continuing I would happily do the job for a lot less than my current salary, but this was not considered an option. I knew then that the FAI no longer wanted me. Before leaving, however, I pointed out that my contract stated that reasonable compensation for me would be discussed in the event of the role being terminated.

'It's a Board decision. We can't offer you any financial compensation but we would like to present you with a crystal vase at Ireland's next home game, as a special thank you from the FAI.' After all the years that I had given to the Irish game, my contract was to be ended without any financial settlement but, instead, with a piece of crystal.

I was not feeling particularly gracious. 'I don't need any crystal, John. I've got plenty of it at home already. I would like to be able to continue my work and, if that is not possible, to be given some sort of reasonable redundancy package.' I had worked for the FAI, in my current role, for thirteen years. That surely counted for something. I wanted to be treated fairly and that the effort I had put in for the Association would be properly recognised and remunerated.

I then explained a preliminary legal view I had obtained was that the FAI's proposed move could amount to unfair dismissal. At this, the strained air of civility vanished. Delaney intimated that if I were to go the legal route with this, then he would take it personally. I said that if I had a legal right, then surely I was entitled to pursue it, especially given that it was the only option I had. We parted without shaking hands.

On 7 May 2013, the legal arguments began. My case against the FAI was heard before a Rights Commissioner. My contention was that, since I began in the role in 1999, I had at all times been an employee of the FAI and so was entitled to the same redundancy payment that any other FAI employee would get on losing their job. The FAI argued that I was merely a consultant and not an employee, an external party who was providing them with a service and who, furthermore, had no intrinsic relationship with the organisation.

As I understand it, such cases turn on the concept of 'control'. If the body, in this case the FAI, exerts sufficient control over a worker, then it is deemed that a relationship of employer and employee exists. This means that the employee benefits from the protections of employment legislation. Consequently, it confers rights on him or her, one of them being, where appropriate, the entitlement to redundancy. If, however, there is little or no control applied, and the worker is more like an independent service provider, he or she is deemed in law to be a consultant, and, if dismissed, has no right to a redundancy package. Obviously, it was in the interests of the FAI for me to be a 'consultant'. With such a verdict, they would incur no financial obligations to me.

My wishes were simple: either to be reinstated to my old position or, if that was not possible, to receive ordinary statutory redundancy pay. My preference was to return to work, even if not on rearranged terms as I had initially sought with the FAI. It was a job that needed doing and one whose importance had been clearly established over the previous thirteen years.

Thankfully, before the Rights Commissioner, I succeeded. My legal team successfully established that there was sufficient control over me and my actions during my time working with the FAI. The organisation told me where to be and when to be there and I did as I was told. I had also been offered, but had declined, office space at the FAI's new Abbotstown headquarters, in west Dublin, when it moved there in 2007. Furthermore, I had an FAI business card that the organisation had given me. The Rights Commissioner ordered that I be reinstated to my previous role with immediate effect. In short, I was considered an employee and the FAI was my employer.

I was delighted with the ruling but the matter did not end there. The FAI appealed: a stay was put on the Rights Commissioner's ruling, and a year later the hearing of the appeal began on 13 March 2014, this time at the Labour Court, where the case ran for two days. The FAI had changed its legal team for the hearing of the appeal.

Although they stuck to the same approach – that I was a consultant and at no time an employee – they presented their case differently. Because I also earned an income from my work as a RTÉ football analyst, reference was made to my so-called 'business empire'.

Issue was also taken with the fact that, from 1999 onwards, I advised Fintan Drury's sports agency and that this represented a conflict of interest with my FAI role. When Fintan, who was a long-time acquaintance, originally sought my help, I had asked Bernard O'Byrne if he had any problem with this and the answer was no. My work with Fintan was no more than a case of being on the end of the phone if he ever had a question on any aspect of football regulations.

From my perspective, there was no empire, nor any intention to build one. There was my day job with the FAI, and limited sidelines with RTÉ and Fintan Drury's sports agency. My business relationship with Fintan had, in any case, long since finished. I stopped doing the work in 2005 to focus solely on my FAI role, and once Fintan's agency had become firmly established.

The significance of my work concerning the FIFA compensation rules was examined by the FAI. It was, they argued, a mere case of interpreting the regulations and, moreover, that that was no difficult task.

To me this was an irrelevant point and I had never taken that tack. My view was that, over more than a decade's work (in a position created and funded by the FAI since 1999) I had won the trust of countless British professional clubs, as well as building up valuable contacts in the FA and at FIFA headquarters in Zürich. This experience had given me the know-how needed to negotiate with powerful British outfits. That part *was* surely going to be difficult to replace because I was the first person to do this work in Ireland.

Over the two days in the Labour Court it was clear to me that the tide was going against me. I lost the case, with the three-person panel of adjudicators ruling against me. The day of the verdict was a bitterly disappointing one for me. I would never have imagined that my forty-five years of involvement with Irish football, stretching back to my first international cap in 1969, should end in the cold environs of Dublin's Labour Court. I had enjoyed my time working with the FAI immensely. There were, and still are, many great people working in the organisation and, if you want to make a meaningful difference to Irish football, with its resources and infrastructure, it is obviously the best place to work. My only issue was with a part of management.

I have not heard of a specific person having been assigned to the work that I did on the application of the FIFA compensation regulations. From what I have gleaned, Irish clubs are having to get by as best they can in their discussions with British clubs. If that is the case, the potential losers in this are the young players whose path to Britain is being jeopardised by the lack of a transparent and fair process being in place. Likewise, the schoolboy clubs will find it much more difficult to obtain the level of compensation they deserve. When I met with Graham Noakes, a high-ranking official in the English FA, in March 2016 in London, he told me that there were numerous problems, with many discussions between British and Irish clubs encountering difficulties. He explained that, in some cases, the Irish clubs, failing to understand the regulations, have been asking for unrealistic sums and driving off the bigger clubs' interest.

I lost in the Labour Court, and although I disagreed with the outcome, I have accepted the verdict and moved on.

Since the verdict of the Labour Court, press contacts have told me that I am effectively *persona non grata* in FAI circles, and I am sad to say that the privilege of being invited to attend home international matches, as previously provided, has been withdrawn.

In late September 2016 I received a call from a retired journalist who does freelance writing for the FAI. He was, he told me, contributing to the official match-day programme for Ireland's forthcoming home World Cup qualifier against Georgia on 6 October and, furthermore, that he would like to do a feature piece on me. It was going to be an article framed as 'Irish World Cup Heroes of the Past' and would focus on my performance as a player against France in our 2-1 victory over the country in the 1974 World Cup qualifiers. I said, 'Fine. If you want to do the article I will help.' A date for an interview was organised but, just as the conversation was about to wrap up, the journalist grew hesitant. He alluded to my falling-out with the FAI, and began to ask if everything was OK between me and the organisation. He also wondered whether or not such a piece would be acceptable to the FAI.

The next day we did the interview on the basis that my interviewer would follow through with his original concept. I gave him the details he wanted and he went away to write the piece. Some hours later, he rang me. Things had changed again. Now he told me that the article would go ahead but that it was likely that it would focus on the team as a whole and not on my performance. The conversation ended with no real clarity as to what would eventually be published.

When the match programme was finally written, I was not surprised by the contents. There was nothing at all about the victory over France, neither about me nor any of the players in that game.

Although, overall, it was not a happy incident, I know what I have achieved in my football career and what I have given to Irish football. I do not need an official seal of approval from anyone to legitimise that.

The view from the gantry. (*L–r*): Con Murphy, me and Gabriel Egan working for RTÉ Radio at the 2002 World Cup in Japan and South Korea.

Throughout my time working with the FAI, I had continued to work as a radio analyst with RTÉ and, in earlier years, as a television co-commentator with the station. My RTÉ work, however, effectively ended in 2012 when the station changed my contract to a per-game basis. The new terms stipulated that they would contact me as and when they needed me but, as of the time of writing, five years on, there have been very few calls.

On the radio, invariably my co-commentator during my fourteen-year stint was Gabriel Egan, while on television it was usually Jimmy Magee or George Hamilton. Together we covered League of Ireland and Irish international matches. These men were unfailingly professional, always did their homework on players and clubs, and were great company. They were accomplished broadcasters and it was a pleasure to work with them.

When any action took place on the pitch, Gabriel, Jimmy and George would paint the scene for the listeners and viewers at home and I would supply the analysis. It was a good combination.

With George Hamilton
(*left*) in Slovakia
in 2007

I had known George since the early 1980s, when he, on occasion, would interview me as Ireland manager for RTÉ Sport. George is a fair and balanced interviewer. He would ask you the tough questions, sure, but his interviews invited detailed football analysis – the kind that football managers love giving. My subsequent work with RTÉ allowed me to get to know George far better. As a conversationalist, there are not many better than him. With his wide-ranging interests, he has enlightened me on so many topics over the years.

Gabriel Egan and I spent many a wintry Friday night hunched at the back of the stand somewhere in rural Ireland covering League of Ireland games for RTÉ Radio. I first got to know Gabriel in 1984 when I scouted some players at a Second Division match involving Fulham, played at the club's Craven Cottage stadium. I was there on Ireland duty while Gabriel was on an assignment for RTÉ radio. Throughout the rest of my time as Ireland manager, he would often interview me before and after games. Gabriel has, over the decades, become a close friend.

When Ireland qualified for major tournaments, Gabriel and I would travel with the squad. Interacting with the many journalists covering these tournaments was always an enjoyable experience. A regular event was to arrange a football match between the Irish and British journalists with myself as the referee.

My broadcasting work took me to Japan and South Korea for the 2002 World Cup and to Poland and Ukraine for Euro 2012. This brought me near to many major events affecting Irish football and none more than the Saipan affair in 2002.

When the news broke in May of that year that Roy Keane was being sent home from the World Cup, my overriding feeling was one of deep disappointment. A player of Keane's calibre should have been enjoying the pinnacle of his career when leading out the Republic of Ireland at only its second World Cup. Instead, he ended up walking the dog at home while the rest of the football world had its eyes on the World Cup.

The facilities on offer at the Saipan training camp were lamentable and, in my opinion, Keane, as had happened on previous trips, should have been excused by McCarthy from attending what was little more than a relaxing week before the real training would begin in Japan. Keane, finding himself in Saipan, was certainly correct in his assessment of the island's unsuitability and he was right to protest. However, after first threatening to go home and then deciding to stay, he shot himself in the foot by subsequently giving the renowned and controversial interview to Paul Kimmage of the *Sunday Independent* and Tom Humphries of *The Irish Times*. Keane chose the wrong way to handle the situation. True to his personality, he went for the nuclear option. After that, there was no way back. By publicly criticising and so undermining Mick McCarthy there was only one possible outcome. Their subsequent bust-up at the now infamous team meeting was inevitable and, once that played out, Mick had to send Keane home. There were no winners in the situation: not Roy, not Mick and certainly not Irish football. Ireland reached the second round of that World Cup, but it could have been so much better with Keane on board. It was a shame.

Inevitably, the fallout divided opinion amongst the press pack. I recall plenty of heated, but good-natured arguments on the topic between myself and RTÉ's Tony O'Donoghue. Tony, as you might expect from a proud Cork man, stood squarely in Keane's corner. Roy could do no wrong!

In January 2016 I boarded a flight to Durban. I was on my way to see my brother Eamonn. I knew that he was not well and I was afraid that he would not live much longer. Eamonn had first moved to South Africa in 1969 when he was only twenty-five and on his honeymoon. It was meant to be nothing more than an extended holiday but he never came back. After seeing an advertisement looking for a junior architect on a temporary basis, Eamonn applied and got the job. Beginning on the bottom rung of a large architectural firm in Durban, he gradually worked his way up to becoming the owner of the business. Eamonn always said that he was a prisoner in paradise. Although he had a comfortable house, selling up and coming back home was never really an option. The weakness of the rand meant that the proceeds of any sale would not have taken him very far in Ireland. Eamonn was, in effect, the main reason why I first started playing football in South Africa in 1973.

While I was en route to South Africa, and two hours before landing, I received a text message on the plane. It was Eamonn's son, Damian, telling me that my brother had passed away minutes earlier. I had thought that I was heading to Durban to visit my brother but now I was going there to help arrange his funeral. Once again, just as in the passing of my mother, death had robbed me of the chance to say goodbye. Memories came back of us running carefree in County Kerry as children and growing up together in Drumcondra. We were close in age: Eamonn was only eighteen months older than me. You always hope that you will be by the side of your loved ones when they face their own death, but life rarely satisfies our neatly arranged expectations. It felt like the end of an era.

Things have come full circle for me. Some of the best times of my youth were spent in Glenalappa in Moyvane and now I am back here living with Pauline, near the same fields that myself and Eamonn spent so many happy summers playing in. We have made new friends in a place where the people have a natural generosity and where there is a genuine community spirit.

The move has also been a chance for me to try out things that I would never have even considered doing before. In Listowel, a town known for its participation in the arts, I have acted in two plays. In one I played a policeman, in the other, a drug dealer! Although I am certainly no late-

(L–r): Jimmy Keaveney, Paddy Cullen, me and Eoin Liston at the 2015 Irish Independent Sport Star awards.

blooming Laurence Olivier, I thoroughly enjoyed the experience that the play's producer, Denis O'Mahony, afforded me.

The town's John B. Keane pub, run by the late writer's son and my friend, Billy Keane, has become a favourite haunt. This has allowed me to indulge my lifelong love of singing, with the many talented musicians in the area, as well as performing in pub theatre there. I am also a member of a musical group called The Bog Hole Boys in Moyvane, with, among others, the writer and poet Gabriel Fitzmaurice. We get together on occasion whenever there is a fundraising initiative and always finish up in Máiréad's bar in Moyvane village. Gabriel was a very welcoming presence when we first arrived in Kerry. Gabriel, who is a fine poet, also has an eye for the funny side of life. After I had got to know him better, and had told him a few stories from my past, he decided to write a poem about me. He called it 'Strimming the Grass' and it was inspired by one of the more humorous moments from my past. During my second stint at Portsmouth, in the late 1970s, after being away from home for a longer period, the grass in the back garden had become

The likely lads: (l–r): Billy Keane, owner of John B. Keane's pub in Listowel, County Kerry, me, songwriter Mickey MacConnell and poet Gabriel Fitzmaurice.

very long. I took out the strimmer and, with my boys Gary and Warren looking on, set to work. It was a beautiful summer's day and I was in high spirits, so I started to sing away as I went about my work. Then, before I could react, some cat droppings flew up from the grass and went straight into my open mouth. It all happened so quickly that I actually swallowed it. I ran into the house to try and wash it out somehow, but it was too late. To this day, whenever the incident is brought up, Gary, Warren and I end up in knots of laughter.

There is a slower pace to the way of life in Kerry and a down-to-earth humour that I thoroughly enjoy. In 2002, when I was driving around the Dingle Peninsula with Pauline on a blistering hot day, we met some fishermen unloading their day's catch at Ballydavid pier. I decided to give my passable Irish a try out. I said hello in Irish, and, recognising me as a former Ireland manager, one of the men responded in Irish and told me that I was not the only past Irish international manager on the peninsula in recent times. Mick McCarthy, he explained, had been playing golf with Páidí Ó Sé at Ceann Sibéal in the previous weeks. Knowing full well, of course, that Mick McCarthy did not have a word of Irish, and bragging about my own *cúpla focal*, I said cheekily: '*Níl aon Ghaeilge ag Mícheál MacCártaigh.*' As quick as you like, he retorted: '*Níl aon Bhéarla ag Mícheál MacCártaigh.*' Mick, whenever I remind him, always finds this story particularly funny.

Since moving to Kerry I have also recorded two CDs. For the first, my friend Mickey MacConnell wrote a wonderful song for me about my mother and The Brazen Head called 'Monica's Song'. The other CD was a collection of traditional songs recorded live in John B. Keane's, the proceeds from which went to St John's Theatre in Listowel and Irish Guide Dogs for the Blind.

I have finally taken up the banjo again – some sixty years after giving it up as a child. If I am to be honest, I am not all that good but I take inspiration from the exemplary banjo players that I have been lucky enough to know over the years: Gerry O'Connor, Sean McGuinness, Brian Furlong and John O'Brien being foremost on that list.

Kerry is a county of Gaelic footballers and few come greater than Mick O'Connell. When myself and Pauline were exploring his native Valentia Island some years ago, we ran into him. He invited us to his home and proceeded to amaze me with his in-depth knowledge of soccer. Mick, renowned as perhaps the greatest Gaelic footballer of them all, was, it turned out, an expert on the 'garrison game'!

In April 2013 I was inducted into the Portsmouth Hall of Fame. Coming in the midst of my ongoing legal dispute with the FAI, it was a welcome recognition of my long connection with the club. At Portsmouth I fought my kind of fight: the contest between myself, my opponent and a football – life at its most simple!

The award was presented to me by the former Portsmouth player Steve Foster. During my second spell with the club, from 1977 to 1979, Steve was one player in particular to whom I became something of a mentor. At that time, Steve was a young, raw, combative centre half but I could see that he had genuine potential. In later years I was delighted to see him realising

My induction into the Portsmouth Hall of Fame in April 2013. After my long association with the club, throughout the 1960s and 1970s, it was an honour to receive the accolade.

that promise: throughout the 1980s Steve would go on to play for Brighton and Hove Albion, Aston Villa and Luton Town in the First Division, as well as being capped three times for England, including travelling to the 1982 World Cup with the national side.

Although football will always be my first game, I have to admit that I have fallen out of love with watching the modern game. The sport has changed a lot since my time as a professional footballer but I cannot say that all those changes have been positive. Diving, for example, is, for me, a blight on the current-day game and something that must urgently be tackled by the powers that be. It is shameful when you go along to an underage match and sometimes see kids diving to win penalties and free kicks. And, what is more, on occasion, you will hear their coaches encouraging them to do so. This behaviour, of course, all starts with the bad example being offered up on our television screens every week: the sight of professional players trying to con referees with their diving antics.

Players are highly paid entertainers in the modern game. They earn huge salaries that supposedly reflect their status. These salaries, however, must come with responsibilities, chief among them not to bring the game into disrepute.

During my own playing days in England you would be open to ridicule from your own teammates if you threw yourself down as easily as some modern players do. I remember the great Frannie Lee of Manchester City and England fame being accused of diving to earn penalties. He didn't – rather his ploy was to run the ball at pace into the penalty area and then draw a clumsy challenge. Very effective but, crucially, fair.

Even in the late 1990s things were not as bad as they are today. I recall vividly how Robbie Fowler fell in the box in a vital match away to Arsenal in 1997. The referee awarded a penalty but Fowler, instead of celebrating, jumped back up and remonstrated with the referee, insisting that he was not fouled. Would that happen today? Not likely. Instead, it has reached the stage where basic integrity and rules are being challenged on a weekly basis. Cheating has almost been elevated to an art form.

Everyone would acknowledge that sport is a way of moulding character through fair competition. Do we want to educate our kids that winning is all that matters and that cheating is a normal part of that process?

It is surely time for the authorities to get serious about punishing simulation. This behaviour needs to be disincentivised and the only way to do that is with effective penalties. A points' deduction for clubs for identified instances of diving would reap immediate benefits.

There is so much talk about the billions flowing into football from television, its wonderful global brand and the immense value of players. Somehow, somewhere, the 'beautiful game' has been lost in all this.

I have a message for young players: don't copy what you see on television. What is the point in admiring a trophy or a medal if you have not won it by fair means? Would you like this as a reminder every time you look back on your playing career? It is time for the beautiful game to become just that again.

As for most people, life has left its bruises on me. I have won some battles and lost some. I can admit that, but I won the most important one, the one that nearly took my life in the Mater Hospital in September 1997. I don't forget that.

With Robbie Keane at the 2017 Soccer Writers' Association of Ireland annual dinner.

Surrounded by family. On the left, my son Warren, on my right, my son Gary, together with my grandchildren (*l–r*) Aidan, Kylan and Fintan.

Looking back now, I can see that throughout my early life, perhaps, I missed the steadying hand of a father. If I had had a paternal figure to turn to, I might have made different decisions.

In the late 1990s I travelled to London to do something that I had wanted to do for many years: find my father's grave. He had died a lonely death from throat cancer some forty years earlier, an outsider in London. His funeral, from what I know, was not a well-attended affair either. With myself, my mother and my brothers unable to go to his funeral, he could hardly have had a great send-off.

Finally, after a lot of looking, I tracked down his grave at Streatham Cemetery in Lambeth, south London. I found a neglected memorial: no more than a simple, rickety wooden cross almost completely choked by weeds. I had not really known my father in life and so I could only use my imagination to fill in the gaps of his life: to wonder how he had lived and how he had felt in his last days and hours. I cleaned up his grave, had a new cross built and paid a fee to ensure the annual upkeep of the plot. It was fitting.

My life has not followed the straight path. Football is the life less ordinary. Anyone schooled in the game will tell you that. Following its nomadic brief has meant missing out on much time with my children. I can honestly say, however, that my children – Gary, Warren, Jason and Shannon – have, at least, had the opportunity to fulfil their ambitions. I did everything I could along the line to help them.

On the whole, however, I have little to complain about. Football allowed me to earn a living from what I loved doing; it gave me the chance to travel and to be introduced to new cultures; and most of all, through it, I met many great people, both inside and outside the game.

As you get older, memories count for so much – the regrets, the joys, the hopes. It is now time to relax and enjoy what is ahead.

I will do just that.

With (l–r) my granddaughter Leah, daughter Shannon, son Jason and grandson Kinam.

Acknowledgements

I would like to give a special mention to the following: the Ballina Manor Hotel, Ballina, County Mayo; the Croke Park Hotel, Dublin; Pat McCann of the Dalata Hotel Group; the Huggard family at the Lake Hotel, Killarney, County Kerry; the Marylebone Hotel, London; the Rose Hotel, Tralee, County Kerry; the Wesley Boutique Hotel, Johannesburg, South Africa; James O'Dowd at the Golf Doc, Tralee, County Kerry; Kane Tuohy Solicitors, Dublin; Listowel Printing Works, Listowel, County Kerry; Ray McManus of Sportsfile; Oliver and Ciaran Barry of Hollystown Golf Club, Hollystown, Dublin 15; TNT Express; Frank Hogan; and my agent Jonathan Williams.

Pauline and I have integrated well in the local community, thanks to the natural kindness of our good friends Damian and Joan Stack, and many others. David Fitzmaurice makes sure we attend the Listowel Races every September.

A close friend, Mary Nolan, who, more than anyone else, along with her husband Connie, helped us to settle in Kerry, sadly passed away during the writing of this book. She had vowed that she would be around to read it but lost her battle with illness.

As much as Pauline and I love the south-west of Ireland, we do, like most people, need an injection of sunshine every now and then. A favourite holiday destination of ours is Lanzarote in the Canary Islands. Over the years, we have enjoyed exploring the island and sampling the craic and the ceol at night-time. We often met up with the former Dublin City Ramblers frontman Sean McGuinness and his dearly departed wife, Breda. I have enjoyed Sean's friendship over fifty years, stretching right back to the Ballad Boom days of mid-1960s' Dublin.

Another musician we regularly meet on the island is Johnny Crowley, a proud Cork man, and former keyboard player with the Tony Stevens Band in Cork city. When I arrived on holiday to Lanzarote in 2006, it was a shock to hear that Johnny had fallen seriously ill with acute pancreatitis – the very same life-threatening condition that I had recovered from in 1997. By coincidence, I was Johnny's first non-family visitor after he came out of a coma. I told him that I had been through this before and tried to reassure him that there could be a good life ahead of him – and, thankfully, so it has transpired. Johnny and his wife, Josie, now run a popular bar in Lanzarote called the Bodhrán Bar, with Johnny himself helping to provide the nightly musical entertainment.

I have been catching up on lost golfing time, playing with friends at Ballybunion Golf Club. There are few more pleasant experiences than looking out at the Atlantic Ocean from this beautiful seaside course.

A long-term ambition of mine has now been fulfilled. I went to the 2016 Ryder Cup at the Hazeltine National Golf Club, Minnesota. This came about through a friendship with Tony McMunn, an American businessman who owns a restaurant-bar in Ballybunion. He kindly provided me and my buddy James O'Dowd with tickets for the event. That really was a once-in-a-lifetime experience.

Kerry is not the only part of Ireland's Wild Atlantic Way that I have taken to, either. Ballina in County Mayo, where Pauline is from, has become a special place to visit. I enjoy my time there, having the chat and games of golf with my brother in-law Pat Doherty, Martin Maguire, Eamonn Bourke and friends. Pat, 'the Ballina Bandit', has a strange way of calculating handicapping – I can rarely beat him. I feel so at home there. I am also delighted that my late mother, Monica, had the opportunity to meet my wife's family, Pat, Claire, Margaret, Nuala and my mother-in-law Clare Doherty. It was a meeting of wonderful people. I have fond memories of the happiness those visits brought to everyone.